Maximilian Reimann
Mediating Geographic Knowledge

AF286435

America ⋯ Culture – History – Politics | 15

The series is edited by Michael Hochgeschwender, Christof Mauch, Anke Ortlepp, Ursula Prutsch and Britta Waldschmidt-Nelson.

Maximilian Reimann is a Research Associate at the Deutsches Museum in Munich. He studied Modern History and completed his doctorate in American Cultural History at LMU Munich. His research focuses on the history of geography and empire, alongside expertise in the digital humanities.

Maximilian Reimann

Mediating Geographic Knowledge

U.S. Geographical Societies, 1888-1914

[transcript]

Die vorliegende Studie wurde 2023 als Dissertation an der Ludwig-Maximilians-Universität München angenommen.

Bibliographic information published by the Deutsche Nationalbibliothek
The Deutsche Nationalbibliothek lists this publication in the Deutsche Nationalbibliografie; detailed bibliographic data are available online at https://dnb.dnb.de

2026 © transcript Verlag, Bielefeld
Hermannstraße 26 | D-33602 Bielefeld | live@transcript-verlag.de

Cover design: Maria Arndt
Cover illustration: Adapted from/Cover image: New American Geographical Society building plan, from "Popular Science Monthly", Vol. 79 (1911)
Printing: Elanders Waiblingen GmbH, Waiblingen
https://doi.org/10.14361/9783839474884
Print-ISBN: 978-3-8376-7488-0 | PDF-ISBN: 978-3-8394-7488-4
ISSN of series: 2702-8046 | eISSN of series: 2702-8054

Printed on permanent acid-free text paper.

Contents

List of Abbreviations

AAG   Association of American Geographers
AAAS American Association for the Advancement of Science
AGS   American Geographical Society
GSC   Geographic Society of Chicago
GSP   Geographical Society of Philadelphia
NGM National Geographic Magazine
NGS   National Geographic Society
RGS   Royal Geographical Society
USGS United States Geological Survey

Introduction: The Politics of Space

Mapping Power at the Paris Peace Conference

At the Paris Peace Conference (1919–1920), where Europe's borders were rene-gotiated after World War I, U.S. geographers exercised considerable influence. Senior figures from U.S. geographical societies served as the American[1] delega-tion's authorities on territorial matters: Isaiah Bowman, director of the Ameri-can Geographical Society (AGS), served as chief territorial specialist; Mark Jef-ferson, former president of the Association of American Geographers (AAG), acted as chief cartographer; and Douglas Wilson Johnson, a prominent mem-ber of both societies, was designated chief of the Division of Boundary Geog-raphy. Their authority stemmed not only from individual expertise, but also from their association with the Inquiry, a geographical "think tank" created by President Woodrow Wilson in 1917 to prepare for postwar negotiations, which convened at AGS headquarters.[2]

Between 1917 and 1918, the Inquiry systematically gathered geographical knowledge in close contact with government departments and the Military In-telligence Division. Its vast output of maps, statistics, and territorial analyses provided the American delegation with a significant advantage. The Inquiry's expertise directly informed policy, including Wilson's *Fourteen Points*, which drew many of its territorial recommendations from an Inquiry memoran-dum.[3] This mobilization of geographical expertise extended well beyond the Inquiry. As AAG president Nevin M. Fenneman remarked in 1920, "nearly one-

---

1 Throughout this dissertation, I use American as the adjectival form for matters per-taining to the United States, while recognizing it is geographically imprecise.

2 Neil Smith, *American Empire: Roosevelt's Geographer and the Prelude to Globalization* (Berkeley: University of California Press, 2003), 120–35.

3 Geoffrey J. Martin, *American Geography and Geographers: Toward Geographical Science* (New York: Oxford University Press, 2015), 589–90.

half of our members have been engaged in some expert capacity during the war."[4] Recent scholarship underscores the significance of geographical knowledge as a source of political authority during the Paris Peace Conference.[5] However, the influence wielded by these geographers in 1919 was not spontaneous, but cultivated through institutional developments over the preceding decades, the period examined in this book.

Wilson's assertion that the American delegation would represent the "only disinterested people"[6] at the conference highlights the central tension explored in this study: the contradiction between geographers' claims to impartial objectivity and the inherently political nature of their work. The participation of U.S. geographers in Paris was the culmination of decades of institutional development, through which U.S. geographical societies crafted an image as authoritative producers of ostensibly objective spatial knowledge. However, geographical knowledge was never purely descriptive; it influenced international relations and territorial decisions through institutional and discursive practices.

Research Questions and Framework

This book investigates how U.S. geographical societies established themselves as authoritative arbiters of spatial knowledge. Specifically, it examines the institutional processes that lent credibility and influence to their claims of scientific objectivity from 1888 to 1914. I argue that U.S. geographical societies emerged during this period as powerful mediating institutions by controlling sites, standards, and circulation, thereby defining and legitimizing what counted as geographical knowledge. By "mediation", I refer to the institutional processes of selecting, transforming, and validating knowledge that enable it to circulate among scientific, governmental, and public audiences. This mediation frequently aligned spatial knowledge with national and imperial ambitions, while the societies claimed scientific neutrality.

---

4   Nevin M. Fenneman, "The Circumference of Geography," *Geographical Review* 7, no. 3 (1919): 170.

5   One recent example is Maciej Górny, *Vaterlandszeichner: Geografen und Grenzen im Zwischenkriegseuropa* (Osnabrück: fibre, 2019).

6   Steven Seegel, *Mapping Europe's Borderlands: Russian Cartography in the Age of Empire* (Chicago: University of Chicago Press, 2012), 268.

This analysis adopts a "history of knowledge" framework that integrates three perspectives: the socially constructed and situated nature of knowledge; attention to diverse actors and practices; and the spatial dimensions of knowledge production. Following Philipp Sarasin's model (see Chapter 1), I analyze four constitutive elements of knowledge production: discursive systems that define what counts as true; media that transport and transform information; actors who legitimize knowledge; and genealogies that reveal power relations. This approach allows me to examine not just the content of geographical knowledge, but also the institutional mechanisms through which it gained authority.

Historiography and Institutional Blind Spots

While histories of major U.S. geographical societies are well documented, a critical analysis of their role as knowledge-producing institutions remains underexplored. The historiography has long been dominated by books written by leading society members, which often privileged institutional self-representation over historically nuanced analyses attentive to political, social, and cultural contexts. This tendency is evident in works such as *The National Geographic Society: 100 Years of Adventure and Discovery*, and the history of the National Geographic Society written by its former president, Gilbert H. Grosvenor.[7] While official histories of the AGS and AAG are more balanced, the authors' insider positions inevitably constrained their critical perspectives.[8] AAG archivist Geoffrey J. Martin's indispensable synthesis *American Geography and Geographers* (2015) exemplifies a historiographical emphasis on largely decontextualized disciplinary narratives, focusing narrowly on the definition

---

7   Gilbert Grosvenor and John La Gorce, *The National Geographic Society and its Magazine: A History* (Washington: National Geographic Society, 1957); Courtlandt Bryan, *The National Geographic Society: 100 Years of Adventure and Discovery* (New York: Abrams, 1987).

8   John Kirtland Wright, *Geography in the Making: The American Geographical Society, 1851–1951* (New York: American Geographical Society, 1952); Preston Everett James and Geoffrey J. Martin, *The Association of American Geographers: The First Seventy-Five Years, 1904–1979* (Easton: Association of American Geographers, 1978). Wright was director of the AGS from 1938 to 1949; James was president of the AAG from 1951 to 1952; and Martin was AAG archivist and Councilor.

and internal development of geography while largely neglecting the field's popular dimensions.[9]

Recent scholarship offers more nuanced perspectives, moving beyond celebratory accounts to critically engage with the history of U.S. geography.[10] Several studies trace American perceptions of the world through the pages of *National Geographic Magazine* (NGM). Tamar Rothenberg analyzes the "strategies of innocence" employed by NGM, using Mary Louise Pratt's analytical framework for European travel writing.[11] Susan Schulten provides a broader survey of popular geographical imagination through maps, atlases, and magazines, including NGM, from 1880 to 1950.[12] Stephanie Hawkins and Lutz/Collins examine how NGM presented the globalized world to its twentieth-century readers, though these studies remain largely focused on photographic analysis and reader reception, respectively.[13]

Despite these contributions, the existing historiography has several gaps that this study addresses. First, an emphasis on prominent figures such as Gilbert H. Grosvenor (NGS), Charles P. Daly (AGS), and William Morris Davis (AAG) has obscured the broader institutional networks sustaining these societies. Scholars have largely overlooked the routine but essential contributions of councilors, editors, secretaries, librarians, and other less visible members. Second, the internal processes by which these societies transformed knowledge as it circulated between scientific, governmental, and public domains require closer analysis. Third, the historiography's focus on finished

---

9   Martin, *American Geography and Geographers.*

10   David N. Livingstone, *The Geographical Tradition: Episodes in the History of a Contested Enterprise* (Oxford: Blackwell, 1992) is an early example of a contextual, critical history of geography; Brian W. Blouet, ed., *The Origins of Academic Geography in the United States* (Hamden: Archon Books, 1981) is one of the few works focusing on geography's origins in the United States.

11   Tamar Y. Rothenberg, *Presenting America's World: Strategies of Innocence in National Geographic Magazine, 1888–1945* (London: Routledge, 2007).

12   Susan Schulten, *The Geographical Imagination in America, 1880–1950* (Chicago: University of Chicago Press, 2001).

13   Catherine A. Lutz and Jane L. Collins, *Reading National Geographic* (Chicago: University of Chicago Press, 1993); Stephanie L. Hawkins, *American Iconographic: National Geographic, Global Culture, and the Visual Imagination* (Charlottesville: University of Virginia Press, 2010). Additional, more popular, works include: Robert M. Poole, *Explorers House: National Geographic and the World it Made* (New York: Penguin Press, 2004); Howard S. Abramson, *National Geographic: Behind America's Lens on the World* (New York: Crown Publishing, 1987).

publications, particularly the NGM, has obscured the collaborative networks underpinning geographical knowledge. Fourth, a predominant emphasis on academic geography has minimized the societies' role in determining what counted as legitimate geographical knowledge and their contributions to the discipline's professionalization.

This study shifts the focus from prominent individuals and finished publications toward the institutional practices, networks, and power dynamics that shaped U.S. geographical societies. While influential individuals such as Davis and Grosvenor remain important, they are treated here not as heroic originators, but as actors operating within and shaped by institutional "networks of opportunities and constraints".[14] This book also treats larger political and historical contexts not as mere backdrops, but as integral forces shaping the production of knowledge. Focusing on institutional practices instead of finished texts or prominent figures, this "mid-picture" approach connects macro-level forces of nationalism and imperialism with micro-level practices of knowledge production.[15] In addition, analyzing geographical societies as interconnected networks rather than isolated entities shows how they collectively shaped U.S. geography.

Geography, Space, and Empire

The practices employed by geographical societies in organizing, producing, circulating, and disseminating knowledge generated powerful "imaginative geographies" that often advanced the interests of an expanding U.S. state. This study argues that U.S. geographical societies enabled and legitimated these imaginative geographies, as shown in Chapter 6 on the Pacific.

Cultural and postcolonial studies have reshaped the historiography of geographical knowledge, culture, and empire. Several influential works highlight the essential role of geographical knowledge in legitimizing imperialism: Edward Said argued that imaginative geographies provided the foundation of imperial power; Mary Louise Pratt analyzed how European travel writing, often explicitly geographical, facilitated conquest; Paul Carter showed that "spatial history" inscribed territories through naming and travel; and Derek Gregory

---

14   Burke, *What is the History of Knowledge?*, 119.

15   Robert E. Kohler and Kathryn M. Olesko, "Introduction: Clio Meets Science," *Osiris* 27, no. 1 (2012): 3.

emphasized the power/knowledge relations inherent in imperial geography.[16] Studies of cartography similarly show that spatial representations were critical tools for imperial control, mapping and surveying spaces to render them legible and governable.[17] As K. Maria D. Lane has argued in her work on astronomical mapping of Mars, even imaginative geographies of extra-terrestrial spaces often blurred the lines between scientific description and imperial projection.[18]

Many historians now argue that imperialism was integral to the formation and institutionalization of modern geography as a discipline.[19] European geographical societies – especially those of Britain, France, and Germany – functioned as essential imperial infrastructure. They supplied imperial powers with the geographical knowledge needed for the expansion and administration of empires, including maps, resource analyses, and statistics.[20] This dynamic re-

16   Edward W. Said, *Orientalism* (New York: Vintage, 1993); Mary Louise Pratt, *Imperial Eyes: Travel Writing and Transculturation* (London: Routledge, 1992); Paul Carter, *The Road to Botany Bay: An Exploration of Landscape and History* (Minneapolis: University of Minnesota Press, 1987); Derek Gregory, *Geographical Imaginations* (Cambridge, Mass.: Blackwell, 1994).

17   Matthew Edney, *Mapping an Empire: The Geographical Construction of British India, 1765–1843* (Chicago: University of Chicago Press, 1997); D. Graham Burnett, *Masters of All They Surveyed: Exploration, Geography, and a British El Dorado* (Chicago: University of Chicago Press, 2000); Robert A. Stafford, "Scientific Exploration and Empire," in *The Oxford History of the British Empire: Volume III: The Nineteenth Century*, ed. Andrew Porter (Oxford: Oxford University Press, 1999), 294–319. On the power of maps, see: J. Brian Harley, "Maps, Knowledge, and Power," in *Geographic Thought: A Praxis Perspective*, ed. George L. Henderson and Marvin Waterstone (London: Routledge, 2009), 129–48; Jeremy Black, *Maps and History: Constructing Images of the Past* (New Haven: Yale University Press, 1997); Ute Schneider, *Die Macht der Karten: Eine Geschichte der Kartographie vom Mittelalter bis heute* (Darmstadt: Primus, 2004).

18   K. Maria D. Lane, *Geographies of Mars: Seeing and Knowing the Red Planet* (Chicago: University of Chicago Press, 2011).

19   Anne Godlewska and Neil Smith, "Introduction: Critical Histories of Geography," in *Geography and Empire*, ed. Anne Godlewska and Neil Smith (Oxford: Blackwell, 1994), 4.

20   Felix Driver, "Geography's Empire: Histories of Geographical Knowledge," *Environment and Planning D: Society and Space* 10 (1992): 23–40; Godlewska and Smith, *Geography and Empire*; Morag Bell, Robin A. Butlin, and Michael Heffernan, eds., *Geography and Imperialism, 1820–1940* (Manchester: Manchester University Press, 1995); Felix Driver, *Geography Militant: Cultures of Exploration and Empire* (Oxford: Blackwell, 2001); Robin A. Butlin, *Geographies of Empire: European Empires and Colonies, c. 1880–1960* (Cambridge: Cambridge University Press, 2009); Iris Schröder, *Das Wissen von der ganzen Welt: globale Geographien und räumliche Ordnungen Afrikas und Europas 1790–1870* (Paderborn: Schön-

flects what David Harvey terms the "deterritorialization" and "reterritorialization" of global spaces to inscribe colonial and imperial needs.[21] Karl Schlögel further argues that modern geography specifically emerged to meet the needs of modern nation-states and empires that required new ways of mastering and representing space.[22] While the link between geography and European imperialism is well-established, the role of geographical knowledge in U.S. imperial expansion, particularly in the strategically significant Pacific, remains comparatively understudied.

This scholarly neglect may stem from the prevailing geographical imagination of the United States itself, reinforced by what Daniel Immerwahr calls the "logo map". By excluding territories beyond the contiguous states, this cartographic convention effectively concealed the extent of the American empire for much of U.S. history. Significantly, Immerwahr notes that around 1900 – precisely the period studied here – American cartographers briefly produced maps explicitly depicting the United States as an empire.[23] This book argues that geographical societies were central to producing and popularizing this temporary but powerful imperial vision.

Reflecting this visual erasure, the historiography of American imperialism has tended to concentrate on the Caribbean, leaving the Pacific relatively neglected.[24] The limited historiography on the Pacific in the American imagination typically emphasizes westward continental expansion to the Pacific coastline, highlighting how nineteenth-century politicians and businessmen perceived the ocean as a commercial and strategic opportunity.[25] Economic histo-

---

ingh, 2011); Carsten Gräbel, *Die Erforschung der Kolonien: Expeditionen und koloniale Wissenskultur deutscher Geographen, 1884–1919* (Bielefeld: transcript, 2015).

21   David Harvey, *The Condition of Postmodernity: An Enquiry into the Origins of Cultural Change* (Oxford: Blackwell, 1989), 264.

22   Karl Schlögel, *Im Raume lesen wir die Zeit: Über Zivilisationsgeschichte und Geopolitik* (München: Hanser, 2003), 46–47.

23   Daniel Immerwahr, *How to Hide an Empire: A History of the Greater United States* (New York: Farrar, Straus and Giroux, 2019), 74.

24   Louis A. Pérez, Jr., *The War of 1898: The United States and Cuba in History and Historiography* (Chapel Hill: University of North Carolina Press, 1998); César J. Ayala and Rafael Bernabe, *Puerto Rico in the American Century: A History since 1898* (Chapel Hill: University of North Carolina Press, 2007).

25   Bruce Cumings, *Dominion from Sea to Sea: Pacific Ascendancy and American Power* (New Haven: Yale University Press, 2009); John Curtis Perry, *Facing West: Americans and the Opening of the Pacific* (Westport: Praeger, 1994); Norman Graebner, *Empire on the Pacific: A Study in American Continental Expansion* (New York: The Ronald Press, 1955); Anders

rians of American empire stand out as an exception, given their stronger focus on the Pacific Ocean.[26] Historians of geography, meanwhile, have predominantly focused on the Arctic.[27] This study addresses the imbalance by centering the Pacific in Chapter 6. Analyzing the role of U.S. geographical societies in this Pacific context illuminates how geographical knowledge underpinned and justified American imperial strategies.

During the nineteenth century, empire and nation grew in tandem. Paul Kramer's framework of a "nation-based empire" that conquered and territorialized the North American continent, wielded power through other nation-states, and pursued overseas colonialism after 1898, is particularly useful here. The framework highlights persistent patterns that legitimized territorial acquisition, whether continental or overseas.[28] Recent scholarship on the American West emphasizes the imperial nature of the dispossession of Native Americans and the territories acquired during the Mexican-American War.[29] Similarly, historians now view the 1898 annexations and occupations of Cuba, Puerto Rico, the Philippines, Guam, and Hawaii as integral to American empire rather than a "great aberration".[30] Niall Ferguson has aptly observed that

---

Stephanson, *Manifest Destiny: American Expansion and the Empire of Right* (New York: Hill and Wang, 1995).

26   One example is: Walter LaFeber, *The New Empire: An Interpretation of American Expansion, 1860–1898* (Ithaca: Cornell University Press, 1963); Walter LaFeber, "A Note on the 'Mercantilist Imperialism' of Alfred Thayer Mahan," *Mississippi Valley Historical Review* 48, no. 4 (1962): 674–85.

27   On the Arctic, see Michael F. Robinson, *The Coldest Crucible: Arctic Exploration and American Culture* (Chicago: University of Chicago Press, 2006); Pascal Schillings, *Der letzte weiße Flecken: Europäische Antarktisreisen um 1900* (Göttingen: Wallstein, 2016); Lisa Bloom, *Gender on Ice: American Ideologies of Polar Expeditions* (Minneapolis: University of Minnesota Press, 1993).

28   Paul Kramer, "Power and Connection: Imperial Histories of the United States in the World," *The American Historical Review* 116, no. 5 (2011): 1371–72.

29   Steven Hahn, *A Nation Without Borders: The United States and Its World in an Age of Civil Wars, 1830–1910* (New York: Viking, 2016) is one recent example; see also Richard White, *"It's Your Misfortune and None of My Own": A History of the American West* (Norman: University of Oklahoma Press, 1991).

30   For an excellent overview of the historiography, see Paul Kramer, "Power and Connection," 1348–91. Some newer works with a focus on the historiography of American Empire include Walter Nugent, *Habits of Empire: A History of American Expansion* (New York: Vintage Books, 2009); Richard H. Immerman, *Empire for Liberty: A History of American Imperialism from Benjamin Franklin to Paul Wolfowitz* (Princeton: Princeton University Press, 2010); Alfred W. McCoy, Francisco A. Scarano, and Courtney Johnson, "On the

the American empire was "as exceptional as all the other sixty-nine empires" in world history.[31] As U.S. territorial aspirations shifted from continental expansion toward overseas empire, geographical societies became important mediators between scientific knowledge production and geopolitical strategy. They reframed expansion in terms of scientific rationality or inevitability, thereby obscuring the political motivations behind it.

Periodizing U.S. Geography, 1888–1914

Between 1888 and 1914, U.S. geography underwent a fundamental transformation in institutional structures, professional identity, and public reach. These decades saw intensive disciplinary formation and boundary-drawing across the earth sciences, creating the institutional landscape in which modern geography was defined. This period marked the founding of the National Geographic Society (1888), the Geological Society of America (1888), and a wider surge in geographical organization and output that saw the discipline evolve from an amateur pursuit into both a professional and a popular science.

Historians label these decades as part of the "Global Age" or "Age of Territoriality", noting an intensified global competition for land and resources that brought spatial questions to the center of political culture.[32] The notion of seemingly infinite space, which expansion narratives depicted as empty despite Indigenous presence in the American West, had long shaped American identity, providing geographical societies with established narratives about space and expansion. By the 1890s, both informal and formal imperialism opened new spaces beyond the North American continent. On a global scale, technological advancements in transportation and communication made

---

Tropic of Cancer: Transitions and Transformations in the U.S. Imperial State," in Alfred W. McCoy and Francisco A. Scarano, eds., *Colonial Crucible: Empire in the Making of the Modern American State* (Madison: University of Wisconsin Press, 2009), 3–33; Frank Ninkovich, *The United States and Imperialism* (Malden: Blackwell, 2001).

31   Niall Ferguson, *Colossus: The Rise and Fall of the American Empire* (London: Penguin, 2005), 15; a "great aberration" coined by Samuel Flagg Bemis, *A Diplomatic History of the United States* (New York: Henry Holt and Company, 1936).

32   Michael Geyer and Charles Bright, "World History in a Global Age," *The American Historical Review* 100, no. 4 (1995): 1034–60; Charles S. Maier, "Consigning the Twentieth Century to History: Alternative Narratives for the Modern Era," *The American Historical Review* 105, no. 3 (2000): 807–31.

it possible to overcome distance at unprecedented speed. This "space-time compression" simultaneously fed fears about a global "closing" of space, which increased demand for spatial and geographical expertise.[33] Historian Stephen Kern emphasizes that between 1880 and 1914, perceptions of time and space shifted dramatically.[34] Within these contexts, geography's capacity to produce authoritative spatial knowledge became indispensable to national and imperial projects, prompting historians to characterize it as the "imperialist science par excellence".[35]

The analysis concludes with the outbreak of World War I (1914), a juncture identified by historians such as Eric Hobsbawm as the end of both the "long nineteenth century" and the "Age of Empire".[36] This juncture was particularly consequential for geographical societies, disrupting their international networks and scholarly communication. It also transformed them from internationally oriented scientific institutions into wartime instruments of national policy. Isaiah Bowman's appointment as AGS director in 1915 signaled a general reorientation of the society and the beginning of a new phase in which geographical knowledge would be more directly mobilized for state purposes.[37] Accordingly, this study examines a critical but historiographically neglected transitional period situated between Karen Morin's analysis of the AGS (ending in 1890) and Neil Smith's study of Isaiah Bowman (beginning around 1915).[38] Although the analysis centers on these years, it occasionally reaches back to earlier decades, especially to the AGS's mid-century origins.

Geographical Societies and the Making of U.S. Geography

While European universities established geography chairs and geographical societies proliferated worldwide during the second half of the nineteenth cen-

---

33   David Harvey, "Between Space and Time: Reflections on the Geographical Imagina-
      tion," *Annals of the Association of American Geographers* 80, no. 3 (1990): 418–34.
34   Stephen Kern, *The Culture of Time and Space, 1880–1918* (Cambridge: Harvard University
      Press, 1983).
35   David N. Livingstone, *The Geographical Tradition: Episodes in the History of a Contested En-
      terprise* (Oxford: Blackwell, 1992), 160.
36   Eric Hobsbawm, *The Age of Empire: 1875–1914* (New York: Pantheon Books, 1987).
37   Smith, *American Empire*.
38   Karen M. Morin, *Civic Discipline: Geography in America, 1860–1890* (Farnham: Ashgate,
      2011); Smith, *American Empire*.

tury, U.S. universities were slower to institutionalize geography as an independent discipline. In the United States, geography was often housed in geology or economics departments, or treated as teacher training rather than a distinct research field. As a result, geography remained a subordinate discipline until the early twentieth century. Due to this delayed academic institutionalization, geographical societies became the principal arbiters of geographical knowledge in the United States. While federal agencies such as the U.S. Geological Survey were significant producers of spatial knowledge, the geographical societies occupied a unique mediating role. Not bound by the same bureaucratic or utilitarian mandates as government surveys and unconstrained by strict academic disciplinarity, these societies bridged scientific, state, and public spheres in ways few other institutions could.

The three most influential societies were the American Geographical Society, the National Geographic Society, and the Association of American Geographers. Together, these organizations shaped the trajectory of U.S. geography in the late nineteenth and early twentieth centuries. Each society performed distinct but overlapping functions: the AAG catered exclusively to professional geographers, the AGS maintained a mixed membership of amateurs and professionals, and the NGS increasingly positioned itself as the leading institution for popularizing geography to a mass audience. In addition to these national bodies, smaller geographical societies were founded in Chicago, Philadelphia, San Francisco, and Seattle, each dedicated to the dissemination and exchange of geographical knowledge through publications, lectures, and research grants. Membership ranged from a few dozen to several thousand, but it was the social composition of these societies that formed the foundation of their institutional power and networks: federal survey personnel, government officials, military officers, business leaders, and professional geographers. While the AAG came to represent professional exclusivity and the NGS championed mass-market popularization, this study pays particular attention to the AGS, arguably the most complex of the three. It was in the AGS's contested "middle ground" – navigating between scholarly ambition, public engagement, and state service – that the idea of geographical societies as mediating institutions comes most clearly into view.

Sources, Methods, and Structure

I treat geography as a cultural product whose institutional practices and representational discourses must be examined together. Thus, this study draws on a broad array of sources to illuminate the inner workings of geographical knowledge production. To trace the relationships between knowledge and power, I examine a diverse set of primary sources, including internal documents that expose decision-making processes and tensions typically invisible in published outputs. These sources encompass the private papers of geographers (manuscripts, correspondence, notebooks); internal society documents (circular letters, minutes of meetings, field trip reports); accounts of society activities from newspapers and other publications; and the societies' own published materials (maps, lectures, journals, and annual reports).[39] This extensive source base moves the analysis beyond published outputs to demonstrate how these institutions constructed and legitimized geographical knowledge. While all three national societies (AGS, NGS, AAG) and many regional ones appear throughout, the AGS offers the most comprehensive and accessible archival record. I therefore use the AGS as a lens through which broader disciplinary patterns become evident, supplemented by targeted analyses of the NGS and AAG where their practices diverged, especially concerning popularization and professionalization.

To capture the overlapping and recursive nature of institutional development, this study is organized thematically rather than chronologically. The chapters analyze how societies organized, professionalized, circulated, disseminated, and represented knowledge. This thematic structure facilitates examining overlapping developments from multiple angles, effectively triangulating the analysis across chapters.[40] Consequently, the chapters intentionally interweave, offering multiple perspectives on shared phenomena.

---

39 Inevitably, archival constraints shape any historical study, and mine is no exception. AGS Council minutes from the 1870s and 1880s have gone missing, while access to NGS institutional records remains restricted. Most smaller societies keep no archives at all. Nevertheless, rare bulletins, yearbooks, handbooks, and pamphlets from the *Geographic Society of Chicago* provide a window into a typical local society, while the University of Chicago's Rollin D. Salisbury papers illuminate the university's geography program and its local society.

40 The idea for this metaphor and aspects of my approach come from David Gugerli and Daniel Speich, *Topografien der Nation. Politik, kartografische Ordnung und Landschaft im 19. Jahrhundert* (Zürich: Chronos-Verlag, 2002).

This approach highlights the historically contingent nature of geographical knowledge by demonstrating how specific practices shaped what counted as legitimate geography at different times. Chapter 1 establishes the theoretical foundations for a history of knowledge centered on geographical societies. Chapter 2 details the organization of U.S. geographical societies, examining their institutional structures, networks, and civic functions as foundational elements shaping knowledge production. Chapter 3 analyzes the uneven process of professionalization, emphasizing boundary-work, disciplinary legitimation, and institutional strategy. Chapter 4 investigates the circulation of knowledge, conceptualizing societies as "centers of calculation" that managed and stabilized knowledge flowing from distant field sites. Chapter 5 examines dissemination through lectures and publications, exploring the negotiation between popularization and scientific authority. Finally, Chapter 6 analyzes how institutional practices culminated in geographical representations legitimizing American Empire, with a case study on constructing the Pacific as an imperial space. Taken together, these chapters reveal the interconnected processes through which U.S. geographical societies mediated knowledge and power at the turn of the twentieth century.

1 Theory and Method: A History of Knowledge

Understanding how U.S. geographical societies mediated knowledge and consolidated authority requires a specific analytical approach. It is not enough to know *what* they produced in their publications; we must also ask *how* their claims accrued credibility and *where* their knowledge was produced. This chapter synthesizes a "spatial history of knowledge" from three theoretical perspectives to establish the analytical framework for this study: (1) the constructed, contingent, and situated nature of scientific knowledge; (2) a history-of-knowledge perspective attentive to practices, actors, and knowledge circulation beyond academia; and (3) a focus on the spatial dimensions of knowledge. Seen through this framework, the societies were not neutral venues for science, but mediating institutions that constructed the knowledge they presented as discovery.

Situated Science, Situated Knowledge

This study builds on a fundamental insight: scientific knowledge, despite its claims to objectivity, is always historically, culturally, and spatially situated, as historians of science and geography have convincingly demonstrated.[1] As historical geographer David Livingstone succinctly argues, "science is not above culture; it is part of culture".[2] This recognition is particularly important

---

1   Steven Shapin, *Never Pure: Historical Studies of Science as If It Was Produced by People with Bodies, Situated in Time, Space, Culture, and Society, and Struggling for Credibility and Authority* (Baltimore: Johns Hopkins University Press, 2010); see also Donna Haraway, "Situated Knowledges: The Science Question in Feminism and the Privilege of Partial Perspective," *Feminist Studies* 14, no. 3 (1988): 575–99.

2   David N. Livingstone, *Putting Science in Its Place: Geographies of Scientific Knowledge* (Chicago: University of Chicago Press, 2003), 13.

for understanding geographical societies, which claimed scientific objectivity while operating as cultural institutions embedded in elite networks with explicit national and imperial commitments. Social constructivist historians have shown scientists to be social actors whose practices, influenced by wider contextual forces, produce knowledge.[3] Bruno Latour, while likewise foregrounding practice ("science in action"), focuses specifically on the networks through which knowledge claims circulate, gain strength, and pass obligatory passage points.[4] This network-oriented perspective is especially illuminating for understanding geographical societies, as their authority rested as much on the effectiveness of institutional networks as on empirical accuracy.

From History of Science to History of Knowledge

Yet the term "science" alone is too narrow a category for capturing the diverse activities and knowledge claims of geographical societies. These institutions published rigorous geodetic surveys, popular travel narratives, statistical compilations, and speculative theories about race and climate – all of which were considered legitimate forms of geographical knowledge by contemporary standards. A conventional history of science might treat these as separate phenomena, whereas a history-of-knowledge perspective recognizes them as parts of a single knowledge-making system.[5] This shift from science to knowledge as the primary analytical category is essential for understanding geographical societies as mediating institutions, whose activities often blurred the lines between scholarly research, state service, and popular engagement. A history-of-knowledge approach thus captures knowledge production and circulation beyond academic institutions. It encompasses a wider range of actors (including amateurs, entrepreneurs, merchants, and state officials) and forms of knowledge (such as popular geography and travel writing). Accordingly, this

---

3   Jan Golinski, *Making Natural Knowledge: Constructivism and the History of Science* (Cambridge: Cambridge University Press, 1998).

4   Bruno Latour and Steve Woolgar, *Laboratory Life: The Social Construction of Scientific Facts* (Los Angeles: Sage, 1979); Bruno Latour, *Science in Action: How to Follow Scientists and Engineers through Society* (Cambridge, Mass.: Harvard University Press, 1987).

5   For an overview of recent developments in the history of knowledge, see Johan Östling, "Circulation, Arenas, and the Quest for Public Knowledge: Historiographical Currents and Analytical Frameworks," *History and Theory* 59, no. 4 (2020): 111–126.

study follows recent scholarship that shifts from an academia-centric history of science toward a more expansive history of knowledge.[6]

This study's analytical framework is guided by Philipp Sarasin's approach to the history of knowledge, which places systems of knowledge at the center of historical analysis.[7] Sarasin argues that historians should "describe the world [...] through the discursive, medial, personal, and institutional forms of knowledge" that connect subjects, artifacts, and actions to social reality.[8] Following Sarasin, this study focuses on the production and circulation of knowledge through institutions, media, amateurs, experts, and publics. The aim is to investigate knowledge as a historical phenomenon by asking how, when, and why certain claims emerge and become authoritative, rather than assessing their ultimate validity. Knowledge is therefore inherently hybrid: even ostensibly objective scientific knowledge retains traces of the conditions that shaped it.[9] For U.S. geographical societies, this hybridity meant that their practices and publications reflected the nationalist currents, imperial aspirations, and elite social networks that constituted their institutional milieu.

Drawing on Fleck's concept of *Denkstil* and Foucault's orders of knowledge, Sarasin proposes four analytical directions that guide this study:[10]

(1) *Systematization and Orders of Knowledge*: Examining the discursive systems that order, produce, and stabilize knowledge, thereby differentiating it from non-knowledge. For geographical societies, this involves analyzing how specific organizational and professional practices created historically contingent notions of objectivity, evidence, and proof (central to the discussion of organization and demarcation in Chapters 2 and 3).

---

6   Jürgen Renn, "From the History of Science to the History of Knowledge – and Back," *Centaurus* 57, no. 1 (2015): 37–53; Lorraine Daston, "The History of Science and the History of Knowledge," *KNOW: A Journal on the Formation of Knowledge* 1, no. 1 (2017), 131–54; Peter Burke, *What is the History of Knowledge?* (Cambridge: Polity Press, 2016), 4.

7   Philipp Sarasin, "Was ist Wissensgeschichte?," *Internationales Archiv für Sozialgeschichte der deutschen* Literatur 36, no. 1 (2011), 159–72.

8   Sarasin, "*Wissensgeschichte*", 172. This and all subsequent translations from Sarasin are my own.

9   Sarasin, "*Wissensgeschichte*", 164–166.

10   Ludwik Fleck, *Entstehung und Entwicklung einer wissenschaftlichen Tatsache: Einführung in die Lehre vom Denkstil und Denkkollektiv* (Basel: Schwabe, 1935); Michel Foucault, *The Order of Things: An Archaeology of the Human Sciences* (London: Tavistock, 1970); Michel Foucault, *The Archaeology of Knowledge* (New York: Vintage Books, 1982).

(2) *Mediality and the Representation of Knowledge*: Investigating how media store, transport, represent, and transform knowledge. These media function as filters that select, emphasize, or suppress information. For example, field notes, map sketches, and magazine articles produced by geographers shaped what could be known about space, particularly as knowledge circulated between expert and popular contexts (informing the analysis of circulation, dissemination, and representation in Chapters 4–6).

(3) *Actors of Knowledge*: Analyzing individuals and the specific functions they perform within knowledge networks. In Sarasin's view, authority derives less from social roles than from an association with valued knowledge, thereby coupling knowledge with power. Expertise in spatial matters thus became a source of political influence, a lens applied in Chapter 3 on professionalization and throughout the study to assess the influence of prominent society members.

(4) *Genealogies of Knowledge*: Conducting discourse analyses that connect media, institutions, actors, and practices to reveal the power relations underlying knowledge systems (particularly relevant to the analysis of imperial dimensions in Chapter 6).[11]

These elements are analytically inseparable: the actors of knowledge (such as explorers), for example, used specific media (such as maps) to conform to the standards of evidence (discursive systems) of their society. Building on Sarasin's model, this study integrates social context with individual agency, acknowledging that individual motivations operated within knowledge systems that Peter Burke has described as "networks of opportunities and constraints".[12] Thus, while individual society members could influence what counted as legitimate geographical knowledge, they could do so only within institutional boundaries.

---

11   Sarasin, "*Wissensgeschichte*", 167–172.

12   Burke, *What is the History of Knowledge?*, 118–19; Suzanne Marchand, "How Much Knowledge is Worth Knowing? An American Intellectual Historian's Thoughts on the Geschichte des Wissens," *Berichte zur Wissenschaftsgeschichte* 42, no. 2–3 (2019): 142.

Geographies of Knowledge

This study incorporates the spatial dimensions of knowledge, stressing the significance of place and space in its production and circulation.[13] Geographical knowledge is spatial in a double sense: it is *about* space, and it is *produced and circulated through* specific networks and sites. For geographical societies, the locations where knowledge was produced – including society headquarters, libraries, and the field – were instrumental in shaping which claims gained credibility and influence. Control over these places thus became essential for commanding knowledge itself.

As historical geographers Livingstone and Withers have demonstrated, "matters of space are fundamentally involved at every stage in the acquisition of scientific knowledge."[14] Starting from the premise that knowledge is inherently "local, situated, and embedded",[15] they assert that "where things happen is crucial to knowing how and why they happen".[16] It follows from this spatial perspective that knowledge does not simply exist, but must be produced *somewhere* and circulated *elsewhere*. This circulation transforms knowledge as each site imposes its own logics, standards, and purposes on the information passing through it. For instance, geographical societies managed their spatial networks to stabilize and validate information flowing between the field and metropolitan centers, a practice examined in Chapter 4. As Livingstone and Withers argue, science has not only a history and a sociology, but also a geography. Scholars exploring "spaces of knowledge" have highlighted how

---

13   James A. Secord, "Knowledge in Transit", Isis 95, no. 4 (2004): 654–672.

14   Livingstone, *Putting Science in its Place*, 12. On the spatial turn in the history of geography see: Steven Shapin, "Placing the View from Nowhere: Historical and Sociological Problems in the Location of Science," *Transactions of the Institute of British Geographers* 23 (1998): 5–12; Diarmid A. Finnegan, "The spatial turn: geographical approaches in the history of science," *Journal of the History of Biology* 41, no. 2 (2008): 369–388; Adi Ophir and Steven Shapin, "The Place of Knowledge: A Methodological Survey," *Science in Context* 4, no. 1 (1991): 3–21; Crosbie Smith, Jon Agar, and Gerald Schmidt, *Making Space for Science: Territorial Themes in the Shaping of Knowledge* (New York: St. Martin's Press, 1998); Diarmid A. Finnegan, ed., *Spaces of Global Knowledge* (Farnham: Ashgate, 2015); Simon Naylor, *Historical Geographies of Science* (Cambridge: Cambridge University Press, 2005); Peter Meusburger, *Geographies of Science* (Dordrecht: Springer Netherlands, 2010).

15   Shapin, "Placing the View from Nowhere," 6.

16   Charles W. J. Withers and David N. Livingstone, "Thinking Geographically about Nineteenth-Century Science," in *Geographies of Nineteenth-Century Science*, ed. Charles W. J. Withers and David N. Livingstone (Chicago: University of Chicago Press, 2011), 2–3.

specific locations and spaces shape scientific practice and claims, informing this study's focus on sites and circulation.[17] Building on this scholarship, this study treats place and space as influential factors in the history of scientific knowledge and examines the dynamic interplay between knowledge, space, and power.

Emphasizing situatedness does not deny the genuine attempts of historical actors to pursue truth. Rather, it underscores the historically and spatially contingent nature of what becomes accepted as valid and authoritative knowledge within specific communities and contexts.[18] Livingstone notes that "at different points in time and in different geographical contexts, people have been justified in holding scientific opinions and beliefs that lack credibility in other space-time circumstances."[19] This contingency helps explain how geographical societies exercised power: not necessarily by discovering objective truths, but by establishing themselves as arbiters of legitimate geographical knowledge.

Framework: Toward a Spatial History of Knowledge

These three theoretical perspectives – situated knowledge, history of knowledge, and spatial dimensions of knowledge – converge on a central insight: knowledge claims gain authority not only from empirical claims, but also through institutional processes that occur in specific places and circulate through networks. This framework analyzes the production and circulation of socially constructed geographical knowledge within U.S. geographical societies, with particular attention to their spatially situated discursive and material practices. It asks not whether the knowledge produced was objectively "true", but how it became powerful by gaining credibility and circulating

---

17   Livingstone, *Putting Science in its Place*, 1; *Geography and Enlightenment*, ed. David N. Livingstone and Charles W. J. Withers (Chicago: University of Chicago Press, 1999); *Geography and Revolution*, ed. David N. Livingstone and Charles W. J. Withers (Chicago: University of Chicago Press, 2005); *Geographies of Nineteenth-Century Science*, ed. David N. Livingstone and Charles W. J. Withers; Charles W. J. Withers, "Towards a History of Geography in the Public Sphere," *History of Science* 37, no. 1 (1999): 45–78; Charles W. J. Withers, *Geography, Science, and National Identity: Scotland since 1520* (Cambridge: Cambridge University Press, 2001).

18   Livingstone, *Putting Science in its Place*, 13–14.

19   Livingstone, *Putting Science in its Place*, 185.

effectively through networks. This approach shows that geographical societies were complex institutions operating at multiple scales, each involving different practices of knowledge mediation. Locally, they functioned as elite social clubs where knowledge production intertwined with civic initiatives. Nationally, they served as nodes in networks linking science, state, and commerce. Internationally, they participated in global networks of scientific institutions that enhanced legitimacy for their claims to spatial expertise. At each scale, societies transformed knowledge, often to serve specific purposes, while presenting their knowledge as objective and universal despite its particular origins. The following chapters develop this argument through empirical analysis of their organizational structures, professional practices, circulation patterns, dissemination strategies, and representational techniques. Ultimately, these analyses provide a reinterpretation of the role U.S. geographical societies played in nation-building and empire-building, contributing new insights into the relationship between knowledge, institutions, and power.

2 Organizing Knowledge

In 1895, the Council of the American Geographical Society (AGS) confronted an apparently minor but telling dispute. A society member had withheld his annual dues, dissatisfied with a recent lecture he felt had unduly popularized and politicized geography.[1] Only after the Council privately assured him that they, too, found the lecturer "objectionable", did he agree to pay.[2] Although seemingly trivial, this incident highlights an inherent contradiction within geographical societies: they were deeply embedded in networks of social power, financial dependency, and politics that constrained their autonomy and shaped their knowledge-making practices. To understand how these societies mediated and organized knowledge, this chapter examines not only their formal structures and constitutions, but also the unwritten rules and informal power dynamics that determined what members could know, discuss, and publish.

The power to mediate knowledge begins with organization: membership rules, venues, and budgets structure who can speak, what counts as evidence, and how claims circulate. This chapter argues that the organizational structures, membership policies, and civic functions of U.S. geographical societies were not simply administrative, but were mechanisms through which societies claimed authority over geography itself. Geographical societies operated as knowledge-producing institutions that shaped U.S. geography through three interconnected processes: first, by establishing the institutional networks that determined who could produce legitimate geographical knowledge; second,

---

1   AGS member to Walter R. T. Jones, Treasurer of AGS, 4.1.1895, Box 15, Folder 13, AGSNY AC 1, *American Geographical Society of New York Records, 1723–2010, bulk 1854–2000, American Geographical Society Library, University of Wisconsin-Milwaukee Libraries* (hereafter AGS Archives).

2   AGS member to A. A. Rave, Recording Secretary of AGS, 25.1.1895, Box 15, Folder 13, AGS Archives.

by regulating access to geographical authority and knowledge through mechanisms such as membership criteria; and third, by grounding geographical knowledge in local and national contexts through civic science. Through a detailed examination of major national societies and smaller local ones, this chapter shows how seemingly neutral organizational decisions had consequences for what counted as authoritative geographical knowledge and who could legitimately claim expertise.

2.1 Institutional Landscape: Metropolitan Centers and Regional Outposts

This section examines U.S. geographical societies as institutions whose organizational forms and spatial distribution were fundamental to their epistemic authority. It situates them within the wider landscape of nineteenth-century American science, tracing their development alongside the global proliferation of learned societies while highlighting distinctive national characteristics. Particular attention is given to the emergence of large national societies alongside local geographical societies, with a focus on their spatial distribution across the United States and the implications of this geography for knowledge production.

As established in the preceding chapter, knowledge production occurs within systems that set standards for differentiating legitimate knowledge from non-knowledge. To understand how geographical knowledge was organized in nineteenth-century America, it is essential to analyze the institutional frameworks that structured its production and circulation, particularly geographical societies. Michael Heffernan defines learned societies as "associations of individuals sharing common intellectual interests and objectives, usually outlined in a formal constitution", a definition that helps differentiate them from clubs devoted only to recreation or exploration.[3] To further distinguish geographical societies from local hiking or exploration clubs, this study focuses specifically on societies that explicitly included "geography" in their name and engaged in disseminating geographical knowledge through publications or lectures. Heffernan regards learned societies as among the "most important creative sites within which scientific theories have developed

---

3   Michael Heffernan, "Learned Societies," in *The Sage Handbook of Geographical Knowledge*, ed. John A. Agnew and David N. Livingstone (Los Angeles: Sage, 2011), 111.

and circulated since the Renaissance".[4] Similarly, Alexandra Oleson concludes that learned societies were "the dominant elements in the organized pursuit of knowledge in America" during the first half of the nineteenth century. This claim remained largely true for U.S. geography through the century's second half, given the comparatively late institutionalization of academic geography.[5]

An institutional lens is essential for several reasons. First, as noted previously, historians of science increasingly advocate a "mid-scale history" approach, which analyzes long-term developments at scientific institutions rather than focusing solely on isolated microhistories.[6] Second, Lisa Malich reinforces this view by highlighting institutions as nodes where discourses and practices intersect, enabling historians to trace knowledge circulation through scientific networks.[7] Third, Martin Daunton emphasizes "the relationship between what is known and how it is organized", proposing that the organization of knowledge influences its content – and vice versa.[8] Institutions that produce, store, and circulate geographical knowledge are therefore central to this history. In nineteenth-century America, geographical societies operated at the center of a wider system of knowledge that included universities, surveys, government bureaus, and other scientific bodies. They often functioned as intermediaries between scientific research and state policy, an important dynamic explored in later chapters.[9] Studying these institutions illuminates the power relations underlying scientific knowledge production and validation. As sites of knowledge production, geographical societies determined the standards, practices, and forms of evidence that constituted legitimate geographical knowledge. Through lectures, publications, and expeditions, and

---

4 Ibid., 111.

5 Alexandra Oleson, "Introduction: To Build a New Intellectual Order," in *The Pursuit of Knowledge in the Early American Republic: American Scientific and Learned Societies from Colonial Times to the Civil War*, ed. Alexandra Oleson and Sanborn C. Brown (Baltimore: Johns Hopkins University Press, 1976), xxiv.

6 Robert E. Kohler and Kathryn M. Olesko, "Introduction: Clio Meets Science," *Osiris* 27, no. 1 (2012): 1–16.

7 Lisa Malich, "Eine Zukunft der Wissenschaftsgeschichte liegt in der Institution," *Berichte zur Wissenschaftsgeschichte* 41, no. 4 (2018): 395–98.

8 Martin Daunton, "Introduction," in *The Organisation of Knowledge in Victorian Britain*, ed. Martin Daunton (Oxford: Oxford University Press, 2005), 10.

9 Mitchell Ash, "Wissenschaft und Politik als Ressourcen füreinander," in *Wissenschaften und Wissenschaftspolitik: Bestandsaufnahmen zu Formationen, Brüchen und Kontinuitäten in Deutschland des 20. Jahrhunderts*, ed. Rüdiger vom Bruch and Brigitte Kaderas (Stuttgart: Franz Steiner, 2002), 32–51.

by controlling membership, these societies shaped whose knowledge claims were recognized. This institutional power positioned geographical societies centrally in the "geography of science", enabling them to influence where, how, and by whom geographical knowledge was produced.

A Geography of American Science: Institutional Centers and Regional Power

The geography of knowledge production is essential for understanding how geographical societies operated. Following David Livingstone's assertion that science has a geography as well as a history, this subsection examines how regional and national patterns of scientific development shaped the institutional landscape of U.S. geography.[10] While scientists typically present their knowledge as universal, it is produced in specific places shaped by regional cultures and distinct "national styles" of science.[11] These influences are not just contextual, but shape scientific practices and knowledge claims.[12] American science in this period was, for example, characterized by national peculiarities that contributed to a delayed formation of scientific societies relative to Europe.[13] During this period, U.S. geography was overwhelmingly practical, empirical, and closely tied to the utilitarian goals of state-sponsored surveys and commercial expansion – in contrast to the more theoretical European traditions.

The spatial organization of American science showed significant regional disparities, most notably the dominance of the Northeast as the nation's intellectual hub throughout much of the nineteenth century. Such regional concentration of scientific institutions shaped who could produce authoritative knowledge and which research questions would be prioritized. Consequently, certain perspectives (urban, northeastern, elite) dominated American geographical thought, while others remained marginalized. As one historian notes in his statistical profile of American scientists, the typical mid-nine-

---

10   See Livingstone, *Putting Science in its Place*, on "geography of science".
11   Livingstone, *Putting Science in its Place*, 15.
12   Livingstone, *Putting Science in its Place*, 88.
13   David E. Allen, "Amateurs and Professionals," in *The Cambridge History of Science*, vol. 6, ed. Peter J. Bowler and John V. Pickstone (Cambridge: Cambridge University Press, 2009), 24.

teenth-century scientist was born in Massachusetts, educated at Harvard, and later taught at a Massachusetts college.[14]

While westward expansion progressed and land-grant colleges facilitated the growth of scientific institutions in the Midwest and West, the South remained comparatively marginal in terms of scientific output and institutional development. Scientific societies followed a similar pattern, with most of them located in the Northeast, a growing number in the West, and very few in the South.[15] The American Association for the Advancement of Science (AAAS), the leading forum for scientists in the mid-nineteenth century, was predominantly composed of Northeastern members.[16] By mid-century, the first scientific societies were established beyond the Appalachian Mountains and, later, beyond the Mississippi River. The South's already low number of scientific societies declined further after the Civil War, limiting the region's scientific contributions.[17] The first sustained geographical society in the South, the Southern Geographic Society in Knoxville, was not founded until 1914.[18] This clustering of the nation's major scientific institutions in the Northeast meant that geographical societies based there initially held disproportionate authority in defining national standards for geographical knowledge.

During the late nineteenth century, Washington, D.C., with its numerous government agencies and scientific bureaus, emerged as a second scientific center of national importance. Robert Bruce identifies a "brain drain" from New England to the North Central states and the capital.[19] Geographers were particularly drawn to Washington, attracted by scientific bureaus and agencies, such as the U.S. Geological Survey, the Coast and Geodetic Survey, and military departments. An 1898 article in the *Journal* of the AGS celebrated the establishment of the Washington Academy of Sciences: "There is probably no

14   Robert V. Bruce, "A Statistical Profile of American Scientists, 1846–1876," in *Nineteenth-Century American Science: A Reappraisal*, ed. George H. Daniels (Evanston: Northwestern University Press, 1972), 91.

15   Ralph Samuel Bates, *Scientific Societies in the United States* (Cambridge, Mass.: MIT Press, 1965), 84.

16   Keith Benson and Jane Meienschein, "Introduction: AAAS Narrative History," in *The Establishment of Science in America: 150 Years of the American Association for the Advancement of Science*, ed. Sally G. Kohlstedt, Michael M. Sokal, and Bruce V. Lewenstein (New Brunswick: Rutgers University Press, 1999), 7.

17   Bates, *Scientific Societies*, 51.

18   "Geographical Record," *Bulletin of the American Geographical Society* 46, no. 9 (1914): 682.

19   Bruce, "Statistical Profile," 80.

city in the country in which there is such a large group of investigators as in Washington, owing to the development there of the many bureaus and offices of the Government having to do with lines of original research."[20] Geographers in Washington became embedded in governmental institutions, positioning geographical societies like the Washington-based NGS as intermediaries between science and the state. Simultaneously, many government-funded scientists moved westward, where they organized local scientific societies and established the short-lived Western Academy of Natural Sciences.[21] In both Washington and the West, geographers followed government funding to regions where their expertise was in demand. Accordingly, the geography of American science, marked initially by Northeastern dominance and later by governmental centralization in Washington, created an uneven institutional landscape that influenced how and where geographical knowledge was produced and validated.

U.S. Societies in Global Context: Models and Operations

U.S. geographical societies looked to European societies as models for legitimacy and organizational structure, but developed their own distinctive identity. Shaped by a unique context of continental expansion, delayed academic professionalization, and reliance on private patronage rather than state support, they developed an institutional hybridity that differentiated them from European societies. This subsection outlines the core components of scientific institutions, such as organizational structure, objectives, membership, publications, and activities, and situates U.S. societies in a global context to highlight similarities and differences.

The number of national learned societies in the U.S. grew steadily throughout the nineteenth century, exceeding 100 by 1900, with one-third located in Washington, D.C.[22] The *Handbook of Learned Societies* listed 120 national and 550 local societies by 1908. Before the Civil War, most scientific societies operated on the local or state level, but toward the end of the century, practitioners in

---

20   "Washington Letter," *Journal of the American Geographical Society of New York* 30, no. 1 (1898): 69.

21   Henry D. Shapiro, "The Western Academy of Natural Sciences of Cincinnati and the Structure of Science in the Ohio Valley," in *Pursuit of Knowledge*, ed. Oleson and Brown, 220.

22   Heffernan, "Learned Societies," 114.

many disciplines formed national associations (e.g., the American Historical Association, founded in 1884; the Geological Society of America, 1888; and the American Anthropological Association, 1902).[23]

While learned societies proliferated globally throughout the nineteenth century, U.S. geographical societies developed relatively slowly, influenced by European precedents yet constrained by the fragmented and decentralized nature of U.S. science. In Europe, geographical societies were founded in nearly all major capitals in the first half of the century, whereas most U.S. geographical societies appeared only in the last quarter of the century, specifically in Washington, San Francisco, Philadelphia, Chicago, Seattle, and Baltimore. The only early exception was the AGS, founded in New York in 1851. By this time, European societies had already developed extensive institutional networks. The British African Association (1788), founded as the Association for Promoting the Discovery of the Interior Parts of Africa, served as the prototype for later geographical societies. It was absorbed into the Royal Geographical Society (RGS, 1830), which became the largest and most influential geographical society in the world, sponsoring costly expeditions as early as the 1830s and 1840s.[24] The first society that explicitly referred to geography in its name was the Paris *Société de géographie* (1821), soon followed by the first German geographical society, the *Gesellschaft für Erdkunde zu Berlin* (1828). Additional societies were soon founded in Vienna (1855), Leipzig (1861) and Munich (1869).[25] Even in the Western Hemisphere, the *Instituto Histórico e Geográfico Brasileiro* (1838) and the *Sociedad Mexicana de Geografía* (1839) both predated the AGS (1851). By 1900, over 120 geographical societies existed worldwide, predominantly in Europe.[26]

European geographical societies served as models for U.S. societies, engaging in activities such as organizing meetings, lectures, expeditions, and publications covering domestic and international geography. In the United States, geographical societies assumed an especially important role in defining legitimate geographical knowledge, given the nation's fragmented scientific landscape and the delayed professionalization of geography. Until 1914, three

---

23   James and Martin, *Association of American Geographers*, 3.

24   Max Jones, "Measuring the World: Exploration, Empire and the Reform of the Royal Geographical Society, c. 1874–93," in *Organisation of Knowledge*, ed. Daunton, 316.

25   WinfriedSchenk, *Allgemeine Anthropogeographie* (Gotha: Klett-Perthes, 2005), 55.

26   Agnew and Livingstone, *Handbook of Geographical Knowledge*, 120.

major societies dominated U.S. geography: The American Geographical Society (AGS, founded originally as the American Geographical and Statistical
Society in 1851), the oldest U.S. geographical society and primary focus of this
book; the National Geographic Society (NGS, 1888), which had become known
for its aggressive popularization of geography by the early twentieth century;
and the Association of American Geographers (AAG, 1904), which presented
itself as a more scholarly alternative to the AGS and the NGS.

The AGS declared its objectives as follows: "to investigate and disseminate
new geographical information by discussion, lectures and publication; to
establish in the chief maritime city of the country, for the benefit of commerce, navigation, and the great industrial and material interests of the
United States, a place where the means will be afforded of obtaining accurate information for public use of every part of the habitable globe."[27] These
objectives reflect the society's early self-perception as a provider of accurate
geographical knowledge, while also highlighting two important contexts: its
close connections to commercial interests and the alignment with national
priorities. Despite these, all societies presented themselves as independent
arbiters of geographical knowledge, stressing their objectivity and impartiality in founding documents, lectures, and publications. The *National Geographic
Magazine* asserted in its guiding principles: "The first principle is absolute
accuracy. Nothing must be printed that is not strictly according to fact [and]
nothing of partisan or controversial character is printed".[28] However, as this
study will show, these claims of pure objectivity frequently stood in tension
with the actual practices of knowledge production within these societies.

The AGS's professed commitment to impartiality is illustrated, for instance, in its handling of the "race for the Pole". In 1904, the AGS Council
declined a request from Robert E. Peary, one of the leading explorers of his
time and then-president of the AGS, to hire a stenographer and administrator,
based at the society headquarters, for his North Pole expedition. Explaining
the decision, Councilor Chandler Robbins articulated the society's desired
self-image, writing: "Ours is a building where prevail the quiet and calm
suited to study and literary composition. To introduce there the bustling ways
of business incidental to the fitting out of expeditions of exploration may in-
terfere seriously with the methodical and regular transaction of the ordinary

---

27   "Front Matter," *Journal of the American Geographical Society of New York* 11 (1879): i–lv.
28   Gilbert H. Grosvenor, "Seven Principles," *National Geographic Magazine* 17, no. 3 (1915):
      318–320 (hereafter *NGM*).

business of the society [...]." Robbins defined the society's work as detached, scholarly contemplation rather than the messy business of exploration. He further cautioned that associating the society too closely with a single expedition would create "a troublesome precedent". He pointed out that another AGS fellow, William Ziegler, was also undertaking an expedition to the North Pole, arguing that "Mr. Ziegler is part owner of the property of the Society and is as much entitled to have the resources and premises used for the purposes of his expedition as Mr. Peary is to have them used for his" (emphasis in original). Instead of taking sides in the rivalry between the explorers, Robbins insisted that the society remain impartial, "concerned only with the increase of knowledge, and must not allow itself to be carried away by any desire to promote the fame of one explorer more than that of another."[29] By placing itself above the ambitions of wealthy members, the AGS projected an image of objective arbitration, even as its authority depended on their financial support, a reminder of the practical limits and strategic uses of neutrality.

Local Societies: Regional Work and National Aims

While national societies such as the AGS, NGS, and AAG were central to the organization and professionalization of U.S. geography, a network of local societies connected geographical knowledge to regional contexts. These local societies disseminated geographical knowledge, often in alignment with specific local commercial, educational, or civic interests. This subsection explores the functions, membership composition, and activities of these smaller societies in chronological order of founding: Geographical Society of the Pacific (San Francisco, 1881), the Geographical Society of California (1891), the Geographical Club of Philadelphia (1891, later renamed the Geographical Society of Philadelphia), the Geographic Society of Chicago (1898), the Alaska Geographical Society (1898), and the Geographical Society of Baltimore (1902). The following analysis examines both the diversity and shared characteristics of these local societies through representative examples in order to illustrate their role within the wider system of U.S. geography.

Founding documents and bylaws illustrate the varying objectives and priorities. The Geographical Society of Baltimore, for example, was explicitly established for "the promotion and diffusion of geographical knowledge, more

---

29   Robbins to Jesup, 22.10.1904, Box 129, Folder 3, AGS *Archives*.

particularly of that which is of commercial importance to Baltimore".[30] In contrast, The Geographic Society of Chicago emphasized education and research, aiming for the "advancement of the science of geography; in exploration and the making of researches; in the discussion of geographic theory and methods of presentation and instruction; and in the interchange of experiences of travel at home and abroad."[31] The Geographical Society of California prioritized acquiring and disseminating geographical knowledge. It hosted monthly lectures by "travelers or qualified scientists", sponsored explorations "on this Coast or elsewhere", invited naval officers to document "points of geographical interest, changes of currents, climatic variations, or other phenomena", and organized a library, a regular publication, and regular meetings. These varied objectives show a shared commitment to dissemination, but also demonstrate how missions were tailored to regional economic or civic agendas, reflecting the situated nature of knowledge production. The California society was highly active in its first year: it attracted 438 members, accumulated over 1,000 books in its library, and established publication exchanges with more than 100 societies in over thirty countries.[32]

The Alaska Geographical Society represents the most explicit fusion of geographical knowledge with territorial and economic agendas. Founded in Seattle in 1898, it rapidly grew to over 500 members in two years. Unlike societies primarily focused on education and outreach, it actively promoted exploration aligned explicitly with U.S. commercial and governmental interests in Alaska and the Pacific. Its objectives included "to encourage Geographical exploration and discovery"; the dissemination of geographical information through meetings, lectures, and publications; the establishment of a library, including a collection of maps, charts, and photographs; as well as establishing correspondence with other societies and geographers. Alongside these standard goals, the society explicitly adopted a commercial mission focused on Alaska and the Pacific: "to foster commerce and navigation; to promote the great industrial, educational and material interests of Alaska and the islands and countries of the Pacific".[33] At the society's inauguration, honorary president John G. Brady (Governor of Alaska), underscored this scientific-commercial mission, stating:

---

30   Brian W. Blouet, "Preface," in *Origins of Academic Geography*, ed. Blouet, x.
31   The Geographic Society of Chicago, "Preliminary Announcement 1907–08," 2.
32   "Annual Proceedings," *Bulletin of the Geographical Society of California* 2, no. 2 (1894): 3–10.
33   "Front matter," *Bulletin of the Alaska Geographical Society* (October 1900), AGS Archives.

"The vast area of unexplored territory within the borders of Alaska, the magnificent results which follow the development of its mineral and agricultural
resources make Alaska an unrivaled field for geographical research and discovery, and your Society is worthy of hearty encouragement and support."[34] More
explicitly than other contemporary U.S. geographical societies, the Alaska Geographical Society linked exploration, governmental support, and economic
goals, illustrating how local institutional actors aligned knowledge production
with political and economic agendas.

The Geographical Society of Philadelphia, initially founded as the Geographical Club of Philadelphia (1891), sought "the advancement of the science
of geography and of geographical studies and exploration, the recording of
discoveries, the presentation of researches, and the accumulation of works on
geography". Like other local geographical societies, it engaged in international
publication exchange, hosted regular meetings, and published scholarly materials. In 1897, the society expanded its objectives to include "the interchange
of experiences of travel at home and abroad", incorporating more amateur
participation in geography. In addition, the inclusion of photographic exhibitions and the "accumulation of [...] photographs of scenery and people"
suggests a move toward a more popular form of pictorial geography.[35] While
this inclusion of popular elements was not unusual, it was rarely formally
codified in the societies' bylaws or charters.

Distinct from geographical societies, though sometimes overlapping in
membership or interest, were associations organized primarily by explorers,
travelers, and mountaineers, often driven more by adventure, sport, or specific exploration campaigns than by scientific motivations. These included
the Appalachian Mountain Club (founded in 1876), the Sierra Club (1892), the
Mazamas (1894; focused on mountain exploration in the Pacific Northwest),
the Peary Arctic Club (1898), the American Alpine Club (1902) and the Explorers
Club (1904).[36] Although often less scientifically inclined, many of these clubs
maintained close contact and regular exchange with geographical societies.
The Appalachian Mountain Club, for instance, was listed as one of the inviting

34   Ibid.

35   Mary Peary Stafford, "History of the Society," in History 1891–1960: Geographical Soci-
      ety of Philadelphia, ed. Geographical Society of Philadelphia (Philadelphia: The Society,
      1960), 5–15.

36   Bates, Scientific Societies, 103.

societies at the 1904 Eighth International Geographic Congress, held in the United States, alongside major geographical societies.

Despite intermittent financial challenges and organizational difficulties, local geographical societies contributed significantly to the production and dissemination of geographical knowledge at both local and national levels. Local societies occupied an ambiguous position: institutionally autonomous with their own governance and finances, yet intellectually functioning as nodes in a national network, hosting traveling lecturers, exchanging publications, and drawing legitimacy from connections to national organizations. Their activities demonstrate the diverse and decentralized nature of U.S. geography, showing that knowledge was shaped not only by elite national institutions, but also by regional civic associations with distinct priorities and knowledge-making practices. Embedded in regional contexts, local societies developed specialized expertise about local environments, while simultaneously connecting these regional landscapes to broader national and imperial narratives. The Geographical Society of the Pacific, for example, positioned San Francisco as the gateway for U.S. interests in Asia, producing geographical knowledge that emphasized transpacific trade (further explored in Chapter 6). Similarly, the Alaska Geographical Society explicitly framed Alaska's development as a national-imperial project requiring scientific expertise. Taken together, these examples illustrate how local societies mediated between regional identities, commercial ambitions, and national projects, operating across the interconnected scales at which geographical knowledge was produced and disseminated.

2.2 Regulating Geography: Membership, Finances, and Governance

The membership policies and financial structures of geographical societies served as institutional gatekeeping mechanisms, shaping access not only to geographical knowledge, but also to geographical authority by determining who could participate in knowledge production, validation, and dissemination. Because membership usually required both nomination and the financial means to pay dues, a society's composition determined whose observations were accepted as data, whose theories merited debate, and whose visions of national space might eventually inform policy. As argued previously, defining the boundaries of a knowledge community is decisive for establishing disciplinary authority and regulating knowledge circulation. Juxtaposing the AAG's strict criteria aimed at professional authority with the NGS's inclusive strategy oriented toward popularization illustrates how different societies influenced the field's development. In both cases, the institutional power to include or exclude shaped what counted as legitimate geographical knowledge.

Membership Patterns: Standards and Composition at AGS and NGS

A large, reputable membership was fundamental to the success of geographical societies, providing their primary source of income and bolstering their public reputation. Across U.S. geographical societies, membership typically rose to a few hundred during their initial years before leveling off between several hundred and roughly a thousand members (with the notable exception of the NGS's later exponential growth). Membership in the AGS, for example, rose from 159 in 1855 to 544 in 1857.[37] In 1902, membership numbers for selected societies were as follows: American Geographical Society (1,310), National Geographic Society (2,600), Geographical Society of California (400), Geographical Society of Philadelphia (480), Alaska Geographical Society (1,200), and Geographical Society of Baltimore (1,725).[38] Given the abundance of learned and geographical societies, many individuals joined multiple associations, linking organizations through overlapping networks. Society members enjoyed benefits such as free society publications, lecture tickets, and library access, as well as letters of introduction to facilitate visits to scientific institutions abroad.[39] Thus, membership criteria and practices functioned as gatekeeping mechanisms by regulating participation in the production, access, and validation of geographical knowledge.

Examining membership standards and their implementation provides insights into the societies' self-perception and the types of members they wished to attract. Membership numbers not only reflect which societies had the widest appeal, but also which had the most lenient criteria. Similarly, the analysis of membership composition reveals the networks and potential influences that shaped the societies' knowledge production and dissemination. Membership requirements varied significantly, with notable discrepancies between official

---

37   AGS Council, "Annual Report of the Council and Officers with Appendix for 1857," Box 98, Folder 1, AGS Archives, 3.

38   James and Martin, *Association of American Geographers*, 187.

39   One example of a letter of introduction: AGS Council Minutes vol. 16, 38, 16.11.1911, Box 106, AGS Archives.

policies and their practical application. Although most societies claimed openness to anyone interested in geography, their bylaws usually required nomination by a current member and often council approval, creating at least a formal barrier to entry and a sense of exclusivity. In practice, at least during its
early years, the AGS accepted almost every nominee, and nominations were
usually a formality.[40] By contrast, the AAG was so selective that it still had only
76 members in 1912.[41] Whereas some European societies excluded women outright until the early twentieth century, many U.S. societies formally admitted
them, though participation levels varied significantly. The Geographical Society of Philadelphia attracted a substantial female membership, which constituted a majority circa 1900, prompting the society to institute a waiting list for
female applicants to restore what it termed a "proper balance".[42] Conversely, of
1,400 AGS members in 1893, only 9 were women.[43]

Early AGS officers came from professions directly connected to territorial
expansion and commercial development, listed here in descending order:
entrepreneurs (telegraph, shipping, land speculation, insurance, manufac-
turing); the Foreign Service; editors and publishers; earth science specialists;
and clergymen, lawyers, judges, and politicians.[44] In 1852, the AGS Council
included three members with banking and shipping interests and seven more
affiliated with publishing, including several associated with Horace Greeley,
a vocal advocate of U.S. empire-building in the American West, and Charles
Dana, a prominent supporter of the Pacific railroad.[45] From the outset, this
membership composition closely linked the society's knowledge production
to territorial and commercial interests that stood to benefit from expansion.

Around 1900, membership across U.S. geographical societies increasingly
comprised teachers, government employees, and military personnel. The

---

40   Dave Benison, "The A.G.S. in the 1850s," unpublished manuscript, Box 43, Folder 5, AGS
      Archives, 26.
41   James and Martin, Association of American Geographers, 43.
42   Geographical Society of Philadelphia, History 1891–1960 (Philadelphia: The Society,
      1960), 18.
43   Wright, Geography in the Making, 119; see also Douglas R. McManis, "Leading Ladies at
      the AGS," Geographical Review 86, no. 2 (1996): 270–77; Janice Monk, "Women's Worlds
      at the American Geographical Society," Geographical Review 93, no. 2 (2003): 237–257.
44   Ernesto Ruiz, "Geography and Diplomacy: The American Geographical Society and the
      'Geopolitical' Background of American Foreign Policy, 1848–1861" (PhD diss., Northern
      Illinois University, 1975), 24; quoted in Morin, Civic Discipline, 31.
45   Blouet, "Preface," in Origins of Academic Geography, x.

NGS, in particular, maintained close ties to the federal government. When the NGS was founded in Washington in 1888, most founding members held government positions. These included Henry Gannett, Chief Geographer of the U.S. Geological Survey; Henry Mitchell of the U.S. Coast and Geodetic Survey; A.H. Thompson of the U.S. Geological Survey; Commodore J.R. Bartlett of the U.S. Hydrographic Office; and A.W. Greely, Chief Signal Officer of the Army.[46] Throughout its early history, the NGS continued to draw its leadership and membership from government and military ranks. The NGS proudly highlighted this in membership lists: one from 1896 included the President of the United States as an honorary member and boasted "sixteen members of the Diplomatic Corps, the Chief-justice and one member of the U.S. Supreme Court, two Cabinet Officers, seven Senators, five members of the House of Representatives". It further reported significant membership numbers from federal bureaus and military branches: "Geological Survey 57, Navy 55, Army 48, Coast and Geodetic Survey 39, Agricultural Department 35, Hydrographic Office 10, Naval Observatory 6".[47] Similar trends are found in European societies, where a close relationship between the state (particularly military and colonial administration) and geographical societies was common. Army and Navy personnel consistently made up about 20% of the London Royal Geographical Society membership throughout the nineteenth century.[48] A 1903 *National Geographic Magazine* issue listed members' occupations and still showed numerous members from the Treasury, Agriculture, and War Departments, alongside personnel from the U.S. Navy and Army, the U.S. Coast and Geodetic Survey, and the U.S. Geological Survey.[49] Such state-society entanglements created channels through which geographical expertise and political power could reinforce one another.

This cultivation of government connections was a deliberate NGS policy designed to attract influential, well-connected members and enhance its institutional standing. In 1898, A.W. Greely, then Associate Editor at NGM and Chief Signal Officer of the Army, wrote to military officers encouraging them

---

46   Abramson, *National Geographic*, 63.

47   Membership List of NGS, dated 17.11.1896, Box 240, Folder 17, AGS Archives.

48   David R. Stoddart, "The RGS and the 'New Geography': Changing Aims and Changing Roles in Nineteenth Century Science," *The Geographical Journal* 146, no. 2 (1980): 190.

49   "Members of the National Geographic Society," *NGM*, no. 1 (1903): appendix.

to join.[50] Subsequently, the NGS actively targeted new educated and well-connected members by extending invitations using membership rolls from the National Education Association, the National Academy of Sciences, and the American Association for the Advancement of Science.[51] Through such a deliberate recruitment strategy, the NGS secured both financial stability and institutional prestige.

Financial Networks: Dues, Donations, and Influence

Closely linked to membership policies was the societies' financial structure, which influenced access to geographical knowledge, shaped institutional priorities, and sometimes constrained intellectual autonomy. For much of their history, geographical societies depended on membership dues as a primary source of funding. Many nominees cited high fees as reasons for declining invitations, and many existing members were removed from membership rolls for failing to pay their annual dues.[52] As a result, geographical societies regularly engaged in aggressive membership drives. Many societies experienced financial difficulties at some point in their history and relied heavily on membership dues and donations. Typically, income barely covered expenses, and budgets remained perpetually tight. An analysis of the 1894 financial report of the Geographical Society of California provides insight into the typical expenditures of a regional U.S. geographical society. Its largest allocations were dedicated to lectures ($509) and staff salaries ($688), followed by the publication of its *Bulletin* ($150) and the acquisition of books and maps ($147).[53] The AGS, despite being much larger and wealthier, exhibited a similar expenditure pattern, with staff salaries as its largest expense, followed by its *Bulletin*, lecture program, and library acquisitions. The cost of maintaining and improving its

---

50   Robert M. Poole, *Explorers House: National Geographic and the World it Made* (New York: Penguin Press, 2004), 41.

51   Philip J. Pauly, "The World and All That is in It: The National Geographic Society, 1888–1918," *American Quarterly* 31, no. 4 (1979): 524.

52   Examples include W.T. Sherman (1874), O.W. Holmes (1888), and G. Eastman (1904); all in Box 9, Folder 13, AGS Archives; A large amount of the AGS's outgoing correspondence regarded unpaid dues.

53   "Annual Proceedings," *Bulletin of the Geographical Society of California* 2, no. 2 (1894): 10.

buildings was another significant expense, but this was managed separately through a dedicated building fund supported by special donations.[54]

This dependence on dues led societies to actively pursue new members. Standard histories of the NGS credit these drives, particularly under *National Geographic Magazine* editor Gilbert Grosvenor after 1899, with significantly bolstering the society financially and expanding its reach.[55] A 1905 letter to NGS members, for example, encouraged them to nominate their peers and colleagues.[56] Another letter, sent to nominees, shows the society's tactics for acquiring members by making membership appear exclusive while promoting its educational benefits: "I have the honor to inform you that you have been recently nominated for membership in the National Geographic Society by a member of the Society, and I have pleasure in sending an outline of the educational work accomplished by this organization. [...] The society possesses an immense amount of exceedingly interesting and original geographical material on all parts of the world which is being given to the members through its magazine."[57] Although the NGS's membership drives are well documented, the AGS employed similar recruitment methods much earlier. As early as 1865, an AGS circular urged its members to recruit others, stating: "The management of the Society during the past year will (I trust) warrant Members in using their exertions to increase the Revenues of the Society – and thus add to its efficiency – by inducing others to associate themselves with us. If each Member would cause a small addition to our Roll of Members [...] few Societies would equal this in usefulness and interest." The letter also reassured members of the ease with which new applications were processed.[58] Thus, formal membership standards were often relaxed in practice to attract paying members. Membership drives thus suggest how scientific authority could be fragile when it depended on voluntary contributions. While their European counterparts often benefited from direct state support, U.S. geographical societies were more dependent on their members, forcing them into a state of constant negotiation over content and priorities to ensure financial survival.

---

54   Account Books, 1874–1899, Box 8, Folder 4, AGS Archives; Ledgers, receipts and disbursements,1863-1898, Box 11, AGS Archives.

55   Poole, *Explorers House*, 41. Grosvenor, *National Geographic Society*, 55.

56   Letter to members of NGS, 1905, Box 240, Folder 17, AGS Archives.

57   O. P. Austin to Alice C. Russell, 26.10.1916, Box 240, Folder 17, AGS Archives.

58   Waddell, Circular to AGS members, "American Geographical and Statistical Society. New York, 1st January 1865," Box 42, Folder 4, AGS Archives.

This financial precarity shaped what kinds of knowledge they could produce and how confidently they could challenge prevailing assumptions.

To escape this financial instability, some societies cultivated another source of income: elite patronage. An analysis of AGS financial records shows that, until the 1890s, its primary sources of income were annual membership dues and one-time payments from life fellows, who contributed $100 upon joining. By the early 1900s, the society had diversified its income through mortgage investments and property sales. During that time, donations became its largest source of income. The main benefactor was Archer M. Huntington, who donated more than $250,000 to the AGS over the years, in addition to purchasing the society's old building and donating land in New York for a new building. The AGS's financial reports also clearly indicate that the society was only able to fund expeditions and construct new buildings due to the generosity of its wealthiest members, who were encouraged to contribute to funds set up for specific initiatives.[59] Further research by Karen Morin documents the close connections between the AGS and New York business interests, primarily in the railroad and shipping industries during its earlier periods.[60] In general, the society's development was enabled and constrained by wealthy patrons, such as Henry Grinnell, AGS President during its first decades; Archer M. Huntington, elected Honorary President in the early 1900s; and influential councilors such as Chandler Robbins and James Ford. This shift offered the society greater autonomy from the immediate pressures of membership numbers, but it did so by deepening its reliance on a small circle of major benefactors. Financial contributions and leadership roles went hand in hand, meaning high-ranking members exerted considerable influence over the society's strategic direction and intellectual priorities. This financial dependence on wealthy members with commercial interests underscores how funding structures could constrain institutional autonomy and influence the types of geographical knowledge societies prioritized.

Legacies and bequests became another major source of income in the 1890s. For example, former President Charles P. Daly left the society $69,000

---

59   Some of the other main financial contributors throughout the society's history until 1914 were James B. Ford, Chandler Robbins, Herman von Post, Archibald Russell, John Greenough, Darius Mills, and Henry Parish; see: Account Books, 1874–1899, Box 8, Folder 4, AGS Archives; Ledgers, receipts and disbursements, 1863–1898, Box 11, AGS Archives.

60   Morin, *Civic Discipline*, 93–126.

upon his death in 1899, and George W. Cullum allocated $100,000 to the AGS in his will. Many of these bequests were left for a specific purpose, such as the construction of a new building or the establishment of a fund for a medal. Until 1909, additional legacies amounting to over $65,000 provided the AGS with substantial capital.[61] This financial stability allowed the society to make long-term investments, and by the early twentieth century, interest from these investments gradually surpassed membership dues as the society's primary source of income.[62]

AAG Membership: Professional Norms and Regional Tensions

Of all U.S. geographical societies, the Association of American Geographers set by far the strictest membership standards, positioning itself as an organization for professional "investigating geographers". Membership was limited to individuals deemed to have published significant original work in geography.[63] Although the AAG initially considered creating an associate membership tier for those "who have specialized less in geography", this tier was ultimately never implemented.[64] These stringent standards also went beyond membership itself. While the AAG constitution promised open attendance at meetings,[65] an internal memo discouraged public access to the 1911 meeting, explaining: "It is not desired that public announcement or general invitation to the public to attend the meetings should be made; but individual invitation to persons seriously interested in the work of the Association should of course be given by local members. The reason for desiring to keep out the 'general public' is that the greater the number of persons present the less is the freedom

---

61   Account Books, 1874–1899, Box 8, Folder 4; for bequests and legacies see (all in AGS Archives): $100,000 from George W. Cullum, Box 4, Folder 15–16; $30,000 from Sarah M. De Vaugrigneuse, Box 4, Folder 18; $25,000 from Darius O. Mills, Box 4, Folder 22; $10,000 from William R. Sands, Box 4, Folder 27. In addition, the AGS received large donations from individual donors like Andrew Agnew ($1,000 in 1909).

62   Interest from the AGS's various investments became the main source of income first in 1904, and continued to overtake membership dues, peaking significantly in 1908 and more dramatically in 1912, after which interest accrued at the same level.

63   William Morris Davis, "The Opportunity for the Association of American Geographers," Bulletin of the American Geographical Society 37, no. 2 (1905): 84–86.

64   Draft for AAG Constitution, 1904, Box 98, Folder 6, AGSL Manuscript Collection 23, Association of American Geographers Records, American Geographical Society Library, University of Wisconsin-Milwaukee Libraries (hereafter AAG Archives).

65   Draft for AAG Constitution, 1904, Box 98, Folder 6, AAG Archives.

of discussion by members."[66] This gatekeeping highlights the AAG's conscious effort to create a selective community of experts distinct from the more open and inclusive models of the NGS or AGS.

The AAG's first membership cohort underwent a rigorous selection process. A committee evaluated whether candidates had published "mature scholarship". Of the 70 proposed founding members in 1904, 12 were ultimately rejected after further deliberation. Ten politely declined membership, but assured the AAG that they supported the association's goals. About half of the founding members held academic positions, while a third were geologists affiliated with the federal surveys.[67] This strong representation from federal agencies, even in this most "professional" of societies, underscores how closely professional geography remained linked to the state. Only one founding member, Martha Krug Genthe, held a Ph.D. specifically in geography (from Heidelberg under Alfred Hettner). She and Ellen Semple were the only female founding members, and Genthe was one of seven who had studied in Europe. Compared to the AGS, the AAG members were relatively younger (between 30 and 49 years), hinting at a generational shift within the discipline.[68]

Due to the AAG's high admission standards, only 130 members were admitted between 1904 and 1923.[69] The nominations process, which required at least one current member's endorsement, provides a window into the society's internal dynamics. Some new members were actively recruited by the AAG, especially those whom William Morris Davis judged to be a good fit. In his nomination of O. E. Baker (Assistant Agriculturist at the Bureau of Plant Industry), for instance, he wrote that "Baker is the kind of man we ought to rope in".[70] Davis's language suggests the extent to which he and the AAG leadership viewed the Association not so much as an open forum, but as a carefully curated community of geographers. Other prospective members withdrew discreetly after receiving negative evaluations, preserving cordial relations among professionals. The selectivity of the AAG is further evident in notable rejections:

66   Document for preparing the AAG meeting in Washington 1911, Box 98, Folder 13, AAG Archives.
67   Herman R. Friis, "The Role of Geographers and Geography in the Federal Government: 1774–1905," in Origins of Academic Geography, ed. Blouet, 46.
68   James and Martin, Association of American Geographers, 36–38.
69   Martin, American Geography, 1025.
70   William Morris Davis to Bowman, 10.1.1914, Box 13, Folder 37, AAG Archives.

In 1913, for example, membership was denied to the well-known explorer Walter Dwight Wilcox, cartographer L. Philip Denoyer, and University of North Dakota geography professor Howard E. Simpson.[71] When Nellie B. Allen, who had published on commercial geography, inquired about membership, the society's reply asserted that publication of original work in the field of geography was essential and that its requirements for membership were "more rigid than in any other geographical society".[72] Yet the application of these criteria could appear inconsistent or arbitrary to outsiders. In 1905, geographer C. H. Gordon attempted to join the AAG, but was offered only an associate role, which he declined, noting that the list of current AAG members included individuals "whose eligibility would seem as questionable as mine".[73]

However, strict admission rules could become more flexible when it served the society's strategic interests. On paper, the requirements for membership in the AAG seemed clear. In practice, admission decisions could be contentious, sometimes influenced by factors unrelated to candidates' published geographic work. For example, William Churchill, primarily affiliated with the AGS, joined the AAG during 1914 negotiations for a financially advantageous partnership between AGS and AAG, even though Churchill's background primarily lay in ethnology. Internal correspondence suggests the AAG was keen to avoid upsetting the AGS while the two societies worked out a lucrative research agreement.[74] Cyrus C. Adams (AAG) also encouraged Albert Perry Brigham (AAG) to co-sign a nomination of Gilbert H. Grosvenor (NGS), the influential editor of NGM. The primary motive behind his nomination was not solely his published geographical work, but his leadership role at the well-funded NGS, which made him a valuable ally. Adams argued: "I believe that a man as prominently identified as he is with the National Geographic Society and its publication should be a member of the Association. This would place us in a position of some influence with regard to his work and strengthen us in our relations with the Washington Society."[75] This explicit acknowledgment illustrates the difference between the AAG's public face as a rigorous professional society and its private calculations of power, funding, and influence.

---

71   AAG to Walter Dwight Wilcox, L. Philip Denoyer, and Howard E. Simpson, 1913, Box 20, Folder 19, AAG Archives.
72   AAG to Nellie B. Allen, 1.2.1914, Box 4, Folder 5, AAG Archives.
73   Gordon to Davis, 14.4.1905, Box 15, Folder 15, AAG Archives.
74   AAG correspondence on Chicago meeting 1914, Box 98, Folder 16, AAG Archives.
75   Cyrus C. Adams to Brigham, 24.5.1907, Box 11, Folder 12, AAG Archives

Further archival material suggests that securing access to NGS resources was a motivating factor in these strategic considerations.[76] Even the most "professional" of the geographical societies could not escape the politics of knowledge production. Despite frequent AAG critiques that popularization would undermine geography as a discipline, the society's leaders were willing to compromise strict professional standards to form a strategic alliance with the main proponent of geography's popularization in the United States.

While the AAG's admission standards regulated who could join, its meeting locations determined who could participate. All three major U.S. geographical societies were located on the East Coast, posing significant challenges to national inclusion and member participation from distant regions. The AAG's experience illustrates how spatial distance shaped engagement and fostered perceptions of exclusion among western members. Multiple AAG members based in the American West expressed frustration over the consistent scheduling of meetings in the East. Apart from a single meeting in Chicago (1907), all AAG meetings were held near the East Coast until 1914. In a 1905 letter to Davis, AAG member Mark Jefferson pointed out that two-thirds of the Association's members would have to travel east to attend that year's meeting at Delaware Water Gap in Pennsylvania and urged a more central location.[77] W. S. Tangier Smith even resigned from the AAG, citing the distance of meetings from Western regions, the lack of distributed proceedings, and the absence of a regular publication.[78] AAG member Fenneman warned that the national scope of the AAG was at risk if its Western members continued to feel marginalized: "It seems to me inevitable that our members who live in the West will gradually drop off and the Society must come to represent only a small group who can get together every year. In that way it would be a very pleasant club but not really a National Society to which every productive geographer might well be expected to belong."[79] This regional imbalance thus mattered not just for participation, but determined whose geographical problems, methods, and expertise would shape the AAG's agenda.

Concerns about regional representation also influenced leadership decisions. The election of Rollin D. Salisbury (University of Chicago) as vice president in 1907 was partly motivated by regional representation, as AAG mem-

---

76   See chapter 3.3.
77   Mark Jefferson to Davis, 7.3.1905, Box 17, Folder 7, AAG Archives.
78   W.S. Tangier Smith to Fenneman, undated, Box 20, Folder 27, AAG Archives.
79   N. M. Fenneman to Brigham, 23.12.1909, Box 14, Folder 20, AAG Archives.

ber Tarr acknowledged privately that "it was felt desirable to have some one from Chicago".[80] When the presidency was under consideration again in 1911, AAG member Alfred H. Brooks recommended a last-minute change to nominate Salisbury again, arguing that "further delay in recognizing him as a leader in American geography might jeopardize the Chicago and Wisconsin men."[81] Consequently, Salisbury was elected AAG President for 1912, a decision influenced by the desire to address regional concerns and reassure members outside the East Coast. After the 1914 cooperation agreement with the AGS solidified ties in New York, AAG activities shifted even more toward the East Coast. However, the agreement also resulted in the AGS funding the AAG *Annals*, a regular publication that helped mitigate the regional disconnect by reaching members nationwide. In 1915, AAG leadership briefly considered organizing regional sections with separate meetings to address these geographical disparities, but the idea was abandoned at that time.[82] Nevertheless, this internal correspondence indicates how geographical location influenced the society's internal participation, its hierarchy and, by extension, its knowledge production. Western members, often excluded from leadership and central events, felt structurally sidelined and warned about the implications for national representation and disciplinary cohesion.

In contrast, the NGS, with its growing national membership base, transitioned more smoothly to a national orientation and structure by amending its bylaws without significant opposition. In 1901, the NGS announced changes to its bylaws designed to "give the Society a more national character, bringing its organization into complete harmony with its title." The society abandoned the distinction between "active" and "corresponding" members, the latter being from outside of Washington. In addition, the NGS added six geographers from outside Washington to its Board of Managers and initiated plans to hold lectures beyond the capital.[83] The society actively expanded participation of its members outside of Washington to substantiate its claim to represent a national society. This strategy proved to be highly successful, as the exponential growth in membership numbers in the following years demonstrated.

---

80   Tarr to Brigham, 7.1.1908, Box 20, Folder 39, AAG Archives.
81   Brooks to Brigham, 18.1.1911, Box 12, Folder 34, AAG Archives.
82   AAG member to Davis, 28.1.1915, Box 4, Folder 13, AAG Archives.
83   *Announcement to the Members of the National Geographic Society of 1901*, Box 240, Folder 17, AGS Archives.

The AAG and the NGS thus pursued two divergent paths to scientific authority. The AAG sought authority through professional closure, defining geography as the domain of a small group of credentialed experts. The NGS, in contrast, sought authority through public reach, defining geography as a popular science whose legitimacy was strengthened by mass membership and a commanding presence in the cultural marketplace.

2.3 Civic Science: Fieldwork, Education, and Nation-Building

Geographical societies linked geographical knowledge to civic life and nation-building, establishing their work as an integral component of scientific and public culture. The societies' civic function was central to their public role and influence. By embedding geographical activities such as lectures, publications, and fieldwork within local civic culture, these societies fostered public engagement with geography. At the same time, their institutional structures shaped how this knowledge was produced and validated, often reflecting and reinforcing the perspectives of their predominantly white, male, and middle class membership.

Smaller local societies often served an essential complementary function in the wider system of geographical knowledge in nineteenth-century America, particularly by promoting regional knowledge and advocating geography as a civic pursuit. Karen Morin's analysis highlights the civic dimensions of geography as practiced by the AGS up until 1890.[84] This section shifts the focus to the turn of the twentieth century and looks beyond the AGS to the local societies, using the Geographic Society of Chicago (GSC) as an exemplary case study. The GSC provides an instructive example of how regional priorities and civic pride could shape knowledge production outside the dominant East Coast centers.

Here, "civic geography" refers to the geographical practices (including lectures, field excursions, publications, and advocacy) through which voluntary associations cultivated informed citizenship, while legitimizing geography as a respected civic discipline. Geography, understood as civic science, relied on "the recognition by contemporaries of geographical knowledge as a form of civil enterprise, and of the institutionalized expression of science as part of civil society."[85] Through voluntary association, local fieldwork, and a shared ge-

---

ographical knowledge of the nation, geographical societies functioned as predominantly middle-class institutions whose legitimacy derived not only from claims to expertise, but also from their embeddedness in local networks and alignment with perceived civic virtues or national goals.

The ties between geography and national identity were strengthened by the inherently civic nature of U.S. geographical societies and their activities. Nineteenth-century voluntary associations functioned as a "mediating layer of civil political activity between state and nation".[86] Johann Neem stresses the reliance of U.S. nationalism on civil society, arguing that imagined communities depend on "local mediating institutions" which perpetuate the collective imagination of the nation through consistent activity at the local level. Voluntary associations thus built civil society "from the bottom up", offering members "concrete settings in which national identification could be constructed and maintained."[87] By the end of the nineteenth century, geographical societies connected citizens nationwide, fostering a sense of collective participation in knowing and shaping the nation's geography. This section explores how geographical societies enacted civic science through three interconnected practices: fieldwork and excursions, the dissemination of geographical knowledge, and educational outreach.

Fieldwork as Civic Practice: Excursions, Observation, and Local Engagement

Civic geography primarily manifested through fieldwork, widely considered a foundational practice for geography as an empirical discipline. Fieldwork and excursions transformed abstract geographical knowledge into embodied practice, allowing citizens to physically engage with their local environments while participating in the scientific enterprise of understanding American space. As Finnegan has shown for Victorian natural history clubs in Scotland, scientific excursions and civic activity complemented each other: "The scientific rationale – systematic description and efficient use of local resources – could be provided alongside the civic rationale – exploring and celebrating the natu-

---

86 Charles W. J., Withers and Diarmid A. Finnegan, "Natural History societies, fieldwork and local knowledge in nineteenth-century Scotland: towards a historical geography of civic science," *Cultural Geographies* 10, no. 3 (2003): 334–353.

87 Neem, "Civil Society," 30–36; quote on 36.

ral riches of a given neighbourhood."[88] Through the observation and interpretation of local (and, by extension, national) environments, civic science took shape. Geographical societies placed great value on local fieldwork, regional knowledge, and publications based on local findings. Such excursions became central to civic science, enabling the collective production of local geographical knowledge. Participating citizens cultivated civic identity by contributing knowledge about their region. Collecting and documenting local geographical knowledge was framed as an act of civic improvement intended to instill participants with pride and shared purpose.[89]

As geography became incorporated into civic culture, community members could enhance their social prestige through involvement with geographical societies. Finnegan emphasizes that fieldwork in this context was less about professional expertise than about the collective undertaking, "a pursuit worthy of responsible and active citizens". Success in this civic context was measured not only by the new knowledge fieldwork generated, but also by the perceived moral, cultural, and civic virtues it cultivated among participants.[90] For nineteenth-century Germany, Andreas Daum similarly shows how science became public knowledge through an expanding network of civic associations, thereby fostering civic identity.[91] In Britain, Withers argues that meetings of the British Association for the Advancement of Science functioned as both scientific forums and informal "civic social gatherings", offering opportunities to cultivate social status.[92]

In the United States, geographical societies similarly nurtured civic culture through local surveying, fieldwork, and excursions. Unlike the national surveys conducted by professional cartographers, local geographic description was a more popular and inclusive pursuit, further embedding geography in civic life. In the inaugural issue of the *Journal of School Geography* (1897), William Morris

---

88   Diarmid A. Finnegan, *Natural History Societies and Civic Culture in Victorian Scotland* (London: Pickering & Chatto, 2009), 15.

89   Withers, *Geography, Science, and National Identity*, 187–88.

90   Finnegan, *Natural History Societies*, 6–8.

91   Andreas W. Daum, *Wissenschaftspopularisierung im 19. Jahrhundert: bürgerliche Kultur, naturwissenschaftliche Bildung und die deutsche Öffentlichkeit, 1848 – 1914*, 2nd ed. (München: Oldenbourg, 2002), 3.

92   Charles W. J. Withers, "Geographies of Science and Public Understanding? Exploring the Reception of the British Association for the Advancement of Science in Britain and in Ireland, c. 1845–1939," in *Geographies of Science*, ed. Peter Meusburger, David N. Livingstone, and Heike Jöns (Dordrecht: Springer, 2010), 190.

Davis published an introduction on "Home Geography", asserting that "geography as a whole is hardly more than a compilation of innumerable local or home geographies."[93] This emphasis on civic science through local engagement was particularly prevalent in smaller societies such as the Geographic Society of Chicago (GSC). From its founding in 1898, the GSC prioritized excursions and field trips, with its first excursion to Stony Island occurring only months after inception.[94] The GSC's constitution stated that one core objective was "to organize and conduct geographic journeys and excursions for members".[95] According to an account published by the society, the motivation for founding the GSC was to establish a community project for geology graduates and the interested public that would satisfy "their interest in nature here in this Chicago region" and thus function as a "geographical society for the people of Chicago".[96] Civic activities such as field trips, excursions, and lectures were consistently the society's largest expenses.[97] Through such civic activities, geographical societies made knowledge production accessible and relevant to local communities.

Each year, the GSC organized five to ten popular field trips exclusively for its steadily growing membership, which from the society's perspective "proved very attractive and successful".[98] These excursions, organized by a dedicated committee, attracted up to several hundred participants. One particular excursion to Starved Rock in 1907 proved so popular that it had to be repeated to give all members a chance to participate.[99] In a later yearbook, the GSC described its numerous field trips as "opportunities for real education".[100] These

---

93   Martin, *American Geography*, 95.
94   Geographic Society of Chicago Handbook 1934–35, F38HS, Geographic Society of Chicago Miscellaneous, Abakanowicz Research Center, Chicago Historical Society Archives (hereafter Chicago Historical Society Archives), 11.
95   Geographic Society of Chicago Year Book 1912–1913, F38HS, Chicago Historical Society Archives, 21.
96   Geographic Society of Chicago Handbook 1934–35, F38HS, Chicago Historical Society Archives, 16.
97   Geographic Society of Chicago Year Book 1912–1913, F38HS, Chicago Historical Society Archives, 5.
98   The Geographic Society of Chicago: Preliminary Announcement 1907–08, F38HS, Chicago Historical Society Archives, 2.
99   The Geographic Society of Chicago: Preliminary Announcement 1908–09, F38HS, Chicago Historical Society Archives, 3.
100 Geographic Society of Chicago Year Book 1912–1913, F38HS, Chicago Historical Society Archives, 4.

trips focused on Chicago and its surrounding areas, including physiography, historical geography, and commercial geography. In addition, the society organized excursions to more distant locations, including Yellowstone, Yosemite, and Glacier National Parks. Starting in 1911, the GSC began publishing *Excursion Bulletins*, which accompanied its trips on *The Rivers and Harbors of Chicago* and *The Rock River, between Rockford and Dixon*.[101] The 1907 excursion to Starved Rock prompted a formal GSC resolution advocating for its preservation as a State Park. The society continued to lobby for the park's conservation and also declared that it played a role in "rousing the present widespread interest in the preservation of Stony Island and the Sand Dunes of Indiana" through excursions and the work of its conservation committees.[102] Thus, the society extended its civic mission into environmental stewardship, linking local geography to public policy and conservation campaigns. The GSC also notes its connection to national conservation efforts, citing member Harriet Monroe's 1909 congressional testimony advocating for the creation of what would become the National Park Service.[103]

Local Findings: Surveys, Bulletins, and National Narratives

While field activities generated local observations, publications and lectures synthesized and disseminated these findings, transforming local knowledge into cohesive representations of regional and national landscapes, often aligned with nation-building narratives. The founding documents of geographical societies all emphasized disseminating geographical information as their primary goal.[104] The AGS charter, for example, explicitly mentioned "the encouragement of explorations for the more thorough knowledge of all

---

101   Geographic Society of Chicago Excursion Bulletin no. 1, *The Rivers and Harbors of Chicago*, 1911, F38HS, Chicago Historical Society Archives; Geographic Society of Chicago Excursion Bulletin no. 2, *The Rock River, between Rockford and Dixon*, 1911, F38HS, Chicago Historical Society Archives.

102   Geographic Society of Chicago Year-Book 1919–21, F38HS, Chicago Historical Society Archives, 7.

103   "History Highlights," Geographic Society of Chicago, accessed May 20, 2023, https://www.geographicsociety.org/about/history-highlights/.

104   See prior chapter and chapter on dissemination of knowledge (5.3); examples include "the increase and diffusion of geographic knowledge" (NGS), "to encourage geographical exploration and discovery" (Geographical Society of the Pacific), "dissemination of such knowledge is consequently the chief aim" (Geographical Society of California), "to disseminate Geographical information by discussions, lectures and publications"

parts of the North American continent" as one objective.[105] Societies regularly organized lectures, published findings, and held meetings, providing
opportunities for members to present their geographical work before an audience. In major cities, lecture halls thus became important civic venues where
citizens could engage with geographical knowledge.

The significance and appropriate emphasis of U.S. geography were frequently debated at society meetings. In 1894, AGS member Henry Holt
asked nine renowned professors by letter if more significant findings could
result from less hazardous, more cost-effective explorations than polar expeditions.[106] William Morris Davis (Harvard) indicated strong support for
domestic geography, remarking that "money and men might be much better
expended in home exploration than in polar exploration." He pointed to the
civic value of producing and disseminating local knowledge in contrast to
distant exploration, stating that "to make a good survey of New York State –
the 'Empire State', unknown to its own citizens – [...] would be vastly more
valuable to New York boys and girls, but it would not put big headlines into
the newspapers." Davis himself intended to continue to focus on local and
national geography: "many persons would risk their lives to penetrate the
Arctic regions, who would not turn a hair in preparing a topographical map
of their own state [...] but when it comes to the application of my own efforts,
I shall carefully reserve them for home work." He concluded that prioritizing
polar expeditions over exploration of the United States would be "beginning
at the wrong end."[107] Davis thus contrasted the civic value of systematic
local knowledge production with the public spectacle surrounding distant,
heroic exploration, highlighting a general tension in U.S. geography between
scientific utility and popular appeal. Reflecting this emphasis on domestic
geography, the relative share of AGS *Bulletin* articles on U.S. geography peaked
in the 1890s, a trend likely tied to the society's stated goal of improving its
publication for geography teachers.[108]

(Alaska Geographical Society), and "promotion of geographical studies" and "the presentation of [geographic] researches" (Geographic Society of Philadelphia)

105   "Amended Charter," *Journal of the American Geographical Society of New York* 11 (1879):
ix–x.

106   Henry Holt to several U.S. Professors, 6.2.1894, Box 271, Folder 21, AGS Archives.

107   Davis to Holt, 8.2.1894, Box 271, Folder 21, AGS Archives.

108   John K. Wright, Materials for a History of the AGS, 1952, Box 43, Folder 22, AGS Archives.

The AGS also lobbied successfully for a comprehensive survey of New York in 1876, aligned with its civic mission to enhance local understanding and the dissemination of regional geographical knowledge. The survey's newly appointed director, James Terry Gardiner, resigned as AGS General Secretary to manage the project. Gardiner's letters to the AGS reflect his dedication to the society's civic mission and his personal sense of pride in charting his home state's geography: "[...] the results of the State Survey which has been fostered by your care may furnish a new proof of the practical value of geographical societies in making large additions to the sum of human knowledge." He also emphasized continued focus on local geographical knowledge, comparing the survey favorably to his prior surveys in the American West: "Colorado was not a greater surprise to me than [...] my native State", adding that Central New York was "as unique and as unknown to science as that of any part of the Rocky Mountains."[109]

The Geographic Society of Chicago further illustrates how disseminating local knowledge strengthened civic culture. All early GSC *Bulletins* focused on the U.S. Midwest, beginning with Rollin D. Salisbury's "The Geography of Chicago and its Environs" in 1899.[110] Its preface stated that the goal was to "present an outline for the geography of Chicago and its immediate surroundings, and especially to sketch in as simple a manner as possible the course of events by which that geography was developed" to ensure that local phenomena were "more easily and more generally understood".[111] Subsequent *Bulletins* echoed this local emphasis by presenting aspects of Chicago's geography accessibly, with issues on topics such as "Plant Societies of Chicago and Vicinity",[112] "Animal Communities in Temperate America – as illustrated in the Chicago Region"[113] and "The Weather and Climate of Chicago".[114] These publications consciously avoided overly technical details, a scholarly tone,

---

109   Wright, *Geography in the Making*, 105.
110   Geographic Society of Chicago Handbook 1934–35, F38HS, Chicago Historical Society Archives, 11.
111   Rollin D. Salisbury and William C. Alden, *The Geography of Chicago and its Environs*, Geographic Society of Chicago Bulletin no. 1 (1899); quote from preface.
112   Henry C. Cowles, *The Plant Societies of Chicago and Vicinity*, Geographic Society of Chicago Bulletin no. 2 (1901).
113   Victor E. Shelford, *Animal Communities in Temperate America – as illustrated in the Chicago Region*, Geographic Society of Chicago Bulletin no. 5 (1913).
114   Henry J. Cox and John H. Armington, *The Weather and Climate of Chicago*, Geographic Society of Chicago Bulletin no. 4 (1914), xxiii.

and rigid disciplinary boundaries in favor of accessible descriptions aimed at helping students and citizens interpret their local environment. The *Bulletin* on Starved Rock State Park exemplifies this emphasis on the local, asserting that "the chief interest of the Geographic Society centers in the geography of the region" and that the *Bulletin* was intended for those "interested in knowing more about the region than can be gathered by personal observation". The *Bulletin* openly acknowledged when it went beyond disciplinary boundaries to advance its civic and educational approach, prefacing an extended section on the history of Chicago with the following remark: "The historical statement has gone beyond the strict limits of geography, but not beyond the limits which seem appropriate in this Bulletin".[115] This intentional blurring of disciplinary lines highlights the GSC's prioritization of civic engagement and local relevance over strict adherence to emerging professional demarcations.

Beyond publishing, the GSC showcased Chicago's geography through curated exhibitions intended to educate citizens and promote the image of a dynamic, cultured city. The society curated a high-quality collection of maps and charts of the local area for exhibition at the Haskell Museum (University of Chicago), which was later exhibited in Cleveland, New York, and Boston.[116] A similarly positive image of Chicago was presented in an address at the 25th anniversary by GSC president J. Paul Goode, titled "Chicago: A City of Destiny", which celebrated Chicago and its distinctive geography.[117] Moreover, in a 1916 speech outline titled "Why Geography is important", former GSC president Rollin D. Salisbury insisted that education must prioritize contemporary local and national geographical issues: "I believe it is a thousand times more important that the boys and girls of this state and country should know its problems, than that they should know the language and problems of Athens and Rome 2000 years ago."[118] Salisbury's remarks plainly expressed the society's civic objective. By disseminating accessible local knowledge, geographical so-

---

115   Carl O. Sauer, Gilbert H. Cady, and Henry C. Cowles, *Starved Rock State Park and its Environs*, Geographic Society of Chicago, Bulletin no. 6 (1918), v.

116   The Geographic Society of Chicago: Preliminary Announcement 1907–08, F38HS, Chicago Historical Society Archives, 3.

117   Geographic Society of Chicago Year Book 1922–1924, F38HS, Chicago Historical Society Archives, 10–16.

118   Rollin D. Salisbury, outline for a speech titled "Why Geography is important," Box 12, Folder 11, Rollin D. Salisbury Papers, 1880–1922, Hanna Holborn Gray Special Collections Research Center, University of Chicago Library.

cieties like the GSC shaped civic identity and bolstered regional pride, linking local concerns to broader narratives of nation-building.

Educational Geography: Schools and Universities

Geographical societies consistently lobbied for strengthening geography teaching in schools and universities. As Brückner shows, early American textbooks promoted nationalism by fostering "geographical literacy" and visualizing the nation.[119] Historian Geoffrey J. Martin contrasts Germany, where geography flowed "down" from university to schools, with the United States, where geography was carried "upwards" from schools to universities by teachers.[120] The influential Department of Geography at the University of Chicago, for example, was established in response to a proposal from educational reformers advocating for improved geography instruction in schools.[121]

Geographical societies positioned themselves as advocates for geographical education. The NGS published an article series specifically for teachers in its magazine and financially supported an international conference on school geography.[122] Similarly, when the AGS solicited contributions to its *Bulletin* in 1897, it encouraged authors to make their work more accessible for geography teachers.[123] The AAG prioritized improving geography education, as the society considered the strengthening of school geography as a potential pathway to establishing geography more firmly at universities.[124] To this end, AAG members contributed articles to the *Journal of Geography* (a magazine intended for schoolteachers), wrote geography textbooks, organized field trips for teachers, and supported the establishment of the National Council of Geography Teachers.[125] There was even discussion of founding a "Geographic Society of North

---

119   Martin Brückner, *The Geographic Revolution in Early America: Maps, Literacy, and National Identity* (Chapel Hill: University of North Carolina Press, 2006).

120   Martin, *American Geography*, 479.

121   Marie-Claire Robic, "Geography," in *The Cambridge History of Science*, ed. Theodore M. Porter and Dorothy Ross, vol. 7 (Cambridge: Cambridge University Press, 2003), 380.

122   Martin, *American Geography*, 83–84.

123   Adams to Hurlbut, 13.1.1897, Box 102, Folder 3, AGS Archives.

124   Gary S. Dunbar, "Credentialism and Careerism in American Geography," in *Origins of Academic Geography*, ed. Blouet, 78.

125   James and Martin, *Association of American Geographers*, 191.

America" to serve as an umbrella organization advocating for geography as a subject in universities and schools.[126]

The Geographic Society of Chicago provides a strong example of this educational commitment at the local level. According to the GSC's constitution, one of its objectives was "to encourage the recognition and establishment of courses in geographic instruction in our universities, colleges and schools."[127] Among the society's first initiatives was a petition advocating a "portable geographic museum for the benefit of the public schools of Chicago".[128] In addition, a committee appointed by the GSC curated a collection of 269 lantern slides (maps, graphs, and other illustrations) to improve meteorology teaching, which was "met with hearty approval by teachers everywhere".[129] The slides were accompanied by a GSC *Bulletin* on "Lantern Slide Illustrations for the Teaching of Meteorology", prepared by a committee of teachers, geographers of the GSC, and meteorologists at the U.S. Weather Bureau.[130] These efforts demonstrate the significance the society attributed to school geography as part of its civic mission. Despite its relatively small size, the GSC made a notable impact on geography education in Chicago and beyond. Former GSC president Rollin D. Salisbury emphasized the ongoing importance of this educational mission in his acceptance speech for the society's Helen Culver Gold Medal, reminding members that promoting "the interests of Geography in the public schools" had always been a primary objective of the GSC. In the same speech, Salisbury summarized his view of geography as a civic science: "Perhaps no science touches human life and interests more closely, or in more ways than this modern Geography. There is, I am confident, no science which, properly developed and utilized educationally, will do more for the development of good citizenship."[131] This statement encapsulates how

---

126   Hubbard to AGS, 22.5.1896, Box 240, Folder 17, AGS Archives

127   Geographic Society of Chicago Year Book 1912–1913, F38HS, Chicago Historical Society Archives, 21.

128   Geographic Society of Chicago Handbook 1934–35, F38HS, Chicago Historical Society Archives, 11.

129   The Geographic Society of Chicago, "Preliminary Announcement 1907–08," F38HS, Chicago Historical Society Archives, 3.

130   Henry J. Cox and J. Paul Goode, eds., *Lantern Slide Illustrations for the Teaching of Meteorology – prepared by a Committee of the Geographic Society of Chicago*, Geographic Society of Chicago Bulletin no. 3 (1906), 5.

131   Rollin D. Salisbury, Manuscript for his acceptance speech for the Helen Culver Gold Medal awarded by the Geographic Society of Chicago, Box 14, Folder 14, Rollin D. Salis-

society leaders explicitly linked geographical education to civic responsibility. The GSC fostered public appreciation for Chicago's local geography through excursions, created resources for teachers, and lobbied to preserve regional landmarks, thereby strengthening both civic identity and individuals' connection to their geographic environment. More generally, geographical societies aimed to strengthen local or national attachment by equipping citizens with frameworks for understanding the geographical foundations of their locality, state, and nation.

bury Papers, 1880–1922, Hanna Holborn Gray Special Collections Research Center, University of Chicago Library.

3 Professionalizing Knowledge

In 1902, Gilbert H. Grosvenor, editor of *National Geographic Magazine*, dismissed a manuscript by Harvard professor William Morris Davis as "exceedingly hard to digest".[1] This seemingly minor editorial judgment crystallized a debate over scientific standards: should legitimate geographical knowledge be defined by popular magazine editors with mass audiences or by academic specialists writing for their scientific community? This chapter argues that competing claims to authority over geographical knowledge drove professionalization, while keeping it contested, uneven, and hybrid. Rather than simply replacing amateur practice with professional practice, this process produced geographical societies as mediating institutions that simultaneously embraced specialized research, popular outreach, and practical application.

3.1 Defining Geography: Amateurs, Academics, and Specialists

Historians of science often portray the nineteenth century as an era of professionalization, a period in which the amateur generalist gave way to the salaried professional scientist. As specialization and academization redefined disciplines, scientific language and practices became increasingly technical and abstract. Around the turn of the twentieth century, geography in the United States emerged as a professional field that offered salaried careers for a small but growing number of specialists. This section tracks this development not as a linear progression toward an ever more professional geography or as a monolithic movement, but as a complex and contested process that unfolded unevenly. This professionalization was punctuated by setbacks and

---

1   Grosvenor and La Gorce, *National Geographic Society*, 27–28.

competing visions of who possessed legitimate authority. Accordingly, understanding this trajectory requires an examination of the specific institutional
and cultural factors that shaped geography's path toward professional status
in the United States.

This section examines how geographers, operating primarily within geographical societies, sought to professionalize their field while negotiating internal tensions over the definition and purpose of geography. Here, "professionalization" refers to a process encompassing the establishment of academic
positions and disciplinary boundaries, the development of specialized institutions, shared standards of practice, and a distinct professional identity. However, this was not a simple replacement of amateurs by academics, but a complex dynamic of interaction, overlap, and mutual influence, particularly within
the mixed memberships of societies such as the AGS and NGS. These dynamics
produced hybrid practices and identities rather than a monolithic professional
identity, further shaping the character of U.S. geography.

Geography in National Context: U.S. and European Models

European developments provide a useful comparative perspective on the professionalization of U.S. geography. Martin and James identify the beginning of
the "new geography" in Germany in the 1870s, when geography professionalized amidst nation-building and imperialism. There, geography departments
and professorships were established, opening opportunities for salaried academic careers. This German model then spread to France, Great Britain, Russia, and eventually the United States. These five nations were especially influential in the emergence of modern professional geography.[2] Martin and James
propose that the formation of a professional scientific field depends on three
key conditions: first, a consensus within a scientific community on practices,
methods, and concepts; second, the establishment of institutions to disseminate these shared standards, such as university departments, scholarly societies, and discipline-specific periodicals; and third, the availability of salaried
positions.[3] In the United States, these conditions were only gradually met in
the early twentieth century, though elements of geography's professionalization appeared earlier. Permanent positions at universities, teachers' colleges,

---

2   Preston E. James, and Geoffrey J. Martin, *All Possible Worlds: A History of Geographical
     Ideas* (New York: Wiley, 1993), vii.
3   Ibid., xiii.

military and naval institutions, and government agencies allowed a growing cohort of practitioners to specialize, while geographical societies offered institutional homes and validation for that expertise.

Many historians regard the period from 1820 to 1880 as a transitional phase for American science, which remained reliant on European models while gradually developing a distinct professional framework.[4] Nathan Reingold argues that by the mid-nineteenth century, the foundations of a U.S. scientific community were in place and by around 1900, American researchers could claim approximate parity with European scientists, although many contemporaries still perceived significant gaps in resources, infrastructure, and prestige.[5] This advancement was substantially supported by the federal government, which outfitted exploratory expeditions and established scientific bureaus. A similar pattern characterized geography, although U.S. geographers remained concerned about their discipline's international standing well into the early twentieth century.[6] For much of the nineteenth century, the federal government rarely funded permanent scientific institutions, with few exceptions such as the Smithsonian Institution.[7] Before the Civil War, the idea of a national academy of sciences was advocated by Alexander Dallas Bache and his circle of well-connected scientists, who aspired to elevate American science to European standards.[8] Federally funded expeditions and surveys created semi-permanent institutions such as the Naval Observatory and the Coast Survey, which carried out a significant share of the nation's scientific

4   Nathan Reingold, "Definitions and Speculations: The Professionalization of Science in America in the Nineteenth Century," in *The Pursuit of Knowledge in the Early American Republic: American Learned and Scientific Societies from Colonial Times to the Civil War*, ed. Alexandra Oleson and Sanborn C. Brown (Baltimore: Johns Hopkins University Press, 1976), 33–69.

5   Nathan Reingold, "American Indifference to Basic Research: A Reappraisal," in *Nineteenth-Century American Science: A Reappraisal*, ed. George H. Daniels (Evanston: Northwestern University Press, 1972), 54–55.

6   Nathan Reingold, *Science in Nineteenth-Century America: A Documentary History* (Chicago: University of Chicago Press, 1964), 45.

7   A. Hunter Dupree, *Science in the Federal Government: A History of Policies and Activities to 1940* (Cambridge: Belknap Press of Harvard University Press, 1957), 114.

8   Axel Jansen, *Alexander Dallas Bache: Building the American Nation through Science and Education in the Nineteenth Century* (Frankfurt: Campus, 2011), 323–24.

work and functioned as de facto national scientific institutions during this period.[9]

One strategy for reducing fragmentation and strengthening institutional cohesion was the formation of a national scientific association. The American Association for the Advancement of Science (AAAS), founded in 1848, became the first national forum for scientific exchange, aiming to overcome the distances separating American scientists and to improve national and international perceptions of U.S. science.[10] But increasing specialization posed a threat to the AAAS's commitment to promote science as a unified enterprise rather than a collection of separate disciplines. By restructuring itself into nine specialized sections in 1881, the AAAS preserved its institutional unity, but this fragmentation created opportunities for geographical societies to position themselves as alternative venues for interdisciplinary exchange, attracting members from multiple related fields. By the late nineteenth century, specialized scientific societies had overtaken the AAAS as the principal venues for disciplinary exchange. Nonetheless, some new societies such as the Geological Society of America (founded in 1888) continued to hold their meetings alongside the AAAS.[11] The AAAS also played a significant role in professionalizing U.S. geography by laying the groundwork for the Association of American Geographers (AAG). The AAG's founding president, William Morris Davis, had served as Vice President of Section E (Geology and Geography) in the AAAS.[12] Frustrated by geography's secondary status relative to geology within Section E, Davis and fellow geographers launched the AAG at the 1904 AAAS meeting. This move was an attempt to distinguish geography from geology and assert an independent scientific identity.

Professional Identity: Founding the AAG

The founding of the AAG marked a decisive moment in the consolidation of professional identity and academic legitimacy in U.S. geography. Led by William Morris Davis, the AAG presented itself as a scholarly alternative to

---

9   Steven J. Dick, *Sky and Ocean Joined: The U.S. Naval Observatory, 1830–2000* (Cambridge: Cambridge University Press, 2003).

10   Kohlstedt, Sokal and Lewenstein, *Establishment of Science*, 7–9.

11   Ibid., 42–47.

12   James and Martin, *Association of American Geographers*, 32.

other geographical societies, especially the NGS with its overtly popular approach. As a professor of physical geography at Harvard, Davis held one of the
most influential academic positions in U.S. geography. Many of his students,
including James W. Goldthwait and Ellsworth Huntington, went on to become
university professors or leading practitioners in the field.[13]

Davis had long expressed discontent with the popularization of geography, especially as practiced by the NGS, creating a conflict between his vision
of geography as a rigorous academic discipline and the NGS's model of geography as mass public education and entertainment. Several of his manuscripts
were criticized or rejected by the National Geographic Magazine's (NGM) editorial
committee, and its editor Gilbert H. Grosvenor dismissed at least one of them
as "exceedingly hard to digest".[14] Grosvenor and his allies at the NGS framed
geography primarily as civic education for a wide readership, even while acknowledging the value of professional expertise. In this view, making geography accessible and engaging for a national audience was a democratic and patriotic duty. In 1902, Davis declined an invitation to join NGM's editorial committee, because he "couldn't approve [a] general policy of popularization at the
expense of science". Rollin D. Salisbury, a geography professor at the University of Chicago who later joined the AAG, turned down an offer to join the NGS
Board of Managers for similar reasons.[15] These incidents illustrate a growing
divide between advocates of specialized, academic geography and those fa-
voring broader public engagement, underscoring fundamental disagreements
over the definition of geographical knowledge and authority.

In a 1904 address before the American Association for the Advancement
of Science, Davis criticized geographical societies with large, mostly amateur
memberships for what he saw as low professional standards. He argued that
the proliferation of amateurs diluted geography's scientific standing and
impeded its development as a "maturely organized science". His speech, later
published in Science, made the case for a new professional society dedicated
to "advancing the more scientific aspects of geography."[16] Davis envisioned
a society with strict membership criteria based on scholarly training and

---

13   Robert P. Beckinsale, "W. M. Davis and American Geography", in Origins of Academic Ge-
      ography, ed. Blouet, 107–22.
14   Grosvenor and La Gorce, National Geographic Society, 27–28.
15   Philipp Pauly, "The World and All that is in it," 530.
16   William Morris Davis, "Geography in the United States," Science 19, no. 473 (1904):
      121–32.

publication, limited to those who had made original contributions to the field. In 1904, Davis discussed the state of U.S. geography and his vision for a professional society with a select group of geographers. In a confidential letter to 30 distinguished geographers, Davis asked if they would support establishing a new, strictly professional geographical society. He planned to convene a private meeting at the Eighth International Geographic Congress in 1904 and asked recipients to keep the proposal confidential. His caution suggests a concern that the NGS might have already been planning a similar initiative to distinguish professionals from amateurs, or that he hoped to pre-empt competing models of professional organization. Davis encouraged recipients to offer their opinions on membership standards, suggest future activities, and nominate additional members.[17] Following this planning phase, work began on drafting a constitution for the AAG. Its constitution explicitly promoted "scientific geography", signaling distance from popular societies: "The cultivation of Scientific Geography in all its branches, especially by promoting acquaintance, intercourse and discussion amongst members, by encouraging and aiding geographical exploration and research, by assisting the publication of geographical essays, by developing better conditions for the study of geography in schools, colleges and universities, and by cooperating with other societies in the development of an intelligent interest in geography among the people of North America." By emphasizing scientific geography and explicit support for educational institutions, the AAG distinguished itself from other societies promoting a more popular conception of geographical knowledge. Membership was to be limited "to persons who have done original work in some branch of geography". In contrast to other societies, the AAG initially refrained from publishing a regular journal, reasoning that for its members "existing geographical journals afford sufficient opportunity for bringing out their essays".[18]

Davis served as AAG president intermittently until 1914 and remained on the Council in intervening years. Even after stepping down from formal leadership roles, he continued to exert considerable influence through his former students who occupied important AAG positions. Albert Perry Brigham, Davis's student and the AAG's first secretary until 1913, shaped many early AAG policies. Subsequent secretaries Isaiah Bowman and Richard E. Dodge, also Davis's former students, steered the AAG until the 1920s and continued to

---

17   Circular Letter by William Morris Davis, 1904, Box 98, Folder 6, AAG Archives.
18   Draft for AAG Constitution,1904, Box 98, Folder 7, AAG Archives.

consult with Davis regularly.[19] Davis's influence is evident in the tone and content of his correspondence, which often included detailed directives. Ahead of the joint 1914 AAG-AGS meeting, he advised Bowman to "run the meeting, don't let it drift" and urged him to "Strike high. Get the very best men you can" (emphasis in original). He outlined specific topics for papers for presentation and advised concluding the dinner "with a fine, well-illustrated exploration story in the last hour". While he conceded that such a presentation "may well be narrative and popular, but good of its kind" (emphasis in original), he cautioned against "showy papers" or "trite subjects".[20] These detailed instructions illustrate Davis's persistent attempts to shape the AAG's scientific culture according to his vision of professional geography, even after he stepped down from official leadership.

Davis's domineering leadership style and degree of personal control over the AAG alienated some colleagues, as private correspondence shows. For instance, geographer William Herbert Hobbs declined an invitation to join the AAG after presenting a paper at a meeting. In a private letter, Ralph S. Tarr, who had extended the invitation, explained why Hobbs declined: "I gathered that he felt that it was a Society for the promotion of Davis, and you know he does not feel over-enthusiastic about Davis."[21] This incident shows how professionalization was not simply an abstract institutional process, but that it was shaped by individual personalities and interpersonal dynamics. Davis's vision for the AAG – focused on rigorous field research and physical geography – marginalized alternative approaches to geographical knowledge and alienated potential allies. However, his insistence on strict standards was also a response to geography's institutional precarity: its lack of distinct university departments, its contested intellectual boundaries, and its struggle for funding and status against more established fields. By emphasizing rigorous field research and professional standards, Davis and AAG leadership aimed to differentiate geography from amateur approaches and to secure scientific legitimacy comparable to established disciplines like geology.

Davis's ambitions for the AAG also raised suspicion among leaders of other societies, who saw the AAG as a direct competitor. Davis declined an invitation to join the American Geographical Society (AGS) in early 1904, only to found the

---

19   Martin, *American Geography*, 64–65.
20   Davis to Bowman, 4.1. 1914, Box 13, Folder 37, AAG Archives.
21   Tarr to Brigham, 18.11.1908, Box 20, Folder 39, AAG Archives.

AAG a few months later.[22] When Cyrus C. Adams, AGS *Bulletin* editor, considered joining the AAG, AGS Councilor Chandler Robbins urged him to remain loyal to the AGS: "I hope you will go a little slow in committing yourself to that proposed Geographical Club which Mr. Davis is getting up. [...] It strikes me that working for that Club, in the way suggested, will be sailing pretty close to the wind, and may be prejudicial to our Society."[23] Nevertheless, Adams became one of the AAG's founding members and later served as its president.

Academic Institutionalization: Geography in Universities

Geography's integration into the American university system occurred relatively late compared to European universities and was shaped by the distinctive structure of U.S. higher education. This created opportunities for geographical societies to act as substitutes for departmental infrastructure and professional networks. Although formal geography departments did not appear until the 1890s, the subject had long been taught in schools and colleges, often within other disciplines. After the Civil War, science thrived at state universities, alongside select private universities and colleges. Amidst rapid urbanization and industrialization, numerous new universities were established in the second half of the nineteenth century. By 1914, these institutions had evolved into modern research universities, many modeled in part on the German university system that U.S. scientists encountered during their studies abroad.[24]

Despite this growth, geography did not emerge as a distinct academic discipline with dedicated departments until the turn of the twentieth century. Prior to that, academic geographers were typically employed by geology or economics departments, or taught at teachers' colleges, where geography was a required subject. The variable institutional placement of geography reflects its contested disciplinary boundaries and its struggle for academic autonomy during this formative period. As with scientific societies, the Northeastern United States emerged as the initial center for academic geography. Geography was first introduced as a subject at Harvard in 1841. By 1875, it was taught at Princeton, Cornell, and Yale, though by faculty from adjacent disciplines.[25] By

---

22   Davis to Henry Parish, 19.1.1904, Box 9, Folder 13, AGS Archives.
23   Robbins to Adams, 7.2.1904, Box 129, Folder 3, AGS Archives.
24   Laurence R. Veysey, *The Emergence of the American University* (Chicago: University of Chicago Press, 1965), 264–302.
25   Beckinsale, "W.M. Davis," 108.

1900, the country still had just five geography professors holding that specific title, all of them leading members of geographical societies, mainly the AGS and, later, the AAG: William Morris Davis (Harvard), Ralph Stockman Tarr (Cornell), William Libbey (Princeton), George Davidson (Berkeley; Geographical Society of the Pacific) and Richard E. Dodge (Columbia). These universities became early centers of academic geography, focusing mainly on physical and commercial geography. Yale soon emerged as another center, educating influential geographers such as Herbert Gregory, Ellsworth Huntington, and Isaiah Bowman.[26]

Academic geography eventually expanded westward and into the Midwest, usually tied to commercial geography or geology. In 1898, the Berkeley College of Commerce established what is often cited as the first independent department of geography (separate from geology) in the United States, headed by George Davidson.[27] Its placement within a business school highlights geography's hybrid disciplinary identity at the time. By 1914, universities in California, Chicago, Nebraska, Miami (Ohio), Minnesota, and Wisconsin each offered at least six courses explicitly labeled geography or closely related fields such as geology.[28] Among these, the University of Chicago stood out, which established an independent geography department in 1903. There, Rollin D. Salisbury developed a highly regarded graduate program that awarded what can be considered the first U.S. Ph.D. in geography granted by a geography department in 1907.[29] Salisbury also served as the founding president of the Geographic Society of Chicago and later as AAG president. The University of Pennsylvania developed a well-known economic geography program, in response to expanding global trade and growing interest in the distribution of raw materials, especially in the American West. Initially, geography was listed as a subject within the Wharton School of Finance and Commerce and later developed into a distinct "Department of Geography and Industry".[30] Emory R. Johnson, who wrote his dissertation on inland waterway transport, led the department. His student J. Russell Smith wrote a dissertation on "The Organi-

26 Martin and James, *All Possible Worlds*, 319.
27 Dunbar, "Credentialism and Careerism," 73.
28 Geoffrey J. Martin, "Paradigm of Change: A Study in the History of Geography in the United States, 1892–1925," *Organon* 20/21 (1984/1985): 275.
29 William D. Pattinson, "Rollin Salisbury and the Establishment of Geography at the University of Chicago," in *Origins of Academic Geography*, ed. Blouet, 151; for "first PhD" see James and Martin, *Association of American Geographers*, 44.
30 James and Martin, *Association of American Geographers*, 20.

zation of Ocean Commerce" and, like Johnson, was employed by the Isthmian Canal Commission to study potential canal routes through Central America.[31] The Isthmian Canal Commission itself was an important node in the U.S. system of geographical knowledge, connecting academic geographers, government funding, and an imperial infrastructure project. Thus, academic geography secured an early claim to legitimacy not just through theoretical research, but by proving its direct utility to a major U.S. imperial infrastructure project: the Panama Canal.

In Britain, geographical societies were instrumental in the campaign to establish geography as a university discipline. Between 1887 and 1900, the Royal Geographical Society (RGS) spent almost half as much on university aid as it allocated to expeditions, illustrating how vital academic geography was to the society. The RGS sponsored lecturer positions for geographers at Oxford and Cambridge to increase the discipline's reach and visibility, and offered scholarships to undergraduates studying geography. This support continued into the early twentieth century.[32] In Germany and France, geography departments were created in the 1870s, in large part to prepare teachers to instill patriotism and geographical understanding in pupils following the Franco-German War. Many early geography professors transferred from adjacent disciplines or had previously worked as teachers. From the 1880s onward, geography professionalized further, and most geographers received formal training at universities.[33] These European precedents served as models for U.S. advocates of university geography, even as political circumstances and funding mechanisms differed significantly. Unlike the RGS, U.S. geographical societies provided little direct institutional support to university positions or departments, but they regularly funded expeditions by academic geographers. They also provided venues for professional discussion of geography at a time when universities lacked the infrastructure and critical mass of academic geographers. The AAG in particular fostered networks among university geographers and provided an outlet for highly specialized lectures and publications.

---

31   Preston E. James, "Geographical Ideas in America, 1890–1914," in *The Origins of Academic Geography in the United States*, ed. Brian W. Blouet (Hamden: Archon Books, 1981), 324.

32   Max Jones, "Measuring the World: Exploration, Empire and the Reform of the Royal Geographical Society, 1874–93," in *The Organisation of Knowledge in Victorian Britain*, ed. Martin Daunton (Oxford: Oxford University Press, 2005), 330–34.

33   Schenk, *Allgemeine Anthropogeographie*, 53–60.

Amateur Persistence: Popular Geography and Hybrid Roles

Despite these strides toward academic institutionalization, geography's professionalization remained incomplete and uneven, as the enduring strength of the amateur tradition demonstrates. This was largely the legacy of natural history as this amateur tradition supplied enduring audiences, methods, and values that professional geographers could neither ignore nor fully displace. However, the persistence of amateurs was not a remnant of an earlier era, rather, it reflected unresolved questions about geography's purpose, audience and epistemic standards that professionalization could not resolve. The AGS's struggles with its own membership standards illustrate this incomplete transition.

Honorary and corresponding memberships, which exempted distinguished members from paying dues in exchange for geographical contributions, carried particular prestige. Originally, the AGS defined corresponding members as individuals recognized for advancing "by their publications or services the sciences of Geography and Statistics".[34] When AGS member L. Bradford Prince was set to be removed from this category in 1898, it became clear that standards for this prestigious category had tightened. Walter R. T. Jones, former AGS treasurer, advocated on his behalf, noting the society's shifting standards for corresponding members over the years: "If his name was before the Society as an original name for action his fitness should by all means be inquired into, but having been once on the Roll puts him in a different position". Jones alluded to the increasing emphasis on professional status for corresponding membership compared to the society's founding years, mentioning that "for certainly in our earlier days many names appeared proposed as you state from the feelings of good friendship and passed without question."[35] Even as the AGS sought to tighten standards for its most prestigious membership tier, it struggled to cleanly separate professional merit from the social networks and friendship ties that had long sustained the society. This tension between merit-based and relationship-based membership exemplifies the hybrid character of geographical societies during this transitional period.

As Philip Pauly has shown, the NGS thrived as an amateur society precisely during a period of growing professionalization in other fields and within geography itself. When the NGS did fund scientific endeavors, it was primar-

---

34   Dave Benison, *The A.G.S. in the 1850s*, Box 43, Folder 5, AGS Archives, 8.
35   Walter R.T. Jones to Robbins, 10.12.1898, Box 124, Folder 9, AGS Archives.

ily motivated by a desire to enhance its public image and provide content for its magazine rather than to advance academic geography.[36] This exemplifies the existence of strong countercurrents and alternative models of geographical practice and dissemination operating alongside professionalization.

During the second half of the nineteenth century, the gap between professional scientists, amateur practitioners, and the public widened. As scientific practices, methods, and terminology became more complex, many amateurs struggled to stay engaged. The evolving character of the American Association for the Advancement of Science meetings reflected this trend, so that by 1875, newspapers noted that the younger scientists used overly technical language. In response, organizers introduced evening sessions with popular lectures to reach a broader amateur audience.[37] Nevertheless, amateurs continued to voice concerns about the perceived elitism of professional scientists, accusing them of attempting to monopolize science. At the same time, certain forms of amateur geography flourished. Nathan Reingold argues that while amateurs were gradually replaced by professionals in many fields, scientific amateurism and applied science persisted longer in the United States than in continental Europe.[38] U.S. geography is better described by a spectrum of scientific participation, within which many geographers continued to operate as amateurs or in hybrid roles. This persistence reflected antebellum intellectual traditions that favored generalist inquiry and permeable disciplinary boundaries.[39] Consequently, professionalization and popularization must be understood as interdependent processes.[40] The increasing specialization of scientific knowledge necessitated popularizers, prompting professional scientists to found exclusive societies (like the AAG) and publications to protect their disciplinary standards. This dynamic made U.S. geographical societies such as the AGS and the NGS, with their mixed memberships, even more important in their function as mediators of geography between expert and lay audiences.

---

36   Pauly, "The World and All That Is in It".

37   Kohlstedt, Sokal, and Lewenstein, *Establishment of Science*, 35.

38   Nathan Reingold, "Reflections on 200 Years of Science in the United States," in *The Sciences in the American Context: New Perspectives*, ed. Nathan Reingold (Washington: Smithsonian Institution Press, 1979), 18.

39   Bates, *Scientific Societies*, 85.

40   Bernard Lightman, *Victorian Popularizers of Science: Designing Nature for New Audiences* (Chicago: University of Chicago Press, 2007), 9–14.

Andreas W. Daum's category of "amateur science", situated between popular and professional domains, captures this intermediary space well.[41] Many nineteenth-century geographers and their practices fit into this middle ground. At that time, most American scientists, and especially geographers, were "amateurs" by institutional status (outside salaried research posts) even when producing rigorous scientific work within Western surveys or government bureaus. They pursued scientific inquiry in their spare time or as part of their official duties.[42] Reingold's typology distinguishes three types of scientists: professional *researchers*, *practitioners* (those in science-related occupations with limited publication records), and *cultivators* (amateurs who conducted applied research). Over the course of the nineteenth century, cultivators became less common, while practitioners grew in prominence, and researchers only began to emerge in greater numbers in the early twentieth century.[43] This trajectory largely maps onto this study's actors, including society-linked survey geologists and naval officers as practitioners, diplomats and merchants as cultivators, and emerging university geographers as researchers.

For many early amateurs, science was primarily a leisurely pastime focused more on collection and description than on the advancement or dissemination of knowledge.[44] Geography's connection to the amateur tradition of natural history enabled societies to maintain inclusive memberships that bridged amateur and professional knowledge, while claiming scientific authority through selective validation of amateur contributions. Reingold identifies natural history as the most widely practiced antebellum science, particularly visible in the Western surveys and U.S. expeditions, where specimens were collected alongside geophysical data. The American West offered abundant material for amateur naturalists, who found in its landscapes a wealth of geological and biological material to collect and study. Natural history allowed these individuals to participate meaningfully in the scientific enterprise, even as professional scientists began to draw boundaries around their disciplines.[45] Importantly, this system allowed amateur explorers to produce reliable and

41   Daum, *Wissenschaftspopularisierung*, 12.
42   Bates, *Scientific Societies*, 30.
43   Reingold, "Definitions and Speculations," 33.
44   Patsy A. Gerstner, "The Academy of Natural Sciences of Philadelphia, 1812–1850," in *The Pursuit of Knowledge*, ed. Oleson and Brown, 175.
45   Reingold, *Science in America: A Documentary History, 1900–1939* (Chicago: University of Chicago Press, 1981), 162.

valuable knowledge that was incorporated into broader scientific fields such as geology, botany, and meteorology.[46] As Theodore Binnema's work on amateur scientists in the Hudson's Bay Company illustrates, lay practitioners frequently published in respected journals despite lacking formal scientific training. While their contributions typically required validation by elite scientists, they nonetheless offered a viable pathway for amateurs to make meaningful contributions to science.[47] Similarly, geographers in the West, the Pacific, and elsewhere submitted their findings to geographical societies, which validated and published their work, thereby bridging the gap between amateur practice and professional science and fulfilling the societies' role as mediators of knowledge.

This persistent tension between the drive for professional exclusivity and geography's amateur and popular appeal fundamentally shaped not only the institutional strategies of the geographical societies, but also the nature of geographical knowledge itself. The field's development was characterized not by a clean break between "amateur" and "professional" geography, but by ongoing negotiations over authority, legitimacy, and disciplinary identity that kept boundaries fluid and contested.

3.2 Disciplinary Boundaries: Geography, Geology, and Authority

The development of geography as a discipline, and the production of knowledge within it, was closely guided by a process of demarcation.[48] Professionalization relied on what Thomas F. Gieryn has termed "boundary-work": the construction of social and epistemic boundaries that legitimize certain forms of knowledge (produced by a specific group, using particular methods, on distinctive topics) while excluding or marginalizing others.[49] In Sarasin's framework (Chapter 1), this boundary-work aligns with constructing

---

46   Vanessa Heggie, "Why Isn't Exploration a Science?," *Isis* 105, no. 2 (2014): 321.

47   Theodore Binnema, *Enlightened Zeal: The Hudson's Bay Company and Scientific Networks, 1670–1870* (Toronto: University of Toronto Press, 2014), 19.

48   Martin has studied the more general "Quest for Definition" of American geography in detail: Martin, *American Geography*, 447–527.

49   Thomas F. Gieryn, "Boundary-Work and the Demarcation of Science from Non-Science: Strains and Interests in Professional Ideologies of Scientists," *American Sociological Review* 48, no. 6 (1983): 781–95.

a system of knowledge by drawing discursive lines that differentiate legitimate knowledge from non-knowledge, and legitimate practitioners from
outsiders. These boundaries had material consequences: they determined
who received funding, whose work appeared in prestigious journals, and
ultimately, whose vision of the world shaped American understandings of
global spaces. Boundaries also helped to distinguish geography from adjacent
fields and to determine who had the authority to produce knowledge. This
"boundary-work" was not only essential for defining geography's intellectual
territory, but also for securing institutional resources, academic legitimacy,
and professional authority against competing claims from adjacent fields or
amateur practitioners. For geographical societies, boundary-work thus served
a dual function: establishing geography's autonomy from related disciplines
while managing internal tensions between academic and popular approaches.
This section analyzes how geographical societies conducted boundary-work
to define the contours of U.S. geography and assert their own institutional
authority in the wider scientific landscape. Through selected case studies, this
section considers how these societies positioned geography as a discipline,
enforced its boundaries through mechanisms such as membership criteria
and funding decisions, and navigated tensions between professionalization
and popularization. Together, these case studies illustrate that demarcation
was not a single, definitive act, but rather an ongoing negotiation through
which geographical societies continually adjusted their disciplinary identity in
response to internal tensions, external pressures, and changing institutional
priorities.

Interdisciplinary Roots: The Nineteenth-Century Scientific Landscape

To understand the boundary-work required to establish professional geography, it is essential first to recognize the field's broad, interdisciplinary origins
in nineteenth-century American science. These origins enabled geographical
societies to position themselves as uniquely qualified mediators between
specialist fields, claiming the authority to synthesize diverse forms of knowledge, while maintaining flexibility regarding what constituted legitimate
geography.

Geography was already fundamental to scientific practice before it became
established in universities. Reingold argues that a proto-geographic influence
permeated American science to such an extent that "scientific fields expanded
in nineteenth-century America [only] if they were part of geography." Unlike

European geography, which developed in close relation to academic history, American geography had its roots in geology, astronomy, geodesy, and topographical mapping, as well as adjacent fields such as anthropology, sociology, and hydrography. As a unified science, geography served as a bridge between the natural sciences and the humanities, bringing together scientists from a variety of specialist disciplines under the umbrella of geography. Reingold identifies four major fields in pre-Civil War American science as proto-geographic: astronomy, taxonomic botany, geology (including paleontology), and meteorology.[50] This assessment aligns with Robert Bruce's statistical analysis of U.S. scientists from 1846 to 1876, which shows that earth sciences constituted the primary field for 25% of U.S. scientists and a secondary field for 31% of those engaged in multiple fields. Earth sciences thus made up the second most common primary field after life sciences and the leading secondary field.[51] Consequently, a large proto-geographic scientific community existed well before geography emerged as a formal discipline, driven in part by specialists from adjacent fields seeking employment opportunities that relied on geographical knowledge. This interdisciplinary context meant that establishing geography as an independent discipline required significant boundary-work to justify its autonomy and secure institutional resources.

Many proto-geographic practitioners were employed in Western surveys or civil engineering projects. For them, science was to be conducted in a practical and utilitarian fashion. Astronomy, for example, was used extensively for surveying and navigation, as precise measurements of the earth depended on accurate astronomical and geodetic data.[52] This emphasis on empirical measurement and applied observation over abstract theory characterized much of nineteenth-century American scientific practice. Indeed, Bruce attributes geography's popularity partly to a distinctively American preference for descriptive, empirical science.[53] Geology dominated the scientific landscape, described by one historian as the "leading antebellum American science – in terms of the number of practitioners and the quantity and quality of the sci-

---

50   Reingold, *American Science*, 60–62.
51   Bruce, "Statistical Profile," 67–68. He based his analysis on a group of "477 American scientists active during any part of the period 1846–76 and distinguished enough to be among the subjects in the Dictionary of American Biography".
52   Reingold, *American Science*, 60–61.
53   Bruce, "Statistical Profile," 67–68.

entific work".[54] As a result, U.S. geography was heavily influenced by geology, especially in academic settings. One historian has characterized geography as an "offshoot" of geology, which gradually evolved from a physical science toward the social sciences.[55] Thus, the nineteenth century saw the emergence of a distinct U.S. geography rooted in Western surveys, which combined geology, cartographic surveying, and economic geography in a highly utilitarian manner. The breadth of contributors – amateurs and professionals alike – eventually necessitated a process of demarcation through which professional geographers sought to institutionalize the discipline on their own terms, often by explicitly defining it in opposition to earlier, more diffuse, interdisciplinary practices.

Disciplinary Borders: Boundary-Work within the AAG

From its earliest days, the Association of American Geographers was preoccupied with defining and demarcating the boundaries of geography. As the society worked to establish itself as the leading professional society for geography, it sought to differentiate it from neighboring disciplines, separate professionals from amateurs, and distinguish scholarly from popular approaches. This process of boundary-drawing influenced the society's membership rules and research priorities. This constructed a particular vision of what constituted legitimate geography in the U.S. in the early twentieth century.

At the AAG's inaugural meeting, its founder and president William Morris Davis articulated a wide-ranging definition of geography in his address "The Opportunity for the Association of American Geographers". He posited that geographical science should bring together the "organic and inorganic sides, the human, economic, zoological, botanical, climatic, oceanographic, and geologic sides of geography".[56] At first glance, this definition appears inclusive, but the AAG's strict membership criteria significantly narrowed who could represent geography: only accomplished and specialized geographers who produced original work were admitted (see section 2.2). This contrast between

---

54   Paul Lucier, "The Professional and the Scientist in Nineteenth-Century America," *Isis* 100, no. 4 (2009): 710.
55   Marvin W. Mikesell, "Continuity and Change," in *Origins of Academic Geography*, ed. Blouet, 4.
56   William Morris Davis, "The Opportunity for the Association of American Geographers," *Bulletin of the American Geographical Society* 37, no. 2 (1905): 84–86.

a wide theoretical scope and exclusive membership criteria became a primary site of boundary-work.

Discussions over membership nominees often came down to the definition and boundaries of geography. In the case of zoologist Alexander Ruthven's candidacy, the AAG was divided over the question of whether his work could be classed as geographical. Nevertheless, his advocate Adams (AAG) defended Ruthven's publications as having "given much attention to the geographic factor" and even insisted that "to rule him out as non-geographic is like ruling out the insurgents as non-republicans!!"[57] Similarly, when Secretary Brigham questioned whether Professor Lindley Keasbey's research on American interoceanic canal projects met the standard for AAG membership, Adams replied that while the work only "treats geography of the subject rather cursorily", it had a strong chapter on commercial geography. He concluded his letter with a paragraph that hints at how malleable conditions for membership in the AAG ultimately were: "I doubt if Prof. Keasbey has specialized in any geographic branch, but at the same time, he may make a very valuable member of the association." Adams added that if commercial geography was to flourish as a subfield, "it will have to be done by the leading teachers in our higher schools and some of their best work should be done in the [AAG]."[58] This implies that strict criteria could be relaxed to strategically admit members in order to associate the AAG with emerging fields of geography and adjacent disciplines, or simply to include influential figures who could lend prestige. These exchanges thus show how membership decisions functioned as ongoing negotiations about geography's boundaries. The society balanced disciplinary coherence against institutional needs for diverse expertise, prestigious connections, and emerging research areas – decisions that ultimately defined what counted as legitimate geographical knowledge.

This tension between wide theoretical scope and narrow professional requirements influenced the society's daily operations. Its leadership took active steps to guard the society's intellectual and reputational boundaries, often through private correspondence. For example, when selecting a chairman for a general meeting, Isaiah Bowman privately urged AAG Secretary Brigham to assume the role, warning that appointing Henry Bryant as chair may compromise the society's reputation, as he supposedly had an undistinguished track record in professional geography: "Unless you come it will be necessary to invite

---

57   Adams to Bingham, undated, Box 11, Folder 11, AGS Archives.
58   Adams to Brigham, 1.3.1905 ; Box 11, Folder 12, AAG Archives.

Bryant to preside. While he makes a dignified presiding officer, I do not like to see him occupy so prominent a position at that time in view of the fact that he does not represent a high grade of geography."[59] Similarly, editorial decisions reflected the society's professional standards. In 1911, geographer Ralph S. Tarr demonstrated sensitivity to the AAG's perceived editorial standards when he inquired about including illustrations in an article for the *Annals* of the AAG: "I am very anxious to have your frank opinion upon the question of the desirability or undesirability of introducing a very limited number of illustrations, not to be described at all, but simply to come in at the proper part of the text which the particular illustration is to illustrate."[60] In another instance, Davis discouraged a geographer from attempts at popularization, writing that "it will not be necessary to popularize your lecture in the least. In fact, the more strictly scientific it is the better liked it will be."[61] Davis's influence also extended to membership decisions. For instance, his own students were readily admitted, whereas figures such as economic geographer J. Russell Smith were initially excluded because they lacked experience in physical geography and fieldwork – both highly valued by Davis.[62] These carefully managed acts of inclusion and exclusion represent a form of professional boundary-work, designed to distinguish the AAG's professional geography from popularization and less favored sub-disciplines.

Some of the most sustained and complex boundary-drawing was centered on the AAG's relationship with geology. While geography initially relied on geology to gain a foothold in academia, the AAG later sought to differentiate geography from geology to establish its disciplinary autonomy. As geography matured as its own discipline, applications from geologists whose work did not align with the AAG's conception of geography were increasingly rejected.[63] Meeting schedules also became contentious: geologists and geographers had once convened every year in the same city, but that arrangement ended in the early 1900s, forcing individuals to choose between the two and thereby reinforcing disciplinary boundaries. In a 1905 letter, AAG member F. P. Gulliver

59   Bowman to Brigham, undated, Box 4, Folder 4, AGS Archives.
60   Tarr to Brigham, 6.11.1911, Box 20, Folder 39, AAG Archives.; article published later as Ralph S. Tarr, "Glaciers and Glaciation of Alaska," *Annals of the Association of American Geographers* 2 (1912): 3–122.
61   Davis to Furlong, 25.11.1913, Box 4, Folder 7, AAG Archives.
62   James, "Geographical Ideas in America," 325.
63   James and Martin, *Association of American Geographers*, 48.

urged a return to joint meetings, arguing that such cooperation would benefit both fields.[64] Despite the gradual separation of geography from geology, such calls for closer ties highlight that the boundaries remained contested and porous. In 1914, AAG member Nevin M. Fenneman similarly advocated for scheduling annual AAG meetings during periods when geologists were not engaged in fieldwork, so that they could participate. His letter shows the AAG's pragmatic ambivalence toward geologists. While asserting disciplinary independence, the association still needed their geological field data and reputation: "We do not want these geologists to tell us where to draw our lines, but we do want from them a lot of first-hand information about the aspect of the regions. Mere geologists can be passed over but not all the men on the survey are mere." (emphasis in original)[65] While geography was asserting its autonomy, the AAG still depended on selective collaboration with field-based geologists, particularly those associated with government surveys, as late as 1914.

Through such forms of boundary-work, the AAG consolidated its professional reputation and defined geography's scope. In doing so, it marginalized aspects of the field that did not align with this specific vision, including certain approaches to geology, economic geography, and popular geography. Instead, AAG-sanctioned geography was to be built on the description and analysis of landforms in fieldwork and physical geography, Davis's favored research areas. Yet the boundary between professional and popular geography was more porous than Davis suggested. The AAG still invited popular explorers like Robert Peary to an annual meeting and counted among its members individuals such as Theodore Roosevelt, Peary, and NGM editor Grosvenor – some of the leading popularizers of geography. Thus, despite its rhetorical commitment to professional exclusivity, the AAG pragmatically engaged with popularizers and prominent public figures when it served institutional interests such as prestige and visibility.

Nonetheless, the definition of geography remained contested within the AAG itself. In his 1918 presidential address, Fenneman remarked that "it is a peculiarity of geography to be always discussing and debating its own content – as though a society were to be organized for the sole purpose of finding out what the organization was for." He criticized geography's tendency to guard disciplinary boundaries and advocated for a more inclusive approach,

---

64   F.P. Gulliver to Brigham, 12.12.1905, Box 15, Folder 23, AAG Archives.

65   N.M. Fenneman to AAG, 24.4.1914, Box 14, Folder 20, AAG Archives.

proposing that geography should have a "central core which is pure geography and nothing else, but there is much beyond this core which is none the less geography, though it belongs also to overlapping sciences." He echoed Grove Karl Gilbert's 1909 AAG presidential address, which introduced the idea of "scientific trespass" as a mode of disciplinary cross-fertilization. Fenneman declared: "In so far as there are frontiers between the sciences, let us have them ungarrisoned and let us have free trade."[66] His call for disciplinary openness stood in stark contrast to Davis's earlier narrow vision. Together, these episodes illustrate how the boundaries of geography were constructed and contested within the AAG. Davis's vision initially prevailed, but debates over disciplinary boundaries remained active, influenced by pragmatic considerations, institutional politics, and the ongoing interplay between professionalization and popularization.

Funding Lines: Expedition Choices at the AGS

At the AGS, the demarcation of geography was frequently negotiated through decisions regarding expedition funding. Selecting which projects to support effectively determined what qualified as legitimate geographical inquiry worthy of the Society's resources, endorsement, and prestige (see section 4.3 on expeditions). The case of Ralph S. Tarr's Alaska expeditions illustrates this point. When Tarr planned a U.S. Geological Survey (USGS) research trip to Alaska, he requested AGS funds for a scientific associate who would conduct supplementary research. Tarr deemed this extra work to be of "high value", but noted in his letter to the society that the USGS had refused to financially support the work as it lay outside of the limited resource-oriented mandate.[67] The AGS granted Tarr $750 on the condition that the research results would first be published in the society's *Bulletin*, which shows the AGS's desire to control and disseminate the knowledge it funded.[68] The advocacy of AGS Councilor Robbins and *Bulletin* editor George C. Hurlbut was likely instrumental in securing the ap-

---

66   Nevin M. Fenneman, "The Circumference of Geography," *Geographical Review* 7 (1919), 168–174; Gilbert's 1909 presidential address was printed as: G. K. Gilbert, "Earthquake Forecasts," *Science* 29, no. 734 (1909): 121–38.; "scientific trespass" on 122.
67   Tarr to Hurlbut, 28.3.1905, Box 164, Folder 27, AGS Archives.
68   Hurlbut to Tarr, 7.4.1905, Box 164, Folder 27, AGS Archives.

proval for Tarr's funding request.[69] Grateful for the assistance, Tarr honored the agreement by submitting an article based on his AGS-funded research.[70]

Several years later, the disciplinary boundary between geography and geology became a point of contention when Tarr sought financial assistance for another expedition, this time to Alaska's Malaspina Glacier, which he described as the "largest and most interesting glacier on the American Continent".[71] Tarr emphasized the project's scientific significance and noted that the USGS would not fund it due to its lack of immediate economic value, implicitly criticizing the government's utilitarian approach to research.[72] The AGS Council responded that the expedition, while "interesting and instructive to geologists", did not qualify for funding "from a *geographical* point of view" (emphasis added).[73] Tarr strongly contested this decision by insisting that "it is not geology but geography that I wish to do – not exploration merely, which I consider of minor importance, but scientific geography." He argued that its exclusion from AGS support was based on an overly narrow view of the discipline.[74]

Learning from this rejection, Tarr framed a $4,000 funding request he made in the following year more strategically. He presented his glacier studies as addressing "a *geographical* problem of the very highest importance" (emphasis added), intentionally employing the society's preferred disciplinary language, and again emphasized that the USGS would not support research outside its resource-driven mandate.[75] Although the society recognized his research as indeed "of the highest scientific interest and importance", it nonetheless maintained that the study was in the field of geology and should therefore be carried out by the USGS.[76] A committee ultimately denied his request.[77] Nevertheless, Tarr's allies in the society attempted to persuade the

---

69   Robbins to Council Members of AGS, 31.3.1905, Box 164, Folder 27, AGS Archives; Council Minutes Vol. 14, 136–137, 20.4.1905, AGS Archives.

70   Tarr to Hurlbut, 20.9.1905, Box 164, Folder 27, AGS Archives; article published as Ralph S. Tarr and Lawrence Martin, "Glaciers and Glaciation of Yakutat Bay, Alaska," *Bulletin of the American Geographical Society* 38, no. 3 (1906): 145–67.

71   Tarr to Robbins, 8.12.1905, Box 164, Folder 27, AGS Archives.

72   Tarr to Robbins, 5.3.1906, Box 164, Folder 27, AGS Archives.

73   Robbins to Tarr, 6.3.1906, Box 164, Folder 27, AGS Archives.

74   Tarr to Robbins, 9.3.1906, Box 164, Folder 27, AGS Archives.

75   Tarr to Secretary of the AGS, 25.1.1907, Box 164, Folder 27, AGS Archives.

76   Robbins to Tarr, 25.2.1907, Box 11, Folder 35, AGS Archives.

77   Archer M. Huntington to Robbins, 23.2.1907, Box 164, Folder 27, AGS Archives.

USGS to support the project by offering to publish an endorsement in the *Bulletin*.[78] In addition, they lobbied for Tarr's research through a letter addressed to the Superintendent of the Coast and Geodetic Survey, written in the AGS's name.[79] Tarr later reciprocated the favor by contributing another article for the *Bulletin*.[80]

These episodes from the AAG and AGS suggest that disciplinary boundaries were not stable and fixed by broad consensus, but that they could be enforced by influential groups in society councils and committees. Researchers like Tarr learned to navigate these institutional definitions through strategic framing of their proposals. In this case, the AGS used its funding decisions to demarcate geography by advancing specific areas of research while sidelining work that it deemed to be geological.

3.3 Negotiating Alliances: Competition and Cooperation

Professionalization posed a strategic paradox for geographical societies: while competition was necessary to establish institutional legitimacy, cooperation was essential to build sufficient authority to compete with established sciences. Thus, pragmatic alliances balanced rivalry with mutual benefit. The formation of a professional geography in the United States required a pooling of resources, such as funding, expertise, and scientific reputation. This culminated in the 1914 strategic alliance between the American Geographical Society and the Association of American Geographers. This section first examines instances of cooperation and competition between U.S. geographical societies in organizing the 1904 International Geographic Congress. It then explores the AGS-AAG collaboration manifested in the transnational excursion of 1912 and their ensuing joint research fund. These efforts illustrate how competition and cooperation together advanced the professionalization of geography.

---

78   Robbins to Tarr, 25.2.1907, Box 11, Folder 35, AGS Archives.
79   Hurlbut to Superintendent of the Coast and Geodetic Survey, 31.1.1907, Letterpress Books Vol. 19, Box 82, AGS Archives.
80   Ralph S. Tarr, "The Malaspina Glacier," *Bulletin of the American Geographical Society 39*, no. 5 (1907): 273–85.

Competing for Prestige: The 1904 Geographic Congress

In the history of science, cooperation and competition often appear as intertwined forces driving institutional development. Perhaps more than any other event in the period, the planning of the Eighth International Geographic Congress (1904) in the United States exemplifies how both cooperation and competition steered the professionalization of geography. In 1903, the National Geographic Society unilaterally invited the Congress to convene in Washington, bypassing the AGS, which had earlier stated that "the time was not ripe" for the Eighth Congress to meet in the United States.[81] As early as 1900, the AGS had informed the Permanent Bureau of the Congress of its preference for the 1904 meeting to be held in St. Petersburg, while declaring its intention to host the subsequent Congress in New York.[82] The NGS's move to sideline the AGS took many geographers by surprise and threatened the AGS's perceived leadership role in U.S. geography.

For professional U.S. geographers already self-conscious about their scientific standing in comparison to their European counterparts, the Congress represented a critical opportunity to project scientific legitimacy on an international stage. Privately, many prominent geographers, particularly those aligned with the more academic visions of the AGS (and soon the AAG, founded in 1904) were dissatisfied that the NGS, widely known for emphasizing popularization, had taken the lead in organizing such a high-profile international event. In this way, the disagreement between the two societies was over competing visions of U.S. geography on the world stage. The NGS's approach represented a modern, popularizing, and Washington-centric model, while the AGS advocated an older, more elite, New York-based model of scholarly leadership.

These tensions are well-documented in AGS-NGS correspondence, which shows an uneasy mix of competition and cooperation between the societies. When the NGS asked the AGS to participate in the Congress's planning, the AGS refused to take a leading role, citing the lack of prior consultation: "[...] it would hardly become the American Geographical Society, which was not consulted as to the expediency of sending the invitation, to intervene now in the arrangements for greeting and entertaining delegates." Still, the AGS affirmed

---

81   Hurlbut to Greely, 24.9.1903, Box 9, Folder 27, AGS Archives.
82   AGS to Libbey, 7.3.1900, Letterpress Books Vol. 14, 430, Box 81, AGS Archives.

that it would participate as a guest, having a track record of accepting every invitation to the congress since 1871. At the same time, the AGS opened the door to some degree of cooperation to prevent any potential damage to the reputation of U.S. geography before European geographers: "Of course the subject is an extremely delicate one and we must proceed with great discretion lest the impression arise that the welcome of our foreign contemporaries is less hearty than most of us think it ought to be."[83] The NGS responded positively and urged all U.S. geographical societies to assist with preparations where possible: "In any event, so long as we are all disposed to extend a warm welcome and cordial hospitality to our foreign brethren, any minor misunderstandings will soon pass into oblivion."[84]

A compromise was reached to designate it the "Washington-New York" International Geographic Congress, with scientific sessions taking place in both cities, to project a joint NGS-AGS endeavor.[85] Yet this agreement quickly faltered and disputes over financial arrangements reignited tensions. Although the NGS secured government support for printing proceedings, it expected local societies to finance the entertainment of delegates.[86] The AGS reiterated that it would assist with the scientific aspect of the congress, but not with its financing or organization.[87] The AGS refused to take on any financial responsibilities, rejected the "Washington-New York" designation, and reaffirmed its decision to participate only as a guest.[88] Even the wording of the Congress's invitation became a point of contention. The inclusion of exploratory and mountaineering clubs as "geographical societies" prompted resistance from geographers who preferred a more restricted definition of geography. The final invitation omitted the word "geographic" before "societies" altogether.[89] University geography departments did not appear on the host list, highlighting the leading role that the societies took in representing U.S. geography.[90]

83   Robbins to Greely, 12.3.1903, Box 9, Folder 27, AGS Archives.

84   McGee to Hurlbut, 28.9.1903, Box 9, Folder 27, AGS Archives.

85   McCormick to Hurlbut, 3.11.1903, Box 9, Folder 27, AGS Archives.

86   Adams to AGS Council, 6.11.1903, Box 9, Folder 27, AGS Archives.

87   Robbins to McCormick, 13.11.1903, Box 9, Folder 27, AGS Archives.

88   Robbins to McCormick, 25.11.1903, Box 9, Folder 27, AGS Archives.

89   McCormick to Hurlbut, 3.11.1903, Box 9, Folder 27; the published Preliminary Announcement referred to "societies", not "geographic societies".

90   J. Russell Smith, "American Geography, 1900–1904," The Professional Geographer 4, no. 4 (1952): 6.

William Morris Davis brokered a compromise: a "Plan for United Action", through which he persuaded the AGS to host a scientific session in New York and thereby contribute to the academic portion of the Congress as an organizer.[91] Davis's intervention was motivated by concern for the international reputation of American geography. His effort to preserve unity and ensure a respectable scientific showing may also have reflected growing frustrations with the field's organizational fragmentation and a perceived lack of professionalism, foreshadowing the founding of the AAG several months later. Thus, the Congress episode demonstrates how competing visions of geography created organizational conflicts with long-term consequences for disciplinary development, while simultaneously revealing how competition for prestige could induce tactical cooperation when reputational stakes were high.

International Cooperation: The International Membership Card Initiative

Beyond ad hoc collaborations, geographical societies also sought institutional mechanisms for promoting sustained international cooperation. One ambitious cooperative initiative was the proposal to create an international membership card, which would allow members of geographical societies to access the facilities and privileges of other societies abroad, such as reading rooms, libraries, and attendance at lectures and meetings. This mutual recognition of membership was explicitly seen as part of a larger effort "to secure the co-operation of the Geographical Societies of the World in a plan to bring about closer affiliation between these separate organizations."[92] In the plan, approved through a resolution at the Eighth International Geographic Congress (1904), the AGS was tasked with coordinating the initiative. In 1905, the AGS sent a circular letter to geographical societies worldwide, inviting their participation. Responses were overwhelmingly positive, with more than thirty societies expressing enthusiasm.[93] However, the proposed policy also raised concerns over women's access to these benefits. The AGS circular included a clause stating that visiting members should be afforded "the same footing as an ordinary member at such social functions as may be organized by the Society."[94] While reciprocal membership privileges were widely endorsed,

---

91   Davis to members of *Committee of Arrangements, International Geographic Congress,* 7.12.1903, Box 9, Folder 27, AGS Archives.
92   Circular to international geographical societies, 1905, Box 88, Folder 1, AGS Archives.
93   Responses to Circular, 1905, Box 88, Folder 1, AGS Archives.
94   Circular to international geographical societies, 1905, Box 88, Folder 1, AGS Archives.

some societies had rules barring female members from certain events. In an otherwise positive reply, Hugh Robert Mill of the Royal Geographical Society (RGS) in London identified a potential complication: not all societies granted equal privileges to women. He cited the case of Ellen Churchill Semple, a prominent female American geographer, who could not participate in the RGS dinner, as these were reserved for male fellows only. Mill diplomatically warned that, despite endorsing the membership card in principle, some geographical societies might limit the benefits extended to women due to existing rules: "One difficulty that may arise is that lady members of such societies as concede equal rights might be unable to receive the same privileges as would be gladly offered to men in a Society which excludes or limits the privileges of ladies."[95] This exchange shows how efforts at transnational cooperation could clash with existing gendered institutional norms.

Building Reputation: The 1912 Transcontinental Excursion

One notable example of successful national cooperation and international network building between geographical societies was the 1912 Transcontinental Excursion planned by William Morris Davis. Jointly organized by the AAG and AGS, it brought together leading members of U.S. geographical societies along with more than fifty geographers from abroad for a cross-country scientific tour from New York to the West Coast. Davis had long envisioned such a tour, drawing on the European tradition of accompanying geographical congresses with scientific field excursions. These excursions offered an opportunity to showcase a host country's geographical features and to promote its scientific standing. Davis intended the U.S. tour to serve two aims: introduce international geographers to American landscapes and highlight recent scientific contributions by U.S. geographers. He insisted the excursion remain strictly scholarly, hoping it would conduct "as serious and scientific an examination of a selected series of geographical problems as can be planned". Distractions such as "irrelevant sight-seeing and entertainments [...] would detract from the scientific profit of the excursion" and were therefore to be avoided. This insistence reflected Davis's ambition to elevate U.S. geography to the level of European geography. Accordingly, he meticulously curated the itinerary to feature a diverse range of geographical phenomena. Davis anticipated that this would attract renowned European geographers and thereby "greatly

---

95   Hugh Robert Mill to Libbey, 23.5.1903, Box 88, Folder 1, AGS Archives.

promote the scientific study of geography in this country and the appreciation of our country abroad."[96]

Davis had considerable experience with planning field excursions in the United States and had previously toured Italy and France with geography students and professors in 1908.[97] However, the AAG lacked the financial means to realize the 1912 excursion. Davis therefore turned to the AGS and personally persuaded its patron, Archer M. Huntington, to underwrite the entire cost, estimated at $25,000. In doing so, Davis emphasized the national significance of the initiative to Huntington, arguing that it would "certainly increase the knowledge of American geography by Europeans, and it would promote the acquaintance of European geographers with Americans."[98] Invitations were extended to Europe's leading geographical societies, and the response was overwhelmingly positive. Over thirty delegates from Europe joined, including prominent German geographers such as Joseph Partsch (Leipzig), Erich Drygalski (Munich) and Alfred Rühl (Berlin), alongside geographers from France, Great Britain, Austria, Hungary, Italy, Switzerland, Belgium, the Netherlands, Russia, Denmark, Norway, and Sweden.[99] The participation of these distinguished European scholars attests to the success of Davis's strategy, underscoring how the AAG and AGS used financial resources and international networks to strengthen U.S. geography's global standing.

The excursion proved highly successful, as is evident by lasting scholarly connections and extensive publications resulting directly from the event. American and European geographers maintained correspondence for decades afterwards. Several international participants contributed articles to AGS publications and two of them later published full monographs on the United States. This was in addition to the more than 200 essays published by U.S. geographers in direct connection with the excursion.[100] Domestically and abroad, the scientific reputation of U.S. geography was successfully bolstered. Contemporary press coverage further attested to the event's success with headlines such as "European Scientists Have Praise for the Wonderful Sights

96   Plan for "A proposed geographical examination of the United States in 1912," Box 124, Folder 16, AGS Archives.

97   David Lowenthal, "Fruitful Liaison or Folie à Deux? The AAG and the AGS," *The Professional Geographer* 57, no. 3 (2005), 469.

98   Wright, *Geography in the Making*, 159.

99   Wright, *Geography in the Making*, 160.

100   Martin, *American Geography*, 499.

of New York", "Geographers Laud American Society", "Foreigners are astounded", and "Geographers of Europe Amazed by Grandeur of the Mountain Scenery Revealed in Colorado". One participant declared the tour to be a "revelation of the United States' natural resources, something to teach the whole world".[101] The Transcontinental Excursion also formed lasting international friendships. In a 1915 letter, Isaiah Bowman (AAG/AGS) wrote to Eugen Oberhummer, a German-Austrian geographer who had participated in the excursion, but had postponed a return visit due to the outbreak of World War I. Bowman expressed personal warmth and respect despite political tensions: "Though, in common with almost all Americans, I have no sympathy with the Austrian government or with the German militarist doctrines, yet at the same time I have still only the warmest respect and personal friendship for men like yourself and the other German members of our great excursion of two years ago."[102]

Strategic Partnership: The 1914 AGS-AAG Research Agreement

The culmination of these inter-institutional dynamics, and an important moment in consolidating professional geography, was the strategic alliance formed between the AGS and AAG in 1914. Under their agreement, the AAG received a permanent room and administrative support at the AGS headquarters, as well as financial backing for the *Annals* of the AAG. In return, the AAG committed to hold its annual meeting at the AGS headquarters. Both societies would otherwise retain their independence. Even though the arrangement was financially advantageous for the AAG, the agreement sparked considerable internal debate. The agreement took months to finalize, largely due to disagreements over the composition of a "Committee on Cooperation". The arrangement was initiated by William Morris Davis (AAG), who had already discussed the plan with AGS patron Archer M. Huntington before proposing it to AAG leadership. In a confidential letter to AAG leaders, Davis emphasized the plan's strategic advantages and dismissed concerns about a potential

---

101   "The Transcontinental Excursion," *New York Times*, October 19, 1912, 11; quoted in Wright, *Geography in the Making*, Plate XV.

102   Bowman to Oberhummer, 3.2.1915, Box 4, Folder 14, AGS Archives.

"absorption" by the AGS as "apparent – but not real". The only drawback he foresaw was the requirement to hold an annual joint meeting in New York.[103]

Despite these reassurances and the obvious benefits of cooperation, reactions within the AAG were mixed, reflecting underlying tensions about disciplinary identity and regional representation. In an internal letter, Brigham expressed concern that the proposed agreement was too far-reaching and required caution. He anticipated opposition from some AAG members, particularly given the society's more rigorous academic profile compared to the AGS's broader, and at times more popular, approach. He also worried that the agreement might alienate AAG members from the western United States and deepen existing regional divisions within the society.[104] Writing to fellow AAG member Bryant, Brigham asked whether affiliation with the New York-based AGS might give the impression that the AAG was too closely tied to East Coast institutions: "Is there any danger that members of our Association [...] will feel that we are making too local an affiliation in New York? Will the Western members feel that we are becoming anchored too much in the East, and putting ourselves unduly under obligation to another organization?"[105] These concerns proved to be justified, as many Western members were indeed skeptical about the proposal. Responding to Brigham, Dodge downplayed this issue, arguing that the partnership was clearly beneficial. Interestingly, his letter also alluded to internal tensions and personal rivalry *within* the AAG: "The only thing that I can see that will arise in the future is the use that we will put our income to. Davis will want to use it for the furtherance of some scientific research by one of his pets. He thinks the Association is his and we are all kids. Time will settle that however and in the right way."[106] Dodge's frustration underscores that the process of disciplinary professionalization was entangled with personal power dynamics and struggles for control over an institution's direction and resources. Despite his irritation with Davis's domineering attitude, Dodge supported the cooperation in a subsequent letter, emphasizing that the AAG would maintain

---

103   Davis to Dodge, Brigham, Fenneman, and Bowman, 17.1.1913, Box 13, Folder 37, AAG Archives.
104   Brigham to Davis and Dodge, 30.1.1913, Box 12, Folder 31, AAG Archives; on the issue of the AAG's Western members, see chapter 2.3 on membership in the AAG.
105   Brigham to Bryant, 6.3.1913, Box 12, Folder 31, AAG Archives.
106   Richard E. Dodge to Brigham, 2.2.1913, Box 14, Folder 1, AAG Archives.

its independence and that the agreement held significant institutional advantages.[107]

Other responses were more cautious, but still recommended moving forward. Ellsworth Huntington (AAG) warned of a "practical merging" of both societies, in which the AAG would become "merely the scientific branch". He feared that, as the AGS would "hold the purse strings", its views on geography and which geographic research was worthy of support would become dominant. Huntington noted the AGS's more popular orientation toward geography and speculated that it might one day become "necessary again to organize an entirely independent association of a strictly scientific character." Nonetheless, he conceded that increased funding for research was urgently needed and that the agreement was the most promising avenue for securing it.[108]

Meanwhile, some AGS Council members grew impatient with the AAG's delayed response and expressed concern over the composition of the proposed research committee. The clash in institutional culture is illuminated in a letter from AGS Councilor Robbins to AGS Chairman Greenough. He warned against letting academics dominate the proposed research committee: "The A.A.G. will furnish all the scientists needed; it is for us to furnish hard headed men of the world who can distinguish between words and wisdom! If our committee as well as theirs should be composed of scientists, they might all be carried away by 'the exuberance of their own verbosity' and let us in for extravagant schemes of great promise and small value." For Robbins, the role of the AAG's scholars was to provide ideas, while the role of the AGS was to provide capital and exercise prudence: "After all, what our society will be called upon to do is <u>pay</u> and to veto impracticable schemes" (emphasis in original).[109] This comment reveals lingering mistrust and differing priorities between the more academic AAG and the practically minded AGS leadership, which guarded its funds carefully.

After extended deliberation, the AAG unanimously approved the cooperation agreement, although regional divisions resurfaced in subsequent votes. The proposal to hold an annual AAG meeting in New York passed by a narrower margin (26 to 9), underscoring the regional tensions Brigham had anticipated. To address these tensions, the AAG scheduled its next meeting "at some point

---

107   Dodge to Brigham, 27.2.1913, Box 14, Folder 1, AAG Archives.
108   Ellsworth Huntington to Brigham, 14.4.1913, Box 16, Folder 37, AAG Archives.
109   Robbins to Greenough, 27.1.1914, Box 129, Folder 5, AGS Archives.

West of Pittsburgh" to accommodate its Western members.[110] In the end, the push for cooperation was driven by the increasing professionalization of geography. At a joint AGS-AAG meeting, the "Round-Table Conference on Geographic Research" emphasized the need for a centralized body to coordinate and fund research. Alfred H. Brooks noted that governmental agencies were constrained by legal mandates, and that universities had contributed too little. He called for an "Institute of Geographic Research" to address "specific problems rather than elaborate expeditions having no specific purpose."[111] Brooks's distinction highlights a shift away from the older, exploratory model of geography, valued for its narrative appeal and territorial discovery, toward a modern, problem-oriented model valued for its systematic production of specialized data. The new alliance between the AGS and AAG aimed to provide an institutional home for this problem-oriented scientific geography. The proposed solution was a joint research fund managed by both societies, which the leading AAG member Bowman described as "one of the most important ever adopted by this Association."[112] A subsequent AAG circular praised the AGS's hospitality at the joint meeting and called the event a model for future cooperation.[113] Yet the halfhearted attendance by AGS members hinted at persistent divisions.[114] Nevertheless, the AGS-AAG cooperation strengthened professional geography in the United States. Through joint meetings, co-publication of the AAG *Annals*, and shared research initiatives, the societies combined their strengths: the AGS provided financial and logistical support, while the AAG contributed academic expertise and disciplinary legitimacy.

The professionalization of U.S. geography was thus not a simple triumph of expertise but a contested process of negotiation. Through boundary-work, strategic alliances, and the careful management of institutional rivalries, geographers created a professional identity that was inherently hybrid: balancing scientific aspiration with popular appeal, and academic independence with service to the state.

110   "AAG Round Table Conference," Box 98, Folder 15, AAG Archives.
111   "Round-Table Conference on Geographic Research – Outline for Discussion of Geographic Research by Alfred H. Brooks," Box 98, Folder 2, AAG Archives.
112   Bowman to John Greenough, 1914, Box 12, Folder 25, AAG Archives.
113   AAG, "Circular of Information," 1914, Box 22, Folder 5, AAG Archives.
114   Bowman to Brooks, 4.6.1915, Box 4, Folder 7, AAG Archives.

4 Circulating Knowledge

In 1864, the American consul in Stettin (then Prussia) finally received a request for geographical information from the American Geographical Society that had taken two years to reach its destination. The consul dutifully sent geographical documents in reply, but these took yet another year to arrive in New York.[1] This three-year exchange illustrates a fundamental challenge of nineteenth-century geography: the difficulty of gathering, validating, and circulating knowledge across vast distances at a time when information traveled slowly. Yet this anecdote also shows how geographical societies, as "centers of calculation", built global networks capable of transforming scattered observations into systematic and authoritative knowledge.

The authority of knowledge depends on its circulation, which connects dispersed sites of knowledge production through networks, actors, and artefacts. Yet scientific knowledge does not circulate through space in a universal, transcendent, or neutral form; rather, it is shaped by the spaces it traverses.[2] This chapter traces the practices and infrastructures that enabled such global circulation, focusing on the American Geographical Society. Treating the AGS as a "center of calculation", it analyzes the society's library as an infrastructural foundation, the diplomatic channels and publication exchanges used to acquire geographical knowledge from abroad, and the sponsorship decisions, patronage, and endorsements that determined which expeditions gained legitimacy and support. The chapter then examines the standardization of field practices and the use of "immutable mobiles" to show how credible knowledge could be produced at a distance and stabilized "on the move". Finally, it reconstructs how field records were converted at the society's headquarters into lec-

---

1   Charles Sundell (Consul in Stettin) to AGS, 25.7.1865, Box 5, Folder 15, AGS Archives.
2   Livingstone, *Putting Science in its Place*, 140.

tures, bulletins, and books, thus completing the cycle of circulation from the field back to the center.

4.1 Accumulating Knowledge: Libraries, Consuls, and Exchanges

To analyze how geographical societies managed the flow and credibility of knowledge, I conceptualize them as "centers of calculation" – hubs of knowledge production and dissemination, analogous to universities, museums, and archives. Bruno Latour coined the term in his ethnographic studies of laboratories as part of a larger effort in the history of science to emphasize the social construction of scientific knowledge.[3] More specifically, Latour's actor-network theory foregrounds how knowledge production depends on networks.[4] In this view, societies derived power not from "discovering" objective facts, but from their institutional capacity to fund, collect, combine, and circulate geographical knowledge.

In this framework, centers of calculation construct knowledge at a distance by assembling networks of human and nonhuman actants. Latour's premise is the "cumulative character of science", which he defines as "a cycle of accumulation that allows a point to become a center by acting at a distance on many other points". This approach has significant implications for the relationship between fieldwork and metropolitan centers of knowledge production: events, places, and people must be brought home through "expeditions, collections, probes, observatories and enquiries". To describe the resources that enabled this process of accumulation, Latour coined the term "immutable mobiles", resources which needed to remain stable (to stay unchanged), mobile (to be transported) and combinable (to be connected to other resources). Maps, photographs, specimens, instrument readings, and field notes functioned as immutable mobiles. Through the mobilization of these actants in repeated "cycles of accumulation", knowledge was aggregated in centers of calculation. At the center, these materials were classified, systematized, and combined to produce

---

3   Golinski, *Making Natural Knowledge.*
4   Jan-Hendrik Passoth, "Aktanten, Assoziationen, Mediatoren: Wie die ANT das Soziale neu zusammenbaut," in *Dimensionen und Konzeptionen von Sozialität,* ed. Gert Albert, Rainer Greshoff, and Rainer Schützeichel (Wiesbaden: VS Verlag für Sozialwissenschaften, 2010), 309–316.

new knowledge claims.[5] The resulting stabilized knowledge is typically a sim-
plified, more coherent version of the phenomena it represents, making it easier to communicate. Such knowledge often takes the form of a "black box", its
constructed nature concealed, and its claims accepted as self-evident.[6] Latour
thus encourages historians to examine "science in the making" – the processes
of production and stabilization – rather than focusing solely on published results.

To ensure the reliability of knowledge gathered remotely, it had to be
obtained systematically and accurately. This necessitated the standardization
of practices in the field – including measurement protocols, the training
of observers' senses, and the provision of instruments and handbooks – all
coordinated from the centers of calculation.[7] Felix Driver's study of the Royal
Geographical Society's guidebook *Hints to Travellers* (first published in 1854)
illustrates how a society could produce credible knowledge at a distance by
disseminating a manual that standardized field-specific practices such as
observing, collecting, and measuring.[8] New knowledge claims produced in
the field were then tested in other settings through "trials of strength" and
were either accepted or rejected. In this way, centers of calculation functioned
both as places where knowledge claims were stabilized and as conduits for
their broader circulation. Typically, knowledge claims from reputable centers
of knowledge production were transformed into accepted facts.[9]

Geographical societies functioned as centers of calculation by relying on
three distinct infrastructures: libraries, diplomatic channels, and publication
exchanges. I adopt Latour narrowly: I use the "center of calculation" concept
to analyze infrastructures and cycles of accumulation, while remaining attentive to human intention. Foregrounding the institutional setting in which
geography was practiced clarifies how networks and infrastructures shaped
the production, validation, and circulation of scientific knowledge. Following the "spatial" and "practical" turns in the history of science, this concept
illuminates how practices and places intersected in constituting knowledge.
Historians of science have applied and expanded this framework in studies

---

5   Latour, *Science in Action*, 220–28.
6   Latour, *Science in Action*, 234–47.
7   Livingstone, *Putting Science in its Place*, 47–49.
8   Driver, *Geography Militant*, 49–67.
9   Latour, *Science in Action*, 247–57.

of botanical gardens, museums, libraries, exhibitions, and universities.[10] Such research often intersects with the history of imperialism by tracing the transnational networks through which these institutions acted as repositories and clearinghouses of colonial knowledge.[11] One example is David Miller's study of Kew Gardens during the age of imperialism. There, Joseph Banks classified botanical specimens collected in imperial contexts according to the Linnaean system, a framework that enabled knowledge to be stabilized and standardized at a distance. In doing so, Banks established Kew Gardens as a reference point for comparing new illustrations with accredited images to classify plants.[12]

U.S. geographical societies mirrored these processes, particularly in their efforts to collect, systematize, and disseminate information. As the Kew Gardens example suggests, producing geographical knowledge depended on accumulating resources via circulatory movements between distant sites and society headquarters. Geographers frequently consulted materials held in these collections before embarking on their expeditions. The following sections examine the specific infrastructures and practices that enabled the AGS to function as a center of calculation and control the knowledge circulating through its networks. The libraries, networks, and institutional exchanges shaped which kinds of knowledge could circulate successfully, how it was validated, and whose perspectives gained authority.

---

10   Ruth Craggs, "Situating the imperial archive: The Royal Empire Society Library, 1868–1945", *Journal of Historical Geography* 34, no. 1 (2008): 48–67; Lawrence Dritsas, "From Lake Nyassa to Philadelphia: A geography of the Zambesi Expedition, 1858–64," *British Journal for the History of Science* 38, no. 1 (2005): 35–52; Nuala Johnson, "Grand design(er)s: David Moore, natural theology and the Royal Botanic Gardens in Glasnevin, Dublin, 1838–1879," *Cultural Geographies* 14, no. 1 (2007): 29–55; Heike Jöns, "Academic travel from Cambridge University and the formation of centres of knowledge, 1885–1954," *Journal of Historical Geography* 34, no. 2 (2008): 338–362.

11   *Science and Empire: Knowledge and Networks of Science across the British Empire, 1800 – 1970*, ed. Brett M. Bennett and Joseph M. Hodge (Basingstoke: Palgrave Macmillan, 2011).

12   David Philip Miller, "Joseph Banks, Empire, and 'Centers of Calculation' in Late Hanoverian London," in *Visions of Empire. Voyages, Botany, and Representations of Nature*, eds. David Philip Miller and Peter Hanns Reill (Cambridge: Cambridge University Press, 1996).

Society Libraries as Knowledge Infrastructure

The libraries of geographical societies were integral components of centers of calculation. As repositories of accumulated geographical knowledge, they acquired books, documents, and maps; processed requests for resources; and subscribed to relevant journals. Using the AGS library as a case study illustrates how societies functioned as central nodes in the production and circulation of scientific knowledge by systematically gathering materials through institutional networks. The AGS library thus served as a mechanism through which the society determined what constituted legitimate geographical knowledge. Through its collection policies, the society library effectively established hierarchies of geographical knowledge, privileging certain types of documents, methodological approaches, and regional focuses over others. Government surveys, military reports, and commercial statistics typically received priority in acquisition, reflecting and reinforcing the society's alignment with state and commercial interests.

An 1865 circular letter from the AGS highlights the significance of the society's library and its collections. In the letter, the AGS secretary asked members for monetary donations to fund improvements, including enlarging the accommodations, binding valuable books, mounting maps for easier consultation, acquiring additional maps to create a properly indexed map room, and expanding the collection of statistical works on U.S. states. The circular emphasized that these changes would transform the library into "a facility, which it is believed does not exist elsewhere in the country", positioning the library itself as a source of institutional prestige and a valuable research resource.[13]

To illustrate the circulation of knowledge into the AGS library, this subsection traces how documents and maps arrived at the library, especially during the society's early years. Like many other geographical societies, the AGS obtained a substantial share of its geographical information from the U.S. government. Society members, many of whom were government employees or closely connected to them, secured reports, documents, and maps from various departments and bureaus. A typical example is found in a 1900 letter from AGS librarian George C. Hurlbut to Henry Gannett of the United States Geological Survey, in which Hurlbut inquires on behalf of the society: "Do you feel at liberty to let me know in what way this Society can procure, for issue

---

13   "Newsletter to members, American Geographical and Statistical Society. New York, 1st January," 1865, Box 42, Folder 4, AGS Archives.

to its members as part of its *Bulletin*, the specially interesting maps published from time to time by the War Department and by other branches of the public service?"[14] This request shows the society pursuing specific materials suitable for distribution to its members. Two years later, a representative of the War Department assured the AGS that it "would be pleased to send you from time to time publications bearing on geographical work", indicating an ongoing exchange.[15] Once established, these relationships became reliable channels of information that enriched the library's holdings over time.

High-ranking politicians were also approached through personal or institutional connections. For example, in 1900, Hurlbut wrote to Senator Thomas C. Platt to request a copy of the "Report and Maps of the Interoceanic Canal Commission". This was not the first such interaction with the Senator, as Hurlbut noted appreciatively: "Your kindness on previous occasions is fully appreciated and [...] I venture again to encroach upon your valuable time."[16] Government-employed geographers also alerted the AGS to upcoming publications and advised the society on how to obtain them. In 1905, geographer Emory Johnson wrote: "I think you may be interested in knowing that a quarto edition, with plates and maps, of the *Report of the Isthmian Canal Commission*, of which I was a member from 1899 to 1904, has been printed by the Government." He provided further details about the content of the report, including his own contribution on trade and industry in Pacific countries and the value of a trans-Isthmian canal, noting that 3,000 copies were allocated to members of Congress.[17] With this precise information, the AGS could request the report promptly and efficiently. This systematic acquisition of government documents made geographical societies intermediaries between state knowledge production and public dissemination. They repackaged government-funded information for different audiences while building relationships that provided access to restricted materials.[18]

Through personal requests, government channels, donations, and acquisitions, the AGS library amassed a substantial collection: by 1929, it held 86,000

---

14   Hurlbut to Gannett, 10.9.1900, Letterpress Books Vol. 20A, Box 83, AGS Archives.
15   War Department Library (A.W. Greely) to Robbins 18.2.1902, Box 163, Folder 5, AGS Archives.
16   Hurlbut to Thomas C. Platt, Senate Chamber, 17.12.1900, Vol. 20A, Box 83, AGS Archives.
17   Johnson to Hurlbut, 4.8.1905, Box 163, Folder 5, AGS Archives.
18   For the NGS and the popularization of government publications, see chapter 5.3

volumes, 67,000 map sheets, and over 1,400 atlases.[19] This accumulation depended on the society's extensive networks, which simultaneously elevated the
AGS's scientific reputation and solidified its position as a center of calculation.
Given that many of the library's materials were obtained from external institutions and individuals, the AGS library operated within a wider network of
knowledge production and circulation. The library functioned as an essential
component of the society's infrastructure: it enabled the society to position itself as an authoritative source of geographical knowledge by systematically collecting government reports, international publications, and other geographical information, and to mediate this knowledge by repackaging it for different audiences via its *Bulletin*. The reach of this infrastructure became visible
in wartime: in 1917, when The Inquiry was convened to prepare United States
peace aims, AGS librarian George McBride joined its select group of geographers (see Introduction), underscoring how society libraries could translate
collection and curation work into state expertise.[20] This participation reflected
the AGS library's infrastructural resources such as staff and comprehensive
catalogues, rather than an intrinsic superiority of its geographical knowledge.

Diplomatic Networks and Consular Channels

In addition to its domestic networks, the AGS relied on informal diplomatic
channels and international connections to gather spatially dispersed information and strengthen its function as a center of calculation with global reach.
One strategy involved designating U.S. consuls and foreign legation staff as
"ex-officio" members, who were encouraged to gather and forward geographical materials from their assigned regions. In the 1860s, the AGS sent certifi-
cates to consuls and legations, informing them of their honorary ex-officio status. The goal was to encourage them to provide geographical materials to the
society. Many recipients responded with excitement, expressed pride at their
appointments, and pledged their support. The U.S. Consul in Macao, for example, replied: "I am in full sympathy with the aspirations of this most excellent

19   Pamphlet: The AGS (1929), Box 123, Folder 30, AGS Archives; for the growth of the li-
      brary collection from 1905 to 1930, see also Box 6, Folder 53, AGSL Archival Collection
      2, American Geographical Society Library Records, 1851–2013, American Geographical
      Society Library, University of Wisconsin-Milwaukee Libraries.
20   Smith, *American Empire*, 122.

association and shall deem it a distinction to do service [...]".²¹ Similar enthusiasm was shown by the Consul in Pernambuco (Brazil), who sent statistical
documents on the province and declared that he was "sympathizing heartily
as [...] with the objects of your Society – I shall bear it constantly in mind and
do what I can to promote its interest."²² However, the acquisition of materials through these channels was not always straightforward or immediate. In
one instance, a letter the AGS sent to the U.S. consul in Stettin in 1862 was only
received in 1864. The consul eventually responded and sent a substantial collection of geographical documents, which reached the AGS the following year.²³
This three-year delay highlights the protracted nature of long-distance knowledge circulation through nineteenth-century infrastructures and the critical
role of geographical societies as centers of calculation capable of patiently accumulating geographically dispersed knowledge over long timespans.

The enthusiastic participation by consuls was likely enhanced by the
manner in which the AGS circulated its request. Rather than relying solely
on individual outreach, the AGS persuaded the U.S. Department of State to

Materials sent by these ex-officio members ranged from statistical reports
and newspapers to books and maps, arriving from places such as Brazil, Peru,
the German states, Egypt, Macao, and Belfast. When ex-officio members were
unable to send materials immediately, they often promised to do so at a later
date.²⁴ The U.S. Consul in Bristol, for example, forwarded reports, maps, and
plans of the survey of England as well as additional books on charts, accounts of
voyages, and trade journals, a collection that aptly illustrates the combination
of state-sponsored cartography and commercial maritime knowledge the society valued.²⁵ An 1865 AGS newsletter showcased these contributions, which
were read and discussed at a society meeting: "A Voyage into the Interior of
China" from Consul Jones, "Island of Zanzibar, on Eastern Coast of Africa" from
Consul Hines, and "Notes of Travel" from Consul Perry detailing an expedition
in Tunisia. The society noted that it "anticipate[d] additional interesting data",
indicating its expectation that the correspondence would continue.²⁶

The enthusiastic participation by consuls was likely enhanced by the
manner in which the AGS circulated its request. Rather than relying solely
on individual outreach, the AGS persuaded the U.S. Department of State to

---

21   W. P. Jones (Macao Consul) to AGS, 30.3.1865, Box 5, Folder 15, AGS Archives.

22   Thomas Adamson Jr. (United States Consulate Pernambuco) to AGS, 4.1.1865, Box 5, Folder 15, AGS Archives.

23   Charles Sundell (Consul in Stettin), 25.7.1865, Box 5, Folder 15, AGS Archives.

24   Over 30 replies in Box 5, Folder 15, AGS Archives.

25   Z. Eastman (Bristol) to AGS, 1865, Box 5, Folder 15, AGS Archives.

26   AGS Newsletter 1865, Box 42, Folder 4, AGS Archives.

distribute its requests for information as an official circular and to forward the replies on behalf of the society. Diplomatic mail also spared the AGS any postage or customs fees. This approach gave the AGS's request a sense of official legitimacy and urgency. A letter from the State Department confirmed its willingness to forward several hundred copies of the AGS's appeal to U.S. diplomatic representatives abroad.[27] The society's main point of contact at the State Department was Acting Assistant Secretary Clarence A. Seward, nephew of William H. Seward, one of the principal architects of American imperial expansion in the Pacific. Clarence A. Seward facilitated the distribution of the circulars and provided the AGS with a list of American consuls and legation staff.[28] The plan was formalized in an AGS Council meeting in 1864, during which the Secretaries of Legation abroad were officially designated "ex-officio" members. According to AGS President Daly, international document exchanges passed through the AGS before being forwarded to "our sister institutions, branches of Government, etc. at Washington", positioning the AGS as a key intermediary for geographical knowledge entering the United States.[29] Whether or not this was consistently the case, the claim reveals the society's ambition to function as the nation's preeminent center of calculation and clearinghouse for geographical knowledge.

The integration of geographical societies into diplomatic networks also indicates the political dimensions of knowledge circulation in the United States. Whereas many European geographical societies could draw on colonial administrative networks, U.S. societies relied more heavily on diplomatic channels, a distinction that produced different, though still state-shaped, geographical knowledge. This ex-officio membership arrangement was mutually beneficial: consuls gained prestige through association with a respected scientific body, while the AGS gained privileged access to official channels of information gathering. This system ensured that geographical knowledge flowing into the society was already diplomatically filtered by U.S. state priorities, structuring what

---

27   Department of State to AGS, 18.5.1865, Box 5, Folder 16, AGS Archives; W. Hunter to Waddell, undated, Box 5, Folder 15, AGS Archives.

28   Clarence A. Seward to William Coventry H. Waddell, 29.6.1865, Box 5, Folder 15, AGS Archives; Seward to Waddell, 27.7.1865, Box 5, Folder 15, AGS Archives.

29   "Discussion in Council meeting of American Geographical and Statistical Society, October 20, 1864, as regards ways of extending the scope of and interest in the Society", Box 43, Folder 5, AGS Archives.

could be known about foreign territories even before materials reached the society's headquarters. Some of the knowledge societies processed and recirculated thus tended to reflect American political and commercial interests rather than neutral geographical facts.

By orchestrating an international network that used diplomatic infrastructure, the AGS gradually extended its global reach, functioning as a central node in the global circulation of geographical knowledge. Even in its earliest years, the society was already operating as a center of calculation, an institutional hub capable of collecting, storing, and redistributing knowledge. However, as the society's reliance on state infrastructure suggests, the circulation of geographical knowledge was fundamentally shaped by institutional structures and power relations rather than flowing freely according to purely scientific considerations. The AGS's strategic cultivation of relationships with government agencies, diplomatic officials, and international societies created pathways through which certain kinds of geographical knowledge could travel efficiently (particularly data relevant to trade, resources, and geopolitics), while others remained marginalized.

Publication Exchanges and Transnational Networks

The circulation of knowledge in the nineteenth century depended on close cooperation between institutions. Geographical societies established a global network of publication exchanges (the systematic exchange of bulletins and geographical reports) with numerous institutions. This subsection examines the mechanics, scope, and strategic purposes of these exchanges, focusing on the types of knowledge circulated through these transnational channels. From its inception, the AGS pursued a deliberate, systematic approach to publication exchange. Within a few years of its founding, the society had established contact with 33 international geographical societies, according to the *Report of the Foreign Corresponding Secretary*. The AGS regularly sent copies of its *Bulletin* to these societies, often accompanied by additional materials such as reports on railroads, patents, Arctic exploration, or general statistical data concerning the United States. In return, by 1857, the AGS library had already received documents from government agencies in Austria, Chile, Sardinia, Portugal, and Belgium, as well as from geographical societies in Berlin, Paris, and London.[30]

---

30   "Council, Annual Report, 1857: Annual Report of the Council and Officers with Appendix for 1857," 34–36, Box 98, Folder 1, AGS Archives.

These exchanges were strategically cultivated and maintained, as the Foreign Corresponding Secretary noted: "the system of Foreign Correspondence and Exchange is at length successfully inaugurated, and only requires diligent attention in the selection of suitable works as donations on our part to ensure very valuable Volumes in return." To encourage reciprocal contributions, the AGS also solicited publications from the U.S. government that were likely to be valued abroad, specifically reports on meteorology, geology, or medical and commercial statistics.[31] The AGS thus positioned itself as a recipient of foreign knowledge and also as a distributor of authoritative U.S. geographical knowledge. In this way, it shaped the transnational flow of information and promoted a particular image of U.S. science.

The global demand for such materials is evident in correspondence with the German cartographer August Petermann, an honorary AGS member. In an 1857 letter, he praised U.S. government reports, reprinted in the AGS *Bulletin* as "truly magnificent works", and contrasted the American openness in sharing scientific information with the reluctance of European governments. From Petermann's vantage point, U.S. geography stood on par with European geography and "a surprising ignorance prevails in Europe, respecting the astounding activity and productiveness of your Country in this respect". Petermann attributed this ignorance to a lack of knowledge about U.S. geography and suggested sending more publications for distribution in his network. He specifically inquired about U.S. expedition reports (e.g., Wilkes on the Antarctic, Lynch on the Dead Sea, Perry on Japan, Kane on the Pole), railroad surveys, coast surveys, patent office reports, and meteorological registers.[32] Petermann's specific requests highlight the forms of U.S. geographical knowledge considered valuable internationally at mid-century, notably large-scale surveys and exploration reports, often linked to resource assessment or territorial expansion. Petermann's enthusiasm also served as a form of validation as European recognition legitimized U.S. geographical work and his requests indicated international demand for American geographical knowledge.

The geographical societies deliberately managed these publication exchanges to circulate and acquire knowledge. These international scientific networks also served domestic functions: European validation provided credibility, global networks demonstrated expertise, and international exchanges positioned U.S. societies as equal participants in global science. Through

---

31   Council, Annual Report, 1857, 34–37, Box 98, Folder 1, AGS Archives.
32   Council, Annual Report, 1857, 39–40, Box 98, Folder 1, AGS Archives.

ex-officio members, foreign correspondents, and carefully maintained institutional contacts, geographical societies built transnational and transimperial networks that enabled knowledge to flow beyond national borders. These exchange networks formed a crucial part of the knowledge infrastructure, allowing societies to function as effective centers of calculation by systematically gathering and disseminating information on a global scale.

4.2 Authorizing Exploration: Patronage, Funding, and Endorsement

Sponsoring expeditions allowed geographical societies to direct how expedition knowledge was produced, circulated, and aligned with institutional agendas. The AGS regularly received expedition funding requests, but it denied most due to limited resources and strategic or disciplinary preferences. To a considerable degree, the AGS's expedition funding decisions shaped the boundaries of legitimate geographical knowledge. By selectively supporting certain expedition proposals while rejecting others, the society determined which regions, phenomena, and methodological approaches would receive institutional validation. Analysis of funding requests and corresponding responses sheds light on which types of expeditions were more likely to be funded by the AGS, and why.

Council members sometimes interpreted funding applications as challenges to their authority, fostering a defensive stance toward applicants they considered presumptuous or overly ambitious. In 1904, AGS Councilor Chandler Robbins captured this attitude in an internal letter: "Undoubtedly the little capital which the American Geographical Society has accumulated is looked at with longing eyes by many who are eager to start an exploring expedition. They fret at what they consider the sluggish conservatism and lack of enthusiasm and enterprise of the Society. They think they could manage the affairs of the Society much better than the Council manages them. If they could only get their hands into our purse, they could accomplish great things in the way of increasing the world's stock of knowledge, etc. etc."[33] This defensive attitude suggests protectiveness over funds, resentment toward a perceived sense of entitlement from applicants, and the political tensions applicants faced in navigating the society's power structures.

---

33   Robbins to Jesup, 22.10.1904, Box 129, Folder 3, AGS Archives.

Personal networks were instrumental in securing expedition support, as demonstrated by AGS-funded expeditions to Alaska (Ralph S. Tarr), the Arctic (Ejnar Mikkelsen), Syria (Ellsworth Huntington) and the Andes (Isaiah Bowman). To obtain funding for his 1905 Alaska Expedition, Tarr enlisted the support of Councilor Robbins and *Bulletin* editor Hurlbut, whose advocacy proved decisive. The Council funded the expedition under the condition that "the scientific results [were] to be first published in the Bulletin", thus asserting the society's control over knowledge dissemination.[34] When Tarr applied for funds for an additional expedition, the AGS could not financially support it. Nevertheless, Robbins and Hurlbut supported Tarr, sending a letter in the AGS's name to the Superintendent of the Coast and Geodetic Survey, suggesting it would benefit the survey to fund Tarr's work, which shows how the society could use its reputation and networks even without direct funding.[35]

In 1907, Ellsworth Huntington requested financial assistance for an expedition in the Ottoman Empire. His application detailed plans for a 100-day expedition across Syria and Palestine and listed the expected costs. To strengthen his request, Huntington referred to his earlier expeditions in the region, the results of which had already been published in the AGS *Bulletin*, demonstrating his track record and alignment with the society's interests.[36] According to AGS regulations, expedition funding decisions were formally made by the Council or an appointed committee.[37] However, personal relationships between influential members and expedition applicants were equally important. A 1908 letter from AGS Councilor Robbins to Ellsworth Huntington (the applicant) suggests that personal meetings with influential and wealthy men such as AGS patron Archer M. Huntington mattered as much, and at times more, than the decisions of the society's Council. Robbins even suggested that Ellsworth Huntington should meet with AGS patron Archer M. Huntington *before* submitting the request to the Council, as his opinion would be decisive.[38] Archer M. Huntington subsequently informed Robbins that the "matter will be placed before

---

34   Council Minutes Vol. 14, 136–137, 20.4.1905, AGS Archives.
35   Hurlbut to Superintendent of the Coast and Geodetic Survey, 31.1.1907, Letterpress Books Vol. 19, Box 82, AGS Archives.
36   E. Huntington to Adams, 13.7.1907, Box 271, Folder 13, AGS Archives; Ellsworth Huntington to Robbins, 8.11.1908, Box 271, Folder 13, AGS Archives.
37   Robbins to Adams, 17.6.1909, Box 129, Folder 4, AGS Archives.
38   Robbins to E. Huntington, 10.11.1908, Box 271, Folder 13, AGS Archives.

the society", which ultimately denied the application.[39] Although the funding request was denied, the episode suggests that society insiders understood that influential patrons' preferences could predetermine council outcomes.

Isaiah Bowman's funding request for his expedition to South America demonstrates even more clearly how personal networks secured expedition support. In parallel to his official expedition proposal, Bowman approached AGS patron Archer M. Huntington directly, referring to the prior introduction by the influential geographer William Morris Davis.[40] Bowman requested $2,500 from the society, emphasizing "the strictest economy" and promising detailed expense reports. His proposal carefully outlined the expedition route and planned scientific objectives, supported by an accompanying map, thereby demonstrating adherence to AGS standards for credible geographical research. Bowman offered to publish his results as a book with the subtitle "under the auspices of the American Geographical Society" and committed to giving lectures and writing articles for the *Bulletin*.[41] The AGS Council approved the request and raised the money, most of which came from its patron Archer M. Huntington. As Adams conceded in a letter to Bowman, it was advantageous to approach Huntington directly, illustrating "the great advantage of personal contact with the man that holds the purse string."[42] Thus, it was not only Bowman's scientific excellence that qualified him for expedition funding, but also his personal connections to influential AGS officers, renowned geographer Davis, and AGS benefactor Huntington.

Societies also used their institutional reputation to assist expeditions in securing alternative sources of funding or navigating logistical and political obstacles. When unable to provide financial aid, the AGS frequently offered endorsement instead. This was the case with the Parker-Browne expedition, which explicitly indicated that they had already secured external funding, but

---

39   Archer M. Huntington to Robbins, Box 271, Folder 13, AGS Archives; In 1913, Ellsworth Huntington requested funding again, this time $20,000 for his next expedition to Asia Minor – the AGS declined. The geographer then planned the expedition on a smaller scale and asked for additional funds a year later – which the AGS denied, again; see: E. Huntington to President AGS and Council, 13.3.1913, Box 271, Folder 13, AGS Archives; James to Madison, "Draft of the proposed report for committee on E . Huntington", 16.12.1914, Box 271, Folder 13, AGS Archives; E. Huntington to Greenough, 3.7.1914, Box 271, Folder 13, AGS Archives.
40   Bowman to A. M. Huntington, 17.2.1913, Box 265, Folder 42, AGS Archives.
41   Bowman to AGS Council, 17.2.1913, Box 265, Folder 42, AGS Archives.
42   Adams to Bowman, 6.3.1913, Box 265, Folder 42, AGS Archives.

sought official AGS endorsement to frame their adventurous first ascent of a glacier on Mount McKinley as a legitimate scientific expedition. As they framed it, they hoped to conduct a "scientific expedition primarily and in order to give it a cachet it is necessary that they should have the authorization of some recognized society or institution".[43] This language highlights how societies could confer legitimacy and significantly enhance an expedition's credibility and standing. Similarly, after failing to secure direct AGS funding, G. C. Curtis received the society's formal endorsement for his Labrador expedition, which improved his chances of acquiring financial support elsewhere.[44] For an expedition to Bolivia, Annie S. Peck asked the AGS for a financial contribution or, failing that, a letter of endorsement from the society.[45] On another occasion in 1912, the AGS commended Vilhjalmur Stefansson's planned expedition to the Arctic as being worthy of support.[46] There were numerous other instances where the AGS offered similar endorsements to expeditions, so that they could secure external funding. By doing this, the society functioned as a gatekeeper and clearinghouse for expeditions meeting its standards, extending its influence beyond its own budget by providing valuable legitimacy and credibility to select expeditions.

Securing endorsement from geographical societies could be nearly as valuable as direct financial support. The reputation conferred by operating under the auspices of the AGS often expedited access to critical resources, smoothed logistical challenges, and facilitated the processing of their accumulated fieldwork into recognized publications. Expedition leaders often sought society endorsement to overcome political or logistical barriers. In 1912, *Yale Peruvian Expedition* leader Hiram Bingham requested an AGS letter to the Peruvian government attesting to the strictly scientific and non-commercial nature of his archaeological and geographical exploration. This became necessary because previous so-called "explorers" had been searching for gold in the region under the guise of scientific exploration.[47] AGS vice president Greenough obliged with a formal letter to the President of Peru affirming the expedition's scientific

---

43   "F.S. Dellenbaugh about planned expedition of Parker, Browne, Cuntz," undated, Box 271, Folder 15, AGS Archives.
44   Council Minutes Vol. 14, 292–293, 18.4.1907, Box 106, AGS Archives.
45   Council Minutes Vol. 13, 91, 14.3.1901, Box 105, AGS Archives.
46   Council Minutes Vol. 16, 125, 19.12.1912, Box 106, AGS Archives.
47   Bingham to Archer M. Huntington, 29.2.1912, Box 270, Folder 11, AGS Archives.

goals by describing it as being "strictly [for] scientific purpose" and "of educational importance and value not only to Peru but to the progress of science in general."[48] Similar assistance was provided for Bowman's Andes Expedition. Bowman asked the AGS president to use his ties to the U.S. Department of State to contact the ministers of several nations in South America to provide Bowman with letters of introduction, which would exempt him from import duties on his expedition equipment.[49]

Apart from funding and endorsements, the AGS's reputation and extensive networks were critical for obtaining government permissions and diplomatic support. Donaldson Smith's 1898 Somaliland expedition highlights the reach of the AGS's institutional reputation and high-level connections. Smith sought AGS assistance to secure travel permissions through British Somaliland, requesting support in lobbying the British government through U.S. diplomatic channels.[50] In response, AGS officer Adams promptly contacted former AGS president Charles P. Daly, known for his governmental connections. Adams strongly endorsed Smith, citing his publications in the *Journal of the Royal Geographical Society* (RGS), awards from the RGS in London, and cartographic contributions to the renowned mapmakers at Gotha. He predicted Smith's expedition would yield "very noteworthy results" and attract widespread interest among geographers.[51] Within a week, Daly directly petitioned U.S. President McKinley, praising Smith as "one of the very few Americans who have contributed to the advance of scientific geography in Africa", noting that the expedition was to be conducted under the auspices of the AGS.[52] According to the correspondence, the matter was quickly forwarded to the Secretary of State,[53] who then instructed the U.S. embassy in London to request the necessary permissions from British authorities.[54] Even though the British government ultimately denied the request,[55] the incident demonstrates the extent of AGS networks, which reached to the highest levels of U.S. government. Despite this setback, Smith eventually found alternative means to conduct his expedition

---

48   Greenough to Bingham, undated, Box 270, Folder 11, AGS Archives.
49   Bowman to AGS Council, 8.3.1913, Box 265, Folder 42, AGS Archives.
50   Smith to Adams, 13.9.1898, Box 265, Folder 41, AGS Archives.
51   Adams to Hurlbut, 16.9.1898, Box 265, Folder 41, AGS Archives.
52   Daly to McKinley, 22.9.1898, Box 265, Folder 41, AGS Archives.
53   Porter to Daly, 24.9.1898, Box 265, Folder 41, AGS Archives.
54   Alvey A. Adee to Daly, 6.10.1898, Box 265, Folder 41, AGS Archives.
55   Smith to Hurlbut, 8.10.1898, Box 265, Folder 41, AGS Archives.

and continued submitting results to the AGS *Bulletin*, showing his apprecia-tion for the society's efforts and maintaining the relationship.[56]

The 1906 Anglo-American Polar Expedition, led by Danish explorer Ejnar Mikkelsen, further demonstrates the influence of the AGS's networks and rep-utation. Mikkelsen, unable to legally command a U.S.-flagged ship without cit-izenship, appealed directly to President Theodore Roosevelt for an exemption. According to AGS Council minutes, Roosevelt responded favorably after learn-ing that the AGS had endorsed the expedition, prompting special legislation granting Mikkelsen authority.[57] Although Mikkelsen later chose to sail under the British flag on a Canadian ship, this event underscores the impact of the so-ciety's reputation in influencing government action.[58] The AGS also frequently used its reputation and networks to assist explorers. In 1903, during Francis H. Nichols's Tibet expedition, the AGS wrote to the Chinese minister in Washing-ton to support Nichols's request for passage into Tibet via China.[59] Similarly, in 1910, the AGS provided letters of introduction and recommendation addressed to the Turkish government for another expedition.[60] In each case, the society's institutional reputation opened doors otherwise closed to individual explor-ers.

Through these various forms of non-material support, ranging from diplo-matic letters and government lobbying to public endorsements and institu-tional affiliation, the AGS played an essential role in sustaining the infrastruc-tures of geographic exploration. Drawing on its reputation and extensive net-works, the society could overcome political, economic, and bureaucratic ob-stacles to knowledge production. From its metropolitan base in New York, the AGS thus oversaw, legitimized, and stabilized the conversion of field observa-tions into credible geographical knowledge.

4.3 Stabilizing Knowledge: Field Practices, Instruments, and Print

Securing credible knowledge from distant expeditions required not only fund-ing and political negotiation, but also the implementation of standardized

---

56   Brother of Donaldson Smith to Daly, undated, Box 265, Folder 41, AGS Archives.
57   Council Minutes Vol. 14, 204, 15.3.1906, Box 106, AGS Archives.
58   Council Minutes Vol. 14, 218, 19.4.1906, Box 106, AGS Archives.
59   Council Minutes Vol. 13, 257, 12.2.1903, Box 106, AGS Archives.
60   Council Minutes Vol. 15, 211, 17.2.1910, Box 106, AGS Archives.

scientific practices in the field. This section examines how U.S. geographical societies ensured the credibility of expeditionary knowledge as it moved from distant field sites to metropolitan audiences. Recognizing that knowledge is "produced through place as practice rather than simply in place", it foregrounds the spatial practices by which scientific knowledge was stabilized in the nineteenth century.[61] Geographical societies, acting as centers of calculation, played a central role in standardizing, validating, and disseminating field-based knowledge, thus integrating it into existing knowledge systems without losing its credibility. While field observations provided the raw material, the transformation of these observations into authoritative knowledge claims occurred primarily at society headquarters, where they underwent verification, standardization, and incorporation into established frameworks.

By analyzing correspondence, reports, and publications of AGS-sponsored expeditions, this section reconstructs how geographical societies controlled and facilitated the movement of knowledge between the field and the metropole. It begins by outlining a theoretical framework for understanding the stabilization of credible knowledge produced at a distance. Next, it explores the implementation of standardized field practices intended to produce immutable mobiles. Finally, it traces the conversion of field data into validated publications, examining how knowledge was made credible and circulated effectively within broader scientific and imperial networks.

Maintaining Credibility: Field and Metropole

As outlined earlier, this study approaches the history of geographical knowledge by investigating its spatial practices. Systems of geographical knowledge encompass practical and implicit forms of knowing, or, as Peter Burke phrases it, "knowing 'how' to do something, as opposed to knowing 'that' something is the case".[62] Practical knowledge was essential for establishing and maintaining a scientific discipline, because it relied on shared methodologies and practices among community members. What distinguished the geographer from the traveler was the use of specialized practices. In the field, these practices included: collecting, observing, measuring, mapping, drawing,

---

61   Charles W. J. Withers, "Place and the 'Spatial Turn' in Geography and in History," *Journal of the History of Ideas* 70, no. 4 (2009): 653; Also see Livingstone, *Putting Science in its Place*, 5.

62   Burke, *What is the History of Knowledge?*, 37.

and photographing – often performed using instruments deemed capable of imparting credibility to observations.[63] Geographers stressed the field as the site where authentic knowledge could be directly accessed through disciplined scientific practices. For geography especially, fieldwork "seemed to offer the enterprising scientist access to the very source of scientific knowledge, namely nature".[64]

However, in practice, the field was not as pure and detached from metropolitan influences as these scientists often implied. Practices in the field were mediated by previously acquired knowledge, prior training, and by conditions at the metropole. For instance, a study of German colonial geography noted that observation habits frequently relied on recognizing the familiar and creating analogies to previously described phenomena. Thus, expeditions often yielded new information, but rarely produced entirely novel scientific approaches.[65] Geographical knowledge gathered during expeditions had to be circulated from the field to the metropole, where geographical society headquarters, lecture halls, and publishing houses were located. Throughout this journey, geographical knowledge underwent multiple transformations: from measurements into notebooks, from notebooks into letters, and eventually into lectures, magazine articles, and books. Learned societies mediated this entire process, functioning as centers of calculation, through practices such as: standardizing scientific techniques; classifying, cataloging, rewriting, recombining, and editing knowledge; discussing results with peers; engaging in correspondence with other scientists; and printing and distributing publications.[66] Yet the practices employed in the production of knowledge were often rendered invisible in the finished articles to avoid undermining their perceived objectivity. This "black boxing" was essential: it obscured the messy contingencies of "science in the making" and presented the final product as a seamless, objective discovery. Thus, it is essential to look beyond the

---

63   Secord, "Knowledge in Transit," 665; Steven Shapin, "Placing the View," 6; Andrew Pickering, *Science as Practice and Culture* (Chicago: University of Chicago Press, 1992).

64   Alix Cooper, "From the Alps to Egypt (and Back Again): Dolomieu, Scientific Voyaging, and the Construction of the Field in Eighteenth-Century Natural History," in *Making Space for Science*, ed. Crosbie Smith and Jon Agar (New York: St. Martin's Press, 1998), 41–42.

65   Carsten Gräbel, *Die Erforschung der Kolonien. Expeditionen und koloniale Wissenskultur deutscher Geographen, 1884–1919* (Bielefeld: transcript, 2015), 194–95.

66   Burke, *Die Explosion des Wissens*, 83.

final printed version and analyze the interconnected practices of field and metropole to reveal how knowledge was actually *made* credible.

The credibility of geographical knowledge depended not just on the perceived authority of specific sites and actors, but also on maintaining trust as it moved from the field to the metropole. Geographical societies ensured this trust through standardized field practices, reliable communication networks, and immutable mobiles. The following AGS-sponsored expeditions illustrate these processes.

Enforcing Standards: Field Practices for Knowledge Production

To preserve credibility from field to metropole, the standardization of scientific practices was essential. This required a variety of "techniques of trust", including disciplining observers' methods and senses through training and standardized protocols.[67] Geographical societies, operating as centers of calculation, promoted these practices, which included precise methods for taking measurements, calibrating instruments, and observing natural phenomena. Such standardized practices originated in the metropole and were applied in the field under the assumption that their correct application produced credible, usable knowledge that could be readily integrated back at the center.

Standardization steered geographers toward the production of what Latour terms "immutable mobiles". These artefacts guaranteed authenticity: instruments and their readings, drawings and fieldnotes, maps and pictures, or data and statistics. These representations of geographic conditions in the field stood in for larger geographical realities, such as rock samples for a distant mountain, a plant specimen for a region's flora, or a map for entire regions. Immutable mobiles circulated from the field to centers of calculation, often undergoing translation and transformation as they moved toward publication.[68] Standardization enabled societies to claim authority over geographical knowledge by establishing themselves as arbiters of proper scientific practice, while the resulting immutable mobiles served as evidence of empirical accuracy and institutional credibility. The act of standardizing practices and valorizing certain types of immutable mobiles was itself a form of power, privileging particular ways of seeing and recording the world.

---

67   Livingstone, *Putting Science in its Place*, 16.
68   Latour, *Science in Action*, 227; Livingstone and Withers, *Geographies of Nineteenth-Century Science*, 424.

In AGS expeditions, immutable mobiles took various forms: physical specimens (botanical and geological samples); numerical data (measurements, coordinates, altitudes); visual representations (maps, photographs, sketches); and instrumental readings (barometric pressure, temperature logs). Immutable mobiles also took center stage in exhibitions and scientific debates, which highlighted their importance. At the 1893 World's Columbian Exposition in Chicago, the U.S. Army Signal Corps organized an exhibition displaying, alongside several flags carried by U.S. explorers in the Arctic, a variety of instruments, sketches, pictures, and notebooks on loan from the AGS, attesting to the scientific foundation claimed for these expeditions.[69]

Several AGS-sponsored expeditions illustrate how standardized scientific practices were intended to produce credible knowledge in the field and demonstrate adherence to the society's expectations. The 1910 Parker-Browne expedition to Mount McKinley shows clearly how the AGS functioned as a center of calculation by setting expectations for standardized practices and instruments. Expedition leaders stressed the scientific legitimacy of their mission when applying for endorsement from the society. While acknowledging their aim to ascend Mount McKinley, they emphasized that their "principal work will be the scientific exploration of this little-known region". To support this claim, they detailed the instruments they intended to use in order to produce credible scientific knowledge: "we shall be thoroughly equipped with instruments to record the topography and hypsometry of the Mountains and glaciers." Aware of public skepticism regarding prior accounts of the region, they argued that "our data shall carry the weight that our reputations and past efforts on the fields of exploration warrant."[70] The AGS approved the request, permitting them to operate under its auspices and thus affording them the institutional prestige of a recognized scientific body.[71] AGS endorsement validated expeditions by signaling compliance with standardized methods, including specific instruments, data collection, analysis techniques, and reporting protocols.

The Parker-Browne expedition also offers insights into how immutable mobiles stabilized knowledge in transit. Before returning to New York, the geographers, intending to reassure the AGS of the scientific value of their

---

69   Capt. R.E. Thompson to AGS Secretary, 24.2.1893, Box 238, Folder 41, AGS Archives.
70   Parker, Browne, and Cuntz to President and Council of AGS 10.2.1910, Box 271, Folder 15, AGS Archives.
71   AGS Council to Parker, Browne, and Cuntz 24.2.1910, Box 271, Folder 15, AGS Archives.

expedition, sent ahead a botanical specimen from Ruth Glacier collected at an altitude of 5,000 feet.[72] In addition, they forwarded their instruments to the AGS ahead of their arrival, so that their topographical and meteorological work could be verified and certified at the society's headquarters later, asking the society to retain the instruments in their original condition, "without any readjustments or changes, so that we can submit them to your officers with our records". The instruments included a transit-theodolite, a barograph-thermograph, and a stadia hand transit.[73] By sending instruments and specimens – key immutable mobiles – back to the center of calculation before their own return, the explorers demonstrated adherence to scientific protocols and facilitated independent verification. This further stabilized the knowledge they produced and aligned it with the AGS's standards for scientific legitimacy. The emphasis on instruments and standardized observation techniques illustrates how geographical societies could stabilize knowledge at a distance, ensuring that knowledge production occurred according to methodological standards established in the metropole even when conducted thousands of miles away.

Two years later, the same expedition group planned to climb Mount McKinley again, but framed their effort as an entirely new expedition emphasizing surrounding glaciers rather than the summit itself. In their funding request to the AGS, they stressed that their primary goal remained scientific. They outlined the proposed route with an accompanying map, summarized their research objectives, and listed the instruments they would employ. The team reiterated that the purpose of the journey was primarily scientific, aiming to conduct systematic observations and measurements of the region's topography, geology, and glaciology. They promised "careful surveys", "many photographs" and "daily meteorological observations". For these, they specifically requested funds for instruments from the AGS, such as a theodolite, a plane table, mercurial and aneroid barometers, a hypsometer, and thermometers.[74] Additionally, their application included a letter of support from AGS member Alfred H. Brooks of the Alaska Geological Survey, whom they described as the leading authority on Alaska. Brooks recommended that the society support their

---

72   Parker, Browne, and Cuntz to AGS, 28.7.1910, Box 271, Folder 15, AGS Archives.

73   Cuntz to Dellenbaugh, 7.9.1910, Box 271, Folder 15, AGS Archives.

74   The society was generally disposed to fund the use of scientific instruments, for example in Donaldson Smith's expedition to Somaliland, see: Council Minutes Vol. 12, 167–77, 5.11.1898, Box 105, AGS Archives.

plans to the cost of about $7,000. Adopting language with some patriotic undertones, the applicants called on the AGS to assist "complet[ing] the scientific exploration of our wonderful Alaskan territory".[75] After some consideration, the AGS declined to provide financial aid to the expedition, but assured them that they "commend the proposed exploration as practicable and as offering a possible solution of important geographical problems".[76] Despite this denial of funding, the explorers clearly understood that their best strategy for sponsorship was adhering to standardized scientific practices, the specific funding request for instruments, and the cultivation of support from reputable individuals within the society.

The emphasis on standardized scientific practices was similarly important in securing support for the Crocker Land Expedition. In his expedition proposal, Donald B. MacMillan offered detailed descriptions of the scientific methods and instruments planned. The plan specified methods such as soundings and tidal measurements and outlined work across multiple geographical subfields: topography, hydrography, glaciology, meteorology, and oceanography.[77] The AGS Special Committee evaluating the proposal recommended that the society contribute up to $6,000 toward the expedition. What the committee found especially convincing was the "distinct value for the extension of scientific knowledge, the interest of the society particularly centering upon the results of soundings and the actual exploration of Crocker Land". This suggests the expedition's alignment with standardized scientific practices and clearly articulated tangible outcomes were factors in securing institutional support.[78]

From Field to Print: Managing Expedition Knowledge

The final stage in knowledge production involved transforming field observations into published works at the centers of calculation and disseminating them to scientific and public audiences. Geographical societies carefully managed this process to maintain authority over knowledge claims and ensure alignment with institutional priorities and editorial standards, a role that Chapter 5 follows into lectures and periodicals. Both the Lumholtz expedition

---

75   Cuntz to Council, 19.3.1912, Box 271, Folder 15, AGS Archives.
76   AGS Secretary to Cuntz, 19.4.1912, Box 271, Folder 15, AGS Archives.
77   AGS Council Minutes Vol. 16, 61, 18.1.1912, Box 106, AGS Archives.
78   AGS Council Minutes Vol. 16, 62–64, 18.1.1912, Box 106, AGS Archives.

to New Mexico and Ejnar Mikkelsen's Anglo-American Polar Expedition provide evidence of the high value geographical societies placed on knowledge obtained in the field under their sponsorship. These cases highlight the societies' insistence to receive regular expedition reports and retain exclusive first publication rights, asserting their authority over the entire knowledge production cycle.

In 1890, the AGS Council approved $1,000 for Lumholtz's expedition to New Mexico, Arizona, and Northern Mexico, stipulating that "the reports of the expedition shall be sent to this Society for publishing in its Bulletin" to generate public interest in its findings.[79] However, before the AGS could publish anything, an article about the expedition appeared in *Science* magazine.[80] When the AGS sought clarification, Lumholtz denied authorship, affirmed he was "aware of his duty to the AGS" and shortly afterward sent several pages detailing his recent geographical fieldwork. In the same letter, he requested additional funding to complete his expedition.[81] This suggests that expedition leaders were aware of the demand for credible field-based knowledge. Several years later, Lumholtz delivered a lecture at the AGS, accompanied by lantern slides of the expedition.[82]

A similar insistence on exclusive first access characterized the AGS's arrangement with Mikkelsen's 1906 Anglo-American Polar Expedition. The society provided 1,000$ under the condition that his forthcoming book acknowledge the joint auspices of the Royal Geographical Society and the AGS, and that "all scientific results, and notes of progress from time to time, should be given to these two Societies for publication in their respective magazines".[83] Upon discovering that Mikkelsen had shared expedition news with other publications, AGS Councilor Robbins firmly reminded him that according to their arrangement, "the first news, and the scientific results of the expedition were to be sent only to the Royal and the American Geographical Societies."[84] In re-

---

79   Libbey to Lumholtz, 5.4.1890, Box 265, Folder 31, AGS Archives.

80   "Mexican Archaeology", *Science* 17, no. 429 (24 Apr 1891): 232; he mentioned his lack of funding for further exploration, so the main motivation could have been to acquire funding from other donors.

81   Lumholtz to Daly, 30.5.1891, Box 265, Folder 31, AGS Archives.

82   Lumholtz to Hurlbut, 11.1.1894, Box 265, Folder 31, AGS Archives; later published as Carl Lumholtz, "The American Cave-Dwellers: The Tarahumaris of the Sierra Madre," *AGS Journal* 26, no. 1 (1894): 299–325.

83   AGS Council Minutes Vol. 14, 202, 15.3.1906, Box 106, AGS Archives.

84   AGS Council Minutes Vol. 14, 284, 21.3.1907, Box 106, AGS Archives.

sponse, Mikkelsen promptly sent a series of reports to the AGS, along with an article for the *Bulletin*.[85]

Publication and archiving expedition results required careful planning to preserve and present knowledge effectively, as illustrated by the Crocker Land Expedition led by Donald B. MacMillan. Knowledge produced in the field was simultaneously sent to both expedition sponsors, the American Museum of Natural History and the AGS. The two institutions had prearranged how the results – in the form of immutable mobiles – would be divided: scientific specimens would go to the museum, while maps and charts would be deposited with the AGS.[86] Similarly, the Parker-Browne expedition arranged to publish its findings in the AGS *Bulletin*, reserving only "certain material which might be desired for publication in a popular magazine."[87] This arrangement highlighted an anticipated distinction between scientific knowledge suitable for the AGS and more popular content intended for lay public audiences, reflecting pre-established organizing principles and considerations of target audiences in knowledge production.

These cases show sustained institutional demand for field-based knowledge, which societies repackaged for government, academic, and popular audiences to consolidate their own authority. Acting as centers of calculation, geographical societies institutionalized continuous field reporting to secure a consistent flow of credible data.

The transformation of field observations into credible publications required selecting formats that supported geographical claims. Ralph S. Tarr's use of photographs in his AGS Bulletin article on the Alaska expedition exemplifies this practice. Toward the end of the nineteenth century, scientific credibility increasingly relied on visual representations like photographs, valued for their perceived objectivity and precision. They were regarded as more reliable than detailed drawings or lay eyewitness accounts.[88] However,

---

85   AGS Council Minutes Vol. 14, 281, 21.3.1907, Box 106, AGS Archives; the article and short report appeared in the AGS Bulletin: Ejnar Mikkelsen, "The Mikkelsen-Leffingwell Expedition," *Bulletin of the American Geographical Society* 39, no. 4 (1907): 224–31; Ejnar Mikkelsen, "Report of the Mikkelsen-Leffingwell Expedition," *Bulletin of the American Geographical Society* 39, no. 10 (1907): 607–20.

86   AGS Council Minutes Vol. 16, 61, 18.1.1912, Box 106, AGS Archives.

87   "F.S. Dellenbaugh about planned expedition of Parker, Browne, Cuntz," undated, Box 271, Folder 15, AGS Archives.

88   James R. Ryan, *Picturing Empire: Photography and Visualization of the British Empire* (Chicago: University of Chicago Press, 1997), 214.

as the *National Geographic Magazine* increasingly popularized geography in the early twentieth century, the use of photographs gradually became perceived as less scientifically rigorous. Anticipating criticism that his inclusion of numerous photographs might be construed as an attempt to popularize his work, Tarr proactively defended their scientific utility. In a letter accompanying his manuscript, he insisted that "each picture has been selected out of the hundreds which we took to illustrate some specific point of scientific importance" and that he had already discarded pictures "whose main merit is scenic grandeur". Tarr asserted that photographs could substantiate scientific claims in ways textual descriptions could not: "a well selected photograph carries conviction where an ordinary description may fail. There have been numerous instances where failure to illustrate has led to grave doubts in late years as to the accuracy of observation."[89] This conscious justification highlights the ongoing negotiation around visual evidence and popularization of geography.

The AGS's control over publication rights and its insistence on assessing expedition data before public dissemination demonstrate how geographical societies maintained authority over the circulation of knowledge throughout the entire cycle. By managing how field observations were transformed into scientific publications, the societies determined which geographical claims became recognized facts and controlled how these facts were presented to scholarly and public audiences. Their authority stemmed not only from the knowledge they produced, but from their institutional capacity to command its circulation. In this way, geographical societies functioned as centers of calculation as well as mediating institutions. By controlling the circulation of geographical knowledge – gathering information through global networks, validating it through standardized practices, and disseminating it through targeted publications – societies positioned themselves as indispensable intermediaries between field research and multiple knowledge communities: government agencies received information relevant to territorial and commercial expansion, academic communities received publications establishing scientific credibility, popular audiences received lectures and magazine articles promoting geographical exploration, and international scientists received publication exchanges projecting U.S. expertise.

---

89   Tarr to Hurlbut 3.2.1906, Box 164, Folder 27, AGS Archives; the article in question was Ralph S. Tarr and Lawrence Martin, "Glaciers and Glaciation of Yakutat Bay, Alaska," *Bulletin of the American Geographical Society* 38, no. 3 (1906): 145–67.

5 Disseminating Knowledge

When Gilbert H. Grosvenor became editor of *National Geographic Magazine* in 1899, he encountered a society burdened with significant debt and a publication containing technical articles that appealed only to a limited readership. In response, Grosvenor adopted a deliberate strategy of popularization, guided by a feedback loop between content and audience interests. He later recalled: "My theory was that if The Society's Magazine was to succeed, I must find out what kind of geographic magazine the public would buy."[1] Grosvenor's market-oriented strategy demonstrates how editorial decisions, driven by perceived audience demand and institutional financial pressures, shaped what counted as legitimate geographical knowledge for a mass readership.

This chapter addresses a further essential dimension of knowledge circulation: dissemination beyond expert circles to wider professional audiences and the public. U.S. geographical societies significantly contributed to this process through public lectures and widely circulated magazines. Rather than viewing dissemination as a secondary process occurring after knowledge production, this chapter argues that geographical societies influenced what constituted legitimate geographical knowledge by selecting, translating, and presenting knowledge for diverse audiences. Three interrelated arguments illustrate this claim: first, audience demand influenced the content and form of geographical knowledge; second, competition between societies for popular lecturers and readers reshaped disciplinary priorities; and third, editorial decisions themselves constituted a form of knowledge production. The chapter traces how societies balanced scientific authority, public relevance, and financial stability. After outlining the theoretical framework for analyzing popularization, the chapter examines lectures and periodical publications, showing how they sustained the popularization of geography and the societies themselves.

---

1   Grosvenor, *National Geographic Society*, 39.

5.1 Communication Circuit: Geographers, Publics, and Popularization

As previously noted, scientific claims often gain broader acceptance only after circulating beyond expert communities, a process usually requiring mediation for non-specialist audiences.[2] U.S. geographical societies, founded primarily to disseminate geographical knowledge, were central to popularizing geography through public lectures and widely circulated magazines. However, the concept of "popularization" is problematic, as its modern connotations imply oversimplification and a one-way flow of information. Following Bernard Lightman, I therefore treat popularization as an object of historical study rather than applying it uncritically as a historiographical principle.[3] The analysis focuses on the interactions between societies, experts, and audiences within the particular historical context of U.S. geography around 1900.

The nature of science popularization and its relationship to the public has long been debated by historians of science. An older "diffusionist" model conceived of knowledge as flowing in a linear, top-down way from scientific elites to passive lay audiences, with simplification, distortion, or even sensationalism as frequent byproducts. This model presumed a rigid divide between amateur and professional scientists, and between expert and popular knowledge. Recent scholarship challenges this approach, advocating instead interactive models that emphasize the co-production and exchange of knowledge. In these frameworks, scientists, popularizers, and audiences are interconnected actors in a reciprocal "communication circuit", where audience demand shapes what scientists choose to study and publish, just as scientific findings shape what audiences come to know. As Lightman emphasizes, popular science is not a diluted version of expert knowledge, but rather influences elite science itself by affecting research priorities and scientific discourse. He argues that popularization constitutes its own form of knowledge-making, where the selection and framing of scientific content create new meanings and applications.[4] In this sense, public dissemination was not separate from knowledge production, but an integral part of it.

This interactive model is particularly illuminating for understanding geographical societies, which depended on their members not only as recipients

---

2   Golinski, *Making Natural Knowledge*, 34.
3   Lightman, *Victorian Popularizers of Science*, 9–10.
4   Ibid., 13–14.

of knowledge, but as financial supporters, field contributors, and sources of institutional legitimacy. Thus, popularization itself was mediation: selecting, transforming, validating, circulating, and representing knowledge for distinct publics. Consequently, popularization through lectures and periodicals was a constitutive practice shaping geographical knowledge. Whereas British and some continental societies enjoyed substantial state patronage, the heavier reliance of U.S. societies on membership dues and ticket sales meant that audience preferences more directly influenced disciplinary priorities. This market-driven exchange could reinforce existing cultural biases or colonial perspectives, as popular tastes for adventure, exoticism, and national progress significantly influenced what was presented as legitimate geographical knowledge. This theoretical perspective explains why the boundaries between "professional" and "popular" geography remained fluid and contested throughout this period.

Nineteenth-century technological and cultural developments significantly shaped the dissemination of scientific knowledge. Advances in printing technology and the expansion of print culture increased public demand for certain kinds of knowledge on this interactive communication circuit. As science was increasingly consumed through periodicals, it had to compete for public attention. Geography held an advantage over other disciplines, already being among the most widely read scientific subjects of the period.[5] Lectures by explorers and articles detailing foreign countries and peoples were especially popular, positioning geography advantageously. Since geographical societies primarily derived income from lecture tickets and magazine subscriptions, audience demand strongly influenced their editorial choices.

Science popularizers in the late nineteenth century came from diverse backgrounds, motivated by personal prestige, professional recognition, research opportunities, or financial necessity. Identifying a "typical" science popularizer is difficult, but Andreas W. Daum's typology, originally developed for the German context, can be broadly applied to the American scene. He differentiates three overlapping categories: (a) *professional popularizers*, whose principal career and income depended on popularization; (b) *occasional popularizers*, including explorers and early-career academics without permanent university affiliations; and (c) *academic or university popularizers*, professors and

---

5   Angela Schwarz, *Der Schlüssel zur modernen Welt. Wissenschaftspopularisierung in Großbritannien und Deutschland im Übergang zur Moderne (ca. 1870–1914)* (Stuttgart: Franz Steiner, 1999), 50.

lecturers with established academic positions.[6] In practice, boundaries were porous and many actors moved between categories over the course of their careers. Most geographers active in U.S. geographical societies were occasional popularizers, while professional popularizers and popularizing academics formed smaller groups. Academic scientists often had the least to gain from popularizing science, as doing so could negatively impact their professional reputations.[7] This typology helps clarify the motivations and strategies behind dissemination and explain the distinctive form of geographical knowledge produced by U.S. geographical societies at the turn of the century.

5.2 Performing Geography: Lectures and Lantern Slides

Alongside print publications, lectures were central to the popularization of geographical knowledge in the nineteenth century, ranging from small gatherings at society headquarters to public events attracting hundreds or thousands of attendees. As live performances combining talks with visual aids, lectures were an influential medium for shaping public perception and establishing the authority of both speakers and sponsoring societies. At the American Geographical Society, the annual addresses of its President Charles P. Daly were particularly popular social occasions that drew large audiences during the 1870s and 1880s.[8]

Geographical societies tailored their lecture formats to different audiences. Some lectures were reserved for members, others were open to the public for an admission fee. Women regularly attended, as a *New York Daily Tribune* article noted in its coverage of an AGS lecture.[9] Importantly, a majority of articles published in the societies' periodicals were initially delivered as lectures. From the 1890s onward, however, articles increasingly appeared without first being delivered as talks.[10] This shift marked a growing divide between public presentations oriented toward a general audience and special-

---

6   Daum, *Wissenschaftspopularisierung*, 382–83.
7   Daum, *Wissenschaftspopularisierung*, 424–25.
8   Morin, *Civic Discipline*, 11.
9   Clipping "Dr. Hayes Before the Geographical Society", undated, Box 52, Folder 2, AGS Archives.
10   Wright, *Geography in the Making*, 153.

ized publications aimed at a professional readership, reflecting the processes of professionalization discussed in Chapter 3.

Public lectures show the reciprocal relationship between producers and consumers of scientific knowledge, as content often had to reflect audience interests. During conferences of the British Association for the Advancement of Science, for example, attendees often moved between sessions to hear more interesting lectures when speakers failed to hold their attention.[11] Geography, integrating adventure narratives, travel stories, and visual materials such as lantern slides, was particularly well-positioned to attract large audiences. Additionally, owing to a strong amateur tradition in geology and geography, many audience members had a pre-existing connection to these subjects.[12] This section analyzes how societies organized their lecture programs, selected speakers, and competed for charismatic lecturers, demonstrating how anticipated audience demand and institutional strategy shaped the public performance of geographical knowledge.

The National Geographic Society's lecture program for 1896–97 exemplifies how geographical societies organized distinct formats for different audiences. The program distinguished between evening lectures, technical meetings, and afternoon lectures. Evening lectures, delivered by speakers of "national reputation" were designed to "interest and instruct" in a popular style. Technical meetings catered to advanced geographers, providing "the latest results of specialists in the various scientific bureaus, with opportunity for discussion". Afternoon lectures, more accessible than technical meetings, were to be "finely illustrated", featuring "new and original photographs" to appeal to large audiences. This careful segmentation allowed the NGS to simultaneously cater to multiple constituencies: it could attract and retain a large popular membership with its accessible illustrated lectures, while still maintaining a space for technical meetings that preserved its claim to scientific seriousness and its connections to government experts. This segmentation indicates how audience demand, as perceived and catered to by the NGS, shaped both the content and form of the geographical knowledge disseminated. The year's lecture series was

---

11   Charles W. J. Withers, "Geographies of Science and Public Understanding? Exploring the Reception of the British Association for the Advancement of Science in Britain and in Ireland, c.1845–1939," in *Geographies of Science*, ed. Peter Meusburger, David N. Livingstone, and Heike Jöns (Dordrecht: Springer, 2010), 190.

12   Martin J. S. Rudwick, *The Great Devonian Controversy* (Chicago: University of Chicago Press, 1985), 40.

titled "The Effects of Geographic Environment in Developing the Civilization of the World", a title broad enough to appeal to general audiences and suggestive of a teleological narrative of Western progress. It likely appealed to patriotic Americans by emphasizing "the advance of civilization along the shores of the Mediterranean, and finally to its grandest development in America." The NGS highlighted the use of lantern slides in the lecture series as "a special feature" to capture audience attention.[13] The substantial effort that the NGS devoted to organizing these lectures suggests that already in 1896, three years before Grosvenor's popularization initiatives at the National Geographic Magazine, the NGS recognized and accommodated its members' preference for a more topical and visual form of popular geography.

In the mid-1890s, the American Geographical Society considered adopting a similar approach. In an internal document addressing the society's future direction, AGS member Cyrus C. Adams proposed dividing lectures into three categories: (1) popular illustrated talks aimed at younger audiences, (2) short lantern demonstrations and geographical exhibits paired with social events, and (3) scientific meetings.[14] These categories mirrored those of the NGS and differentiated popular and scientific lectures. While the AGS strove to maintain its professional reputation, it recognized the need to remain responsive to demand for popular lectures in order to sustain its membership and influence.

The process of selecting lecturers and lecture topics provides insight into how societies anticipated and responded to audience interests. Correspondence between Adams and librarian Hurlbut, who managed the AGS lecture program, shows that speakers were often selected for topic appeal and presentation style rather than personal renown alone. Adams recommended a lecture on "Storms and Weather Forecasts" by Willis L. Moore, Chief of the Weather Bureau. Although Adams had neither attended the lecture nor seen its visual aids in person, he trusted word-of-mouth reviews and printed materials, especially a pamphlet containing 25 maps, to conclude that it would be "clear and popular". Similarly, Adams suggested a lecture on "Crater Lake, Oregon", by J.S. Diller of the U.S. Geological Survey, describing it as an "admirable topic on one of the natural wonders of the country" and praising its high-quality lantern slides. R. E. Dodge's lecture "How the Earth Grows Old"

---

13   "NGS Lecture Program 1896–97," Box 240, Folder 17, AGS Archives.
14   "Suggestions for Society Work during the coming year," Adams to Peary, Robbins and Hurlbut, 30.11.1896, Box 6, Folder 7, AGS Archives.

was also praised for its strong visual aids and engaging presentation.[15] These choices highlight that lectures were selected not only for scientific merit, but also for their popular appeal, particularly the promise of visual spectacle and accessible delivery. In this way, the audience's demand for specific kinds of geographical knowledge was a significant factor behind the selection of lecturers at the AGS, thereby influencing public geographical knowledge.

As demand for engaging speakers increased, prominent lecturers began charging fees, which altered the relationship between societies and speakers. Initially, paying lecturers was controversial within the AGS. An AGS member remarked in 1896 that "the honor of addressing the Society should be sought, and not paid for", adding that "most geographical societies do not pay lecturers."[16] However, by the early 1900s, the AGS began offering payments of up to $50 for select lecturers.[17] By this time, celebrated popular geographers began to charge ever more substantial fees. For instance, when Annie Peck was invited to lecture at the AGS, she informed the society of her usual rates: $500 in big cities, $200 in small cities, or alternatively, a gold medal.[18]

As audiences grew, competition among geographical societies intensified. Hosting famous polar explorers (often acting as "occasional popularizers" combining scientific reporting with adventure narratives) typically drew large turnouts, and by the early 1900s, the AGS and NGS competed intensely to host these celebrity-geographers. This competitive dynamic appears clearly in the AGS's strategic efforts to secure exclusive lectures from prominent explorers. The society's attempt to secure Fridtjof Nansen's first U.S. lecture following his 1897 polar expedition shows this strategy in practice. The society proposed awarding him a medal on arrival, hoping to induce him to speak at the AGS first. An internal letter reveals this was a deliberate attempt to "not have our Society come behind that of Washington [the NGS], and several other lecture engagements", emphasizing that the AGS was to have its "appropriate place, as the representative American Geographical Society, in receiving him."[19] The explicit framing of this strategy against the NGS underscores how competition

---

15   Adams to Hurlbut, 3.2.1897, Box 102, Folder 3, AGS Archives.
16   Adams to Special Committee of AGS, 1896, Box 102, Folder 3, AGS Archives
17   Council Minutes Vol. 15, 4, 21.11.1907, Box 106, AGS Archives; Council Minutes Vol. 16, 58, 18.1.1912, Box 106, AGS Archives.
18   Peck to Hurlbut, 27.12.1908, Box 10, Folder 42, AGS Archives.
19   Libbey to Robbins, undated, Box 124, Folder 16, AGS Archives.

for celebrity speakers shaped institutional priorities and how public attention increasingly drove societies' programming priorities.

When rumors spread in 1909 that Frederick Cook had reached the North Pole, the AGS again acted quickly, seeking visibility and public attention before its Washington rival could. They proposed presenting Cook with a medal, possibly even involving the U.S. President, in order to "bring the Society prominently before the public and incidentally perhaps getting subscriptions for our new building".[20] This suggests how securing high-profile lectures was linked to institutional prestige and fundraising goals. The rivalry intensified with the visit of explorer Ernest Shackleton to the United States. The AGS sought to host his first appearance, offering a medal and a formal reception.[21] However, the NGS managed to secure his first lecture by offering Shackleton's agent $600 and a gold medal.[22] When Shackleton's agent asked the AGS to match the offer, the society declined. Their internal correspondence expressed dismay: "No explorer like Shackleton would think of charging a price for addressing our society. Do you imagine the R.G.S. paid him for addressing them? The honor of being asked to address them is ample remuneration."[23] The agent informed the AGS that Shackleton stood to lose $1,000 if he lectured for the AGS before speaking at the NGS.[24] This indicates that exclusive contracts had become the norm and that lofty society objectives such as the widest dissemination of knowledge assumed secondary importance. An AGS member complained about NGS tactics, accusing them of "grabbing [Shackleton] on the occasion of his visit to Washington to pay his respects to the President is a new antic on their part simply to get in ahead of us."[25] The AGS ultimately failed to host Shackleton's first U.S. lecture. He delivered his talk first to the NGS, receiving a medal, and spoke at the AGS a few days later, where he was awarded another medal.[26] The AGS's indignation reflects nostalgia for a vanishing, gentlemanly

20   Kean to Robbins, 3.9.1909, Box 129, Folder 4, AGS Archives; Robbins to Adams, 5.9.1909, Box 124, Folder 10, AGS Archives.

21   Robbins to Adams, 31.8.1909, Box 129, Folder 4, AGS Archives.

22   Adams to Robbins, 11.11.1909, Box 129, Folder 4, AGS Archives.

23   Robbins to Adams, 30.9.1909, Box 129, Folder 4, AGS Archives.

24   Robbins to Libbey, 28.1.1910, Box 124, Folder 16, AGS Archives.

25   Libbey to Robbins, 12.2.1910, Box 124, Folder 16, AGS Archives.

26   On NGS, see: *New York Times*, 27.3.1910, p. 24.; on AGS: "Sir Ernest Shackleton Receives the Cullum Geographical Medal," *Bulletin of the American Geographical Society* 42, no. 4 (1910): 241–43.

model of science where knowledge was shared for honor and prestige. In contrast, Shackleton's contract and the NGS's payment represented an explicitly commercial model of geography in which scientific celebrity became a valuable commodity.

The commercialization of geographical lectures and intensified competition mirrored Robert Peary's earlier return from his North Pole expedition. In 1909, NGM editor Grosvenor traveled to Canada to greet Peary upon his return. Anticipating that Grosvenor would secure Peary's first lecture for the NGS, the AGS attempted to intercept Peary by sending a congratulatory telegram ahead of time. In an internal letter, Adams (AGS) criticized Grosvenor, predicting that he "will try to extract from Peary a promise that he will deliver his first lecture before the Washington Society and fill a whole number of the Magazine with his story and pictures."[27] This remark reflects the AGS's frustration with the NGS's increasingly assertive tactics and its unease with how the NGS popularized and commodified geographical knowledge.

Yet the AGS struggled to keep pace. The NGS, based in Washington, well-connected with government officials, and supported by strong magazine revenue, could offer higher fees and greater exposure. Its large subscriber base and broad public appeal allowed it to supersede other societies in the quest for lectures by celebrity explorers, which demonstrates the advantage of its successful popularization strategy. This intense competition had an impact on geography: it accelerated the commercialization of popular geographical knowledge, transforming it from a scholarly pursuit into a valuable entertainment commodity in some areas. Furthermore, it elevated a particular type of geography (especially heroic narratives of polar exploration) to a position of public importance, often at the expense of less spectacular but equally important branches of geography. In this way, the lecture circuit did not just disseminate knowledge, but also shaped the discipline's priorities.

5.3 Periodical Marketplace: Editorial Strategy and Imperial Imaginaries

While lectures provided temporary and localized opportunities for knowledge dissemination, periodical publications offered geographical societies a lasting and widely disseminated medium through which they established insti-

---

27   Adams to Robbins, 10.9.1909, Box 129, Folder 4, AGS Archives.

tutional authority, defined disciplinary boundaries, and shaped geographical knowledge. More than any other activity, publications created the enduring networks through which geographical knowledge circulated and solidified. Indeed, geographical societies generally considered regular publications to be their most important and enduring contribution to knowledge dissemination. Almost all societies listed periodical publication as a primary objective in their founding documents. By the mid-nineteenth century, mass printing had become more affordable, and periodicals surpassed books in popularity as vehicles for science popularization. As historians of print culture have shown, periodicals in the nineteenth century created communities of readers and shaped the meaning of knowledge as it moved through society.[28] For geographical societies, bulletins and magazines were platforms through which they forged their institutional identity, projected authority, and packaged their vision of the world for diverse audiences. This section analyzes how geographical societies negotiated the tension between popularization and professionalization through their periodicals, focusing first on editorial strategies and content acquisition at the AGS and NGS. It then considers the Geographical Society of Philadelphia to show how even smaller societies recognized periodicals as vital to their credibility and international standing.

Competing Strategies: AGS and NGS Editorial Approaches

The divergent editorial strategies of the AGS and NGS show two competing visions for U.S. geography, each responding to different institutional pressures and audience demands. The NGS established the *National Geographic Magazine* shortly after its founding in 1888. During its first eight years, the magazine appeared irregularly and contained often dense technical articles focused on Western surveys, hydrography, or geology. Yet from the outset, the NGS adopted a broad definition of geography as encompassing "anything animal, vegetable or mineral, on the land, in the sea or in the air".[29] In 1896, the maga-

---

28   Geoffrey Cantor and Sally Shuttleworth, eds., *Science Serialized: Representations of the Sciences in Nineteenth-Century Periodicals* (Cambridge: MIT Press, 2004); Susan Sheets-Pyenson, "Popular Science Periodicals in Paris and London: The Emergence of a Low Scientific Culture, 1820–1875," *Annals of Science* 42, no. 6 (November 1985): 549–72; James A. Secord, *Victorian Sensation: The Extraordinary Publication, Reception, and Secret Authorship of Vestiges of the Natural History of Creation* (Chicago: University of Chicago Press, 2000).

29   Poole, *Explorers House*, 28–29.

zine began monthly publication and gradually shifted toward more accessible articles and global coverage. This process accelerated in 1898, when Alexander Graham Bell became NGS president. Facing a $2,000 debt, Bell proposed boosting the magazine's circulation by broadening its appeal.[30] The society consequently adopted a new, all-encompassing definition of geography as "the world and all that is in it", signaling a turn toward popular geography. Under Gilbert H. Grosvenor, editor from 1899, NGM became increasingly accessible and visual. Scientific writing on physical geography gave way to travel narratives and occasional political commentary.

This editorial shift caused internal resistance from prominent members who wished to preserve the NGS's scholarly standards. The Editorial Committee warned that "the excessive use of superficial description and pictorial illustration shall be subordinate to the exposition of relations and principles." As Grosvenor recalled, "the so-called professional geographers say that [NGM] prints too much about flowers and animals and so on. They say that isn't geography."[31] Despite attempts to remove Grosvenor from his position as editor, he prevailed and continued to pursue his popularization strategy. The Editorial Committee's warning was an attempt at internal boundary-work, a losing battle fought against Grosvenor's new, market-driven model of popular geography. The NGS's trajectory thus illustrates a deliberate strategy to prioritize audience growth and financial stability through popularization, even at the cost of internal dissent from more academically oriented members.

Despite its growing popular appeal, NGM aimed to project scientific credibility by carefully balancing accessible content and authoritative sources. By the early twentieth century, NGM had become significantly more accessible, but retained scientific credibility by continuing to publish some professional geography. Grosvenor insisted that popularization would not compromise scientific accuracy: "We did not mean to lower the scientific standard of the magazine and make it simply popular, but we wanted to add certain features that would be of interest to everybody."[32] Many contemporaries still perceived NGM as a serious journal, albeit a more entertaining one, whose reputation also rested considerably on the professional networks cultivated by the NGS.

The success of Grosvenor's popular model was measurable, and the metrics used to track it fed back into editorial selection, privileging topics that

30   Abramson, *National Geographic*, 44.
31   Grosvenor, *National Geographic Society*, 37.
32   "The National Geographic Society," *NGM*, no. 3 (1912): 275.

converted most efficiently into subscriptions. The NGS developed methods
to track reader interests and adapt its content accordingly. To identify which
kinds of geographical knowledge most appealed to readers, NGM editor
Grosvenor printed distinct application codes on the membership forms bound
into each issue, enabling the NGS to track which issues and topics attracted
new members. He recalled: "My theory was that if The Society's Magazine was
to succeed, I must find out what kind of geographic magazine the public would
buy."[33] Geographical societies increasingly competed in a marketplace of magazines and newspapers, giving rise to a direct feedback loop in which audience
reception influenced editorial strategy. As the NGS became more reliant on its
readership for funding, its editorial direction increasingly adapted to readers'
interests. Subscription numbers confirm the success of this market-driven
approach: NGM circulation grew from 1,417 in 1898 to 2,500 in 1899 and then
to 11,000 in 1905. After 1905, circulation increased rapidly to 20,000 in 1907,
74,000 in 1911, and approximately 300,000 in 1914.[34] Actual readership was
likely even higher, as subscribers shared issues and newspapers reprinted and
quoted NGM articles.

In contrast to the extensively studied NGM, the AGS's parallel but distinct
publication efforts have received far less scholarly attention. The following
analysis therefore focuses on the evolution of the AGS's periodical publication,
the *Bulletin*, and examines the society's attempts to balance popular appeal
with scientific credibility. Grosvenor's popular editorial approach created both
a challenge and an opportunity for the AGS. Given the NGM's popular success, the AGS positioned itself as a pragmatic hybrid that balanced scholarly
authority with selective popularization.

The AGS's periodical underwent several changes in title and orientation between 1852 and 1901. It began as the *Bulletin of the American Geographical and Statistical Society* (1852–1856), followed by several name changes: *Journal* (1859), *Proceedings* (1862–1866), the *Journal of the American Geographical Society of New York*
(from 1872), and the *Bulletin of the American Geographical Society* (from 1901).[35]
Internally, the society consistently referred to individual numbers of its periodical as the "Bulletin" throughout, and this study follows that convention. As
the society grew, so did the *Bulletin's* circulation. By 1896, the society distributed

33   Grosvenor, *National Geographic Society*, 39.
34   Grosvenor, *National Geographic Society*, 44; "The National Geographic Society," NGM,
      no. 3 (1912): 272.
35   Letterpress Books Vol. 15, 26, Box 82, AGS Archives.

roughly 2,000 copies per issue to its members described as "people of education and wealth".[36] In the 1890s, the *Bulletin* expanded its content and frequency
and by 1898, it appeared five times a year, more than ever before.[37] By 1903, it
included an additional 16 pages for maps and book notices.[38] From 1904 onward, it was published monthly, each issue spanning approximately 50 pages.
Its budget rose steadily from $2,500 in 1898 to $6,000 by 1912.[39] This steady
growth demonstrates a sustained institutional commitment to the publication
as the AGS's primary vehicle for asserting scientific authority. In addition, the
increased publication frequency (also seen at the NGM) enabled the societies
to respond more quickly to current events.

Although the historiography often highlights the NGS as the primary
driver of popular geography, the AGS also negotiated popularization, particularly how to broaden its appeal without sacrificing scholarly standards. The
AGS's shifting attitude shows an ambivalent and sometimes opportunistic
relationship with popularization, which highlights the fluid boundaries of
what counted as "professional" geography. Early on, members worried that
popularization might compromise scientific quality. In 1864, one Council
member already cautioned that "we must be careful not to popularize at the
cost of sacrificing our scientific character."[40] Despite this warning, the AGS
gradually adopted a more pragmatic stance. When the editor solicited articles
for the *Bulletin* in 1897, he asked contributors to popularize their papers some-
what: "[...] when applying to scientific men for collaboration, we tell them
that while we wish, in no way to impair the scientific value of the articles they
prepare for us, we shall be glad if their material may be adapted to instruct
and interest the mass of our members and teachers who form the larger part
of our readers."[41] Taken together, this 1897 directive and parallel evidence from
the NGS challenge the prevailing historiography of U.S. popular geography. To
a significant degree, the turn toward popularization, so often credited solely
to Gilbert Grosvenor at the NGM after 1899, was in fact already underway at

---

36   Adams to Special Committee of AGS, 1896, Box 102, Folder 3, AGS Archives.
37   Council Minutes Vol. 12, 119, 4.12.1897, Box 105, AGS Archives.
38   Council Minutes Vol. 13, 215, 11.12.1902, Box 105, AGS Archives.
39   Council Minutes Vol. 12, 131, 8.1.1898, Box 105, AGS Archives; Council Minutes Vol. 16,
      57, 18.1.1912, Box 106, AGS Archives.
40   "Discussion in Council meeting of American Geographical and Statistical Society, Oc-
      tober 20, 1864, as regards ways of extending the scope of and interest in the Society,"
      Box 43, Folder 5, AGS Archives.
41   Adams to Hurlbut, 13.1.1897, Box 102, Folder 3, AGS Archives.

both the AGS and NGS. Thus, the shift was not the product of a single editor, but rather a broader response by geographical societies to the demands of their members and the changing cultural marketplace for science.

The AGS strategically positioned its *Bulletin* as both a scholarly geography journal and a widely appealing publication. To this end, Cyrus C. Adams, an influential figure in the society and later editor of the *Bulletin*, presented detailed plans to the AGS Council in the late 1890s. For inspiration, he studied the practices of European geographical societies and identified those with the greatest impact. First, he advocated greater collaboration with unaffiliated geographers to broaden the contributor base. He contrasted the AGS's passive editorial approach with the proactive models of societies in London and Berlin, which actively solicited material for their journals and built photographic archives through open calls for contributions. Second, Adams recommended enhancing the Bulletin's visual appeal by including large-format maps, common in European journals. He also called for expanded publication exchanges with foreign institutions to secure a steady flow of materials for adaptation. Third, he proposed publishing an annual program in the December issue, previewing upcoming lectures, articles, and book and map acquisitions, to give members a strong incentive to renew their membership. Finally, he argued for a bi-monthly publication schedule. Adams's vision was to transform the AGS into the central hub of geographical knowledge in the United States, explicitly linking the *Bulletin's* quality to institutional dominance: "I have yet to meet an American geographer who does not believe that the Society should be and can be made the chief center of geographical interests in this country."[42]

Adams proposed professionalizing the Bulletin by listing book reviews first, assigning authorship to shorter notes, and developing closer ties with federal and state scientific bureaus. He believed these measures would attract high-quality contributions, and ultimately "widen the Society's influence and enlarge its membership".[43] Concurrently, Adams suggested incorporating color map inserts – particularly of Alaska and Antarctica – and outsourcing production to a reputable Leipzig publisher. Each issue, he argued, should feature "a timely and useful map for Americans", intended as a means of at-

---

42   Adams to the Council of the AGS, 30.11.1896, Box 102, Folder 3, AGS Archives.
43   Adams to *Special Committee* of AGS, 1896, Box 102, Folder 3, AGS Archives.

tracting readers and increasing the AGS's visibility. In addition, Adams called for expanding photographic collections for use in the Bulletin.[44]

One year later, internal debates on improving the *Bulletin* further illustrate the society's ambivalent relationship with popularization. Editor Adams suggested printing Peary's photos from Greenland, taking care to specify that these should be presented in a professional rather than popular way, only "to illustrate types of Arctic ice conditions (...) the idea being not to accompany the photos with elaborate letterpress, but to have each phase described concisely and clearly in a few sentences."[45] This proposal suggests the AGS's effort to adopt the visual techniques characteristic of popular geography without compromising its carefully cultivated scientific image.

The NGM remained a point of reference with regard to popularization for the AGS and other societies, who made efforts to differentiate themselves from the NGM's particular brand of geography. In 1907, Robbins (AGS) privately complained that the NGS "with its attractive picture book and $2 membership is hurting us."[46] The remark captures the disruptive influence the NGS had on the field. Robbins complained that scientific authority now competed in a marketplace, where institutional success was being measured not by the scholarly weight of a journal, but by the low price point and visual appeal of publications. The AGS felt compelled to adjust its *Bulletin* strategy in response to the NGM's popular success, which indicates that competition for readership and institutional standing influenced disciplinary priorities with regard to publication content and style. Referencing the NGM in 1912, Bowman at the AGS expressed his discontent that the magazine had "run to pictures and more pictures, with a few isolated pages of text". In contrast, he envisioned the AGS *Bulletin* becoming the serious, scholarly alternative of comparable or even greater stature, asserting that under these circumstances of unrestrained popularization, the AGS would have to "bear the entire responsibility in the matter of American geography".[47] By cultivating a reputation of scientific professionalism while selectively adopting techniques from popular geography, the AGS attempted to consolidate its scholarly reputation without alienating potential supporters or losing members to the NGS.

---

44 "Suggestions for Society Work during the coming year," Adams to Peary, Robbins, and Hulbut, 30.11.1896, Box 6, Folder 7, AGS Archives.
45 Adams to Hurlbut, 1897, Box 102, Folder 3, AGS Archives.
46 Robbins to Ralphs, 13.9.1907, Box 129, Folder 3, AGS Archives.
47 Bowman to Adams, 12.3.1912, Box 182, Folder 7, AGS Archives.

By 1909, Adams reported significant progress: roughly half the Bulletin was devoted to bibliographies and book reviews, which he claimed made it an unmatched geographic resource in the Western Hemisphere. Still, he recommended adding 16 pages dedicated entirely to "reading matter of popular interest, without sacrificing scientific quality", especially exploration accounts.[48] In a 1912 letter to honorary AGS President Huntington, Adams reiterated the need to expand membership through a more popular approach to lectures and publications. He proposed "striving always to combine good geography with entertainment" and suggested frequent exhibits of maps and photographs. In his view, the Bulletin could be "popular in the best sense" without sacrificing scholarly quality.[49] These initiatives show the AGS carving out its unique institutional identity: a pragmatic mediator occupying the contested middle ground between the NGS's mass-market appeal and the AAG's professional exclusivity.

Sourcing Materials: Government, Academy, and Field

Editorial practices at geographical societies shaped the production of geographical knowledge. Both the AGS and NGS strategically determined what appeared in their periodicals through deliberate content acquisition strategies. This subsection examines their proactive approaches to securing material, their use of government sources, and their responsiveness to reader preferences, illustrating how editorial choices influenced the geographical knowledge they disseminated.

Close connections to government agencies provided National Geographic Magazine with valuable content and high-quality photographs, enabling the society to adapt and popularize government-produced materials. A 1905 NGS advertising pamphlet positioned the society as bridging government-produced geographical knowledge and the American public. It promoted the society's support for the "diffusion of geographic knowledge" by financing exploration, holding lectures, and establishing a library. The pamphlet praised NGM for offering "interesting and accurate articles on exploration, travel, the geography of current events, the geography of commerce", reflecting a broad definition of geography aligned with public interests. Most significantly, the

---

48   Adams to Robbins, 5.12.1909, Box 129, Folder 4, AGS Archives.
49   Cyrus C. Adams to Huntington, 19.2.1912, Box 102, Folder 5, AGS Archives.

advertisement presented the magazine's role as repackaging federal publications to provide a "popular and authentic record of the marvelous discoveries
and achievements of the hundreds of workers in the scientific bureaus of
the government." The pamphlet concluded with a striking justification for
NGM's editorial strategy: "Often these results are buried in massive volumes,
which are not available to the public. They are, however, as interesting as they
are valuable and important."[50] This framing positioned the NGS as perform-
ing a vital democratic function – making government knowledge accessible
to citizens – while obscuring how this process selected and transformed
knowledge.

Through its government contacts and its members with official affiliations, the NGS gained access to high-quality geographical knowledge, which it
popularized in its magazine. Thus, the NGS's content acquisition and editorial
strategies were not just acts of popularization, but integral to the production
and mediation of knowledge. Many leading NGS members held government
positions, granting the society privileged access to official materials. For example, in 1904, the magazine printed a detailed war map of Manchuria and
Korea during the Russo-Japanese War, provided directly by the U.S. War Department, followed by similar war maps of South Africa, China, and others.[51]
By publishing official military maps during major international conflicts,
the NGS mediated a state-sanctioned geopolitical perspective, teaching its
readers to see the world through a strategic, military lens.

Collaboration between the NGS and the government reached a high point
with the 1905 NGM special issue on the Philippines. U.S. Secretary of War
William Howard Taft, who had earlier overseen the census of the Philippines
as Governor, provided statistical data and photographic plates for reproduc-
tion. Aware that images of distant and "exotic" regions drew reader interest,
editor Grosvenor dedicated the entire issue to government-supplied photographs of the Philippines. This strategy proved effective: subscriptions
surged from 3,400 to 11,000 members in one year. Grosvenor later cited this
issue as a turning point in the magazine's popularity.[52] This close alignment
with state interests, particularly in the dissemination of information about
U.S. colonial territories such as the Philippines, underscores NGM's role in

---

50   Pamphlet "National Geographic Society," O. P. Austin (NGS secretary) to Libbey,
      30.1.1905, Box 240, Folder 17, AGS Archives.
51   Ibid.
52   Grosvenor, *National Geographic Society*, 43.

producing and circulating an American imperial vision. The presentation of government data and imagery helped naturalize U.S. presence and authority overseas, shaping public perception and fostering acceptance of imperial expansion, a topic explored further in Chapter 6.

Meanwhile, the AGS developed its own systematic approach to content acquisition for its *Bulletin*, employing multiple strategies to secure high-quality material. The society relied on a combination of lecture transcripts, direct solicitations, and international publication exchanges. Before the 1890s, it was common practice to publish lecture content as articles. In addition, the AGS encouraged scientists returning from expeditions to submit short summaries of their findings and issued public calls in magazines seeking contributions from explorers to support its mission of collecting and disseminating domestic geographical knowledge.[53]

By the late 1890s, the AGS had developed a more targeted approach to content acquisition, guided by scholarly standards and reader interests. In 1897, Cyrus C. Adams advised *Bulletin* editor Hurlbut on securing materials for the periodical. The proposed topics demonstrate that the AGS was tracking ongoing work by institutions, survey agencies, and individual researchers. Adams contacted institutions directly, such as the California Academy of Sciences, requesting an article summarizing its expeditions to California and Mexico since 1888. He wrote to the Hydrographic Survey and the U.S. Geological Survey about recent developments and invited Professor George Davidson, President of the Geographical Society of the Pacific, to contribute a review of geographic work along the Pacific Coast.[54] These proactive efforts illustrate the AGS's new strategy of actively pursuing authoritative material aligned with reader interests, rather than passively waiting for submissions.

Adams's correspondence included highly specific requests, reflecting the AGS's thorough knowledge of global research activities. In a letter to Professor Henry A. Ward, Adams asked for a summary of recent explorations of the Great Barrier Reef, including details such as "portions of the Reef visited" and "methods of collecting coral." He even noted the rate of $8 per 1,000 words, indicating that the AGS was prepared to pay contributors to secure high-qual-

---

53   Hurlbut to Leffingwell, 1.10.1908, Box 9, Folder 51, AGS Archives; Clipping from *Overland Monthly* Vol II, no. 5 (November 1873), Box 42, Folder 3, AGS Archives.

54   Adams to Hurlbut, 13.1.1897, Box 102, Folder 3, AGS Archives.

ity content.[55] Similarly, he asked Professor O.J. Storm of the Naval School in Buenos Aires for summaries of exploring expeditions along the Cordilleras, a statement on boundary treaties between Argentina and Chile, and an overview of geographical work by South American states, including surveys, mapping efforts, and institutional activities.[56]

Another important source of content for the *Bulletin* was the AGS's extensive international publication exchange network, conducted through its library. These materials could be used either as reference material or as content for the magazine. In a letter to librarian Hurlbut, Adams listed numerous specific journals to target for exchange, prioritizing European publications in colonial geography and thereby importing their priorities into AGS archives, such as the *Proceedings of the Asiatic Society of Bengal*, *Mitteilungen von Forschungsreisenden und Gelehrten aus den deutschen Schutzgebieten*, *Publications de l'Union Coloniale Francaise*, *Revue maritime et coloniale*, *Journal of the Royal Colonial Institute*, and the *Bulletin de la Societe d'Etudes coloniales*.[57] Adams elaborated that seeking out publication exchanges was also a way of maintaining transnational correspondence that "get[s] us into relations [with] geographic workers and they will begin the habit of sending more of their literary work to us for notion."[58] This exchange shows that networks of knowledge production were built up strategically. Adams also recommended expanding the range of maps featured in the Bulletin, especially those from colonial surveys, including the French *Service geographique de l'Armee* of Tunis, Algeria, Laos and Africa; British Admiralty Charts and surveys of India; Petermann's maps of Africa; and a map of Ethiopia by the Italian *Ministero della Guerra*.[59] In 1897, one year before the Spanish-American War, these priorities reflect not only a pragmatic interest in high-quality cartographic material, but also an implicit alignment with the geographies of contemporary European imperialism, informing American perspectives and the society's own outlook. By systematically collecting and disseminating information on European colonial administration, resource exploitation, and territorial control in Africa and Asia, the AGS implicitly provided its influential readership with models and justifications for overseas

---

55   Adams to Prof. Henry A. Ward, 6.2.1897, Box 102, Folder 3, AGS Archives; according to the letter, this was the usual payment received by all paid writers from the AGS.
56   Adams to Hurlbut, 13.1.1897, Box 102, Folder 3, AGS Archives.
57   Adams to Hurlbut, 21.1.1897, Box 102, Folder 3, AGS Archives.
58   Adams to Hurlbut, 21.1.1897, Box 102, Folder 3, AGS Archives.
59   Adams to Hurlbut, 27.1.1897, Box 102, Folder 3, AGS Archives.

expansion, familiarizing them with the operational geographies of empire-building just as the U.S. was poised to embark on its own.

In sum, geographical publications functioned as important gatekeepers in the circulation of knowledge, determining which geographical facts, theories, and representations reached scientific and popular audiences. Editorial decisions about content acquisition, visual presentation, and article selection shaped not only what counted as important and legitimate geographical knowledge, but also influenced which regions, topics, and approaches received attention.

Publishing for Prestige: Regional Societies and International Networks

While the AGS and NGS dominated the national landscape, smaller geographical societies also used periodicals to establish scientific legitimacy and foster institutional networks. Even comparatively small regional societies participated significantly in global networks. For instance, in 1902, the Geographical Society of the Pacific in San Francisco conducted active reciprocal exchanges with over 100 societies across more than thirty countries, demonstrating the depth and breadth of these networks.[60] The case of the Geographical Society of Philadelphia (GSP) illustrates in detail how local societies viewed periodicals as indispensable tools for upholding their scientific reputation, fostering scholarly networks, and engaging in international publication exchanges. Like their national counterparts, smaller societies faced the challenge of balancing professional standards, popular appeal, and institutional necessities.

The GSP established its Bulletin early in its history, recognizing the importance of a publication for scientific credibility and international visibility. The first volume of the GSP's *Bulletin* was published in January 1893, two years after the society's founding. In its early years, the publication schedule was irregular due to financial constraints and limited material for publication, but the *Bulletin* quickly became central to promoting the GSP's visibility. As one society member observed, the publication helped make the GSP "known to American and foreign learned societies and educational institutions". Another member remarked at the time that "liberal dissemination of the publication would tend to make [the GSP] better known in this country and in Europe."[61] These

---

60   *Transactions and Proceedings of The Geographical Society of the Pacific* 2, no. 2 (1902).

61   Geographical Society of Philadelphia, *History 1891–1960* (Philadelphia: The Society, 1960), 56.

statements attest to the instrumental role of periodical publications in building a society's academic reputation and extending its national and international network.

Despite ongoing financial challenges, the GSP consistently prioritized its publication as it was essential to its scientific standing and international connections. The *Bulletin*'s importance for international publication exchanges was reaffirmed repeatedly in internal discussions. In a 1904 board meeting, member E. R. Johnson criticized the disproportionate allocation of funds to lectures over publishing and urged a more frequent and regular publication schedule for the *Bulletin*.[62] In 1907, amidst ongoing financial difficulties, another member stressed the indispensability of the *Bulletin*, which was still a net loss for the society. He argued that "the maintenance of a regular publication is a distinct advantage to the society in making possible the maintenance of a large and extremely valuable list of regular exchanges, in keeping up interest in the growth of the society, and in maintaining the scientific standard of the society."[63] This view was widely shared among geographical societies, as a periodical publication attracted members and maintained engagement, leading to increased revenue and prestige.

Despite its modest size, the GSP established an impressive international exchange network through its *Bulletin*. The 1907 *Report of the Library Committee* listed 217 different societies and scientific institutions with which the GSP regularly exchanged publications, 137 of which were located abroad. By 1912, the largest number of exchanges were conducted with institutions in France, Germany, South America, Austria-Hungary, England, Russia, and Sweden, in declining order.[64] Alongside its international ambitions, the GSP made efforts to broaden the Bulletin's appeal at home. A committee overseeing the publication sought to make the journal more popular and engaging.[65] Nonetheless, the *Bulletin* still served as a platform for professional geography, as its content was provided by prominent geographers such as Robert De C. Ward, William Morris Davis, R.S. Tarr, C.R. Dryer, D. W. Johnson, Mark Jefferson, J. Russell Smith, and A. P. Brigham. From 1906 onward, the *Bulletin* began including book reviews and further professionalized.[66]

---

62   Geographical Society of Philadelphia, *History 1891–1960*, 60.
63   Geographical Society of Philadelphia, *History 1891–1960*, 67.
64   Geographical Society of Philadelphia, *History 1891–1960*, 67.
65   Geographical Society of Philadelphia, *History 1891–1960*, 57.
66   Geographical Society of Philadelphia, *History 1891–1960*, 61–66.

The publishing strategies adopted by geographical societies, from prioritizing popular appeal like the NGS to balancing professional and popular interests like the AGS and GSP, reflect the interplay among intellectual objectives, audience demand, institutional competition, and financial necessity. Rather than merely simplifying pre-existing scientific knowledge for the public, these societies shaped geographical knowledge through their curatorial and editorial decisions. The choices they made about which topics to feature, which speakers to invite, which visual materials to include, and which government sources to adapt all influenced what constituted legitimate geographical knowledge in the U.S. context and how it was presented. Thus, for geographical societies, dissemination was not separate from knowledge production, but integral to the knowledge-making process itself.

6 Representing Knowledge: The Pacific as American Space

The preceding chapters traced how U.S. geographical societies organized, circulated, and disseminated knowledge. This chapter analyzes the results of these processes: how societies produced authoritative spatial representations that legitimated American imperial interests, particularly in the Pacific Ocean. Given the Pacific's prominence in societies' lectures and publications, the ocean offers an exemplary lens for understanding how spatial knowledge reinforced imperial claims. Between the 1850s and 1914, geographical societies constructed and popularized spatial representations that framed the Pacific Ocean as spatially and geographically connected to U.S. commercial and geopolitical interests, thus making imperial expansion appear both natural and inevitable. These "imaginative geographies" were shaped by the institutional practices explored in earlier chapters. The societies' organizational dependence on commercial and political elites, drive for state-relevant expertise, and control over knowledge circulation fostered an institutional bias toward representing the Pacific as a logical sphere of American influence. Geographical societies often adapted and amplified spatial knowledge originally produced by state actors working within government bureaus and surveys, naval expeditions, and the military. The societies' role was mediation: selecting, framing, and disseminating often state-produced knowledge to legitimize and popularize an imperial vision of the Pacific.

This chapter proceeds in three stages: First, it establishes a theoretical foundation by discussing the representation of space through the frameworks of "imaginative geographies" and "critical geopolitics." It then provides a brief historical overview of federal government expeditions in the West and the Pacific, which generated geographical knowledge that societies adapted and disseminated. In the final part, it analyzes how geographical societies deployed three interconnected spatial arguments to represent the Pacific: as a natural space for American commercial empire, as an ocean made accessible through a transisthmian canal, and as a contested geopolitical space requiring American control. These representational frameworks illustrate how the practices of organization, dissemination, and circulation culminated in specific knowledge claims that presented imperial expansion as a scientifically justified outcome rather than a politically motivated choice.

6.1 Imaginative Geographies: Space, Geopolitics, and Power

This section develops the theoretical framework for analyzing spatial representations by drawing on the concepts of "imaginative geographies" and "critical geopolitics". These concepts help deconstruct ostensibly objective representations of space, revealing their underlying power dynamics and the political projects they legitimize. The section first situates imaginative geographies within theories of space as socially constructed; second, it explores their imperial manifestations, drawing particularly on Edward Said's *Orientalism*; and third, it incorporates insights from critical geopolitics to examine how geographical societies institutionalized spatial discourses.

Representations of space are fundamental to the production of geographical knowledge. Following the linguistic turn, scholars treat geography less as an objective record of physical realities and more as a culturally mediated construct, conveyed through texts and images. Stuart Hall emphasizes that this perspective does not deny the existence of the material world, but rather foregrounds how language systems shape perceptions of reality.[1] Therefore, spatial representations are historically situated expressions of social meaning rather than natural categories, which helps explain why certain representations of space become hegemonic while others remain marginalized.[2] For most nineteenth-century Americans, including many geographers, distant regions such as the Pacific were places they would never personally visit. Instead, knowledge of these places circulated through representations produced and dissem-

---

1   Stuart Hall, *Representation: Cultural Representations and Signifying Practices* (London: Sage, 2007), 25.

2   Iris Dzudzek, "Räumliche Repräsentationen als Element des Politischen – Konzeptionelle Grundlagen und Untersuchungsperspektiven der Humangeographie," in *Die Politik räumlicher Repräsentationen – Beispiele aus der empirischen Forschung*, ed. Iris Dzudzek, Paul Reuber, and Anke Strüver (Münster: LIT Verlag, 2011), 7–13.

inated by institutions such as geographical societies. These spatial orderings of the world constitute "imaginative geographies", defined as "representations of place, space and landscape that structure people's understandings of the world, and in turn help to shape their actions."[3] Thus, imaginative geographies operate as powerful discursive formations linking space, power, and knowledge, legitimizing some political actions while delegitimizing others.[4]

Edward Said popularized the concept of imaginative geographies in *Orientalism*. Said argued that European imperial powers invented the Orient to legitimize and manage imperial conquest by portraying non-Western societies as backward and irrational, in opposition to their own identity.[5] The "Orient" itself became one of the most successful imaginative geographies, constructed as a geographical category that conflated vast and culturally diverse areas into a homogenous entity. Geographers often described the Orient using pre-existing categories and thereby reproduced and institutionalized them.[6] Said emphasized the often-overlooked significance of geographical knowledge for imperialism, arguing that the "struggle over geography" was not only about military actions, but also about "ideas, about forms, about images and imaginings".[7] This insight is particularly relevant for understanding how U.S. geographical societies facilitated American imperialism. According to Said, space is first studied "at home", then appropriated through statistics, surveys, and mapping, and only afterward subordinated through economic means, colonial administration, and military action. Said's three-stage process (study, appropriation, subordination) provides a useful framework for examining how geographical societies facilitated imperial work. By studying and appropriating the Pacific through knowledge production and circulation, they prepared the ground for later political, economic, and military subordination (in which individual amateur geographers also participated). As Said noted: "We would not have had empire itself, as well as many forms of historiography, anthropology, sociology, and modern legal structures, without important philosophical and

---

3   Felix Driver, "Imaginative geographies," in *Introducing Human Geographies*, 3. ed., ed. Paul Cloke, Philip Crang, and Mark Goodwin (London: Routledge, 2014), 246.

4   Julia Lossau, *Die Politik der Verortung: eine postkoloniale Reise zu einer anderen Geographie der Welt* (Bielefeld: transcript, 2002), 76.

5   Edward W. Said, *Orientalism* (New York: Vintage, 1993); similar arguments advanced in Edward W. Said, *Culture and Imperialism* (New York: Knopf, 1993).

6   See also chapter 4.

7   Said, *Orientalism*, 7.

imaginative processes at work in the production as well as the acquisition, subordination, and settlement of space."[8]

The term "imaginative geography" was later elaborated by Derek Gregory, who argues that geography as a discipline was complicit in colonialism and that imperialism itself established geography as a scientific discipline.[9] These imaginative geographies extended beyond the discipline and its associated scientific community. They circulated into a wider public discourse through media such as newspapers and schoolbooks, eventually becoming everyday knowledge. Importantly, imaginative geographies are not simply imagined constructs, but constitute social realities that underpin political practices and actions.[10] In the United States, geographical societies disseminated these imaginative geographies through periodical publications and public lectures, which transformed abstract spatial concepts into seemingly concrete realities that shaped Americans' understanding of their nation's place in the world. The blend of scientific authority, public reach, and elite membership positioned U.S. geographical societies to produce and disseminate imperial narratives that bridged state ambitions, commercial interests, and public sentiment.

To analyze how geographical societies' representations legitimized U.S. imperial expansion, this chapter draws on insights from critical geopolitics, which treats geopolitics not as an objective science, but as a historically situated discourse embedded in particular institutional sites and contexts. Gearóid Ó Tuathail and John Agnew pioneered this approach, illuminating how geographical knowledge functions as a power/knowledge complex that produces, rather than simply describes global spatial hierarchies.[11] Geographical discourses construct territories and borders, marginalizing alternative

---

8   Edward W. Said, "Representing the Colonized: Anthropology's Interlocutors," *Critical Inquiry* 15, no. 2 (1989): 218.

9   Derek Gregory, *Geographical Imaginations* (Cambridge, MA: Blackwell, 1994), 168.

10   Shadia Husseini de Araújo, *Jenseits vom "Kampf der Kulturen": imaginative Geographien des Eigenen und des Anderen in arabischen Printmedien* (Bielefeld: transcript, 2011), 27.

11   Gearóid Ó Tuathail, "Geopolitical Discourses: A New Geopolitics Series," *Geopolitics* 5, no. 1 (2000), 127; Gearóid Ó Tuathail, *Critical Geopolitics: The Politics of Writing Global Space* (London: Routledge, 1996); Simon Dalby, "Critical Geopolitics: Discourse, Difference, and Dissent," *Environment and Planning D: Society and Space* 9, no. 3 (1991): 261–83; Klaus Dodds and James Derrick Sidaway, "Locating Critical Geopolitics," *Environment and Planning D: Society and Space* 12, no. 5 (1994): 515–24; John Agnew, "The Origins of Critical Geopolitics," in *The Ashgate Research Companion to Critical Geopolitics*, ed. Klaus Dodds, Merje Kuus, and Joanne Sharp (London: Ashgate, 2016), 19–32.

visions and hierarchically ordering global spaces and populations.[12] Representations produced by U.S. geographical societies frequently employed what Ó Tuathail terms the "geopolitical gaze", a way of seeing that reduces complex local realities to broad abstractions and thereby naturalizes spatial orders conducive to imperial interests. This gaze operates through "geo-graphing", earth-writing practices that inscribe strategic meanings onto spaces, simplifying complex locales into strategic locations. Such spatial orders appear natural only as long as the criteria and power relations behind them remain obscured, which makes it necessary to critically examine how geographical societies constructed these representations.[13] Thus, the analysis explores how seemingly natural spatial categories and world orders were, in fact, shaped by social and political contexts and the power-knowledge structures enabling them.[14]

Imaginative geographies circulate not only through language, but also through visual media, especially maps. As compressed visualizations of territory and identity, maps were central to imperial and national orderings. Their apparent precision and scientific appearance lent them persuasive power that textual descriptions often lack.[15] Mark Monmonier demonstrates that all maps generalize spatial information by processes of selection, displacement, simplification, or typification.[16] These processes may appear technical, but they always involve political choices about what to include, exclude, and emphasize. In their selection of projections, colors, labels, and lines, maps advocate for a particular way of seeing and ordering the world. Maps reflect the social, political, and cultural contexts in which they are produced. Therefore, maps do not simply represent space, but help produce it, most visibly in national or imperial contexts. Benedict Anderson points to maps, alongside the press, museums, and the census, as the most important tools for visualizing and uniting nations as imagined communities.[17] Cartographic representations

---

12   Lossau, *Politik der Verortung*, 88–89.
13   Lossau, *Politik der Verortung*, 106.
14   *Felix Driver and Gillian Rose, Nature and Science (Cheltenham:* Historical Geography Research Group, *1992*), 4.
15   Livingstone, *Putting Science in its Place*, 154.
16   Mark Monmonier, *How to Lie with Maps* (Chicago: University of Chicago Press, 1991); Mark Monmonier, *Mapping It Out* (Chicago: University of Chicago Press, 1993).
17   Benedict Anderson, *Imagined Communities: Reflections on the Origin and Spread of Nationalism* (London: Verso, 1983).

thus forged a homogenized national space, creating a foundation for territorialization and national identity. Surveying and mapping equated space with nationhood, thereby contributing to the creation of the modern territorial nation-state.[18] Consequently, maps became vital instruments for spatial and cultural self-location within the nation.[19]

In imperial contexts, cartography was necessary not just for navigation, but also to maintain control over colonial territories administratively and conceptually. Maps visualized the extent of territories and could provide an overview of large empires at a glance. As David Harvey pointed out: "in both its iconography and its concrete effects, the map has often been interpreted as one of empire's most powerful imaginative tools".[20] As noted earlier, empires appropriated territories first by knowing them (i.e., collecting data) and then by assuming control and governing them. The maps of trade routes, shipping distances, and strategic positions that frequently appeared in geographical society publications did not simply represent existing realities. Instead, following Thongchai Winichakul, they anticipated future imperial arrangements, even before formal control was established, serving as "a model for, rather than a model of, what it purported to represent".[21]

6.2 State Geographies: Surveys, Expeditions, and Expansion

This section grounds the theoretical framework discussed above and prepares the analysis of society publications that follows. The imaginative geographies promoted by U.S. geographical societies emerged from a long tradition of state-sponsored exploration that linked continental expansion in the West with imperial ambitions across the Pacific. This section details the development of geographic knowledge practices during continental expansion, illustrating how they provided templates subsequently adapted for overseas contexts. By tracing these continuities from westward expansion to Pacific imperialism, it establishes the historical foundation for understanding societies' later representations of U.S. overseas power.

---

18   Schlögel, *Im Raume lesen wir die Zeit*, 72–73.
19   Speich and Gugerli, *Topografien der Nation*, 97.
20   Felix Driver, "Mapping Cultures," in *Introducing Human Geographies*, ed. Cloke et al., 241.
21   Thongchai Winichakul, *Siam Mapped: A History of the Geo-Body of a Nation* (Honolulu, University of Hawaii Press, 1997), 130.

From Continental Empire to the Pacific

By 1900, the United States held noncontiguous and overseas possessions from Alaska and the Caribbean to the western Pacific. Throughout the second half of the nineteenth century, the United States expanded in an imperial manner across the North American continent, employing military force and diplomatic negotiations to displace Native American and other populations. In 1898, following the Spanish-American War, U.S. expansion extended beyond the North American continent, as the United States acquired overseas territories when Spain ceded Guam, Puerto Rico, and the Philippines to it. Cuba gained nominal independence, but later remained under U.S. influence through the 1901 Platt Amendment. During the same imperial moment, the United States also annexed Hawaii (1898), Wake Island (1899), and parts of Samoa (1900).

Although many contemporary Americans perceived these actions as advancing civilization rather than engaging in imperialism, historians now recognize these expansions as fundamentally imperial. Challenging exceptionalist narratives, recent scholarship emphasizes the continuities between continental expansion in the West and overseas imperialism after 1898.[22] Richard Immerman, for example, concludes that by the Civil War, the United States already "fit even the most restricted definition of empire".[23] Similarly, Jay Sexton highlights how anticolonial rhetoric and imperialist ambition coexisted in American political thought.[24] Thomas Bender situates American imperial expansion within a global pattern of the late nineteenth-century "closing of space" that paralleled European colonial empires, challenging exceptionalist narratives that separate American from European imperial histories.[25]

The Pacific had already become central to the American imperial imagination well before 1898, as the United States pursued an informal or commercial empire across the Pacific throughout the nineteenth century.[26] This informal approach prioritized trade rather than outright territorial control, exemplified

---

22   Steven Hahn, *A Nation Without Borders: The United States and Its World in an Age of Civil Wars, 1830–1910* (New York: Viking, 2016), 37.

23   Richard H. Immerman, *Empire for Liberty: A History of American Imperialism from Benjamin Franklin to Paul Wolfowitz* (Princeton: Princeton University Press, 2010), 11.

24   Jay Sexton, *The Monroe Doctrine: Empire and Nation in Nineteenth-Century America* (New York: Hill & Wang, 2011), 5.

25   Thomas Bender, *A Nation among Nations: America's Place in World History* (New York: Hill and Wang, 2006)

26   Mona Domosh, *American Commodities in an Age of Empire* (New York: Routledge, 2006).

by the U.S. Navy's forcible "opening" of Japan and the "Open Door" policy toward China. In addition, the purchase of Alaska from Russia in 1867 enabled the United States to project influence into the northern Pacific. Furthermore, the U.S.-backed construction of the Panama Canal, facilitated by military support for Panamanian separatists in 1903, exemplifies how infrastructure projects supported broader imperial ambitions.[27]

Surveys and State-Building in the West

The spatial logic that underpinned U.S. expansion into the American West increasingly extended into the Pacific Ocean – geopolitically, militarily, and discursively. Government surveys and military expeditions produced the spatial knowledge essential to both continental and overseas imperialism, creating a foundation upon which geographers later constructed their spatial representations. During the first phase of western expansion, geographers employed by military or government survey expeditions were deeply involved in facilitating national expansion. These expeditions and surveys into the American West, typically led by military personnel accompanied by civilian scientists (with many geographers among them), produced extensive geographical knowledge that transformed abstract "space" into surveyed "territory". They gathered data on natural resources and geology, surveyed land to be parcellated for settlement, and produced maps that guided settlement. U.S. national identity was, to a significant extent, forged through geographical knowledge. State-sponsored geographical knowledge of the West supported Manifest Destiny and Turner's frontier thesis, both influential as ideological frameworks for imperial expansion and national identity. Frederick J. Turner based his frontier thesis on data produced by the U.S. Geological Survey, whose work is judged by one historian as among the "key contributions made by science to the realization of the American nation".[28] At the frontier, national identity and geographical knowledge intertwined, with maps, surveys, and statistics functioning as essential tools for the expansion and settlement of the West. Turner himself acknowledged the influence of geography in shaping national identity in his essay "Geographical Interpretations of American His-

27   Anders Stephanson, *Manifest Destiny: American Expansionism and the Empire of Right* (New York: Hill and Wang, 1995), 75.

28   Naylor, "Historical Geographies of Science," 8.

tory", arguing that distinctive spatial conditions in the West fundamentally influenced American character and expansion.[29]

Although Sexton notes the absence of a centralized "master plan" for empire, U.S. expansion was far from spontaneous.[30] Scholars such as Brian Balogh have demonstrated that federal institutions played a larger role in western settlement than the popular notion of a "government out of sight" suggests.[31] Steven Hahn similarly characterizes the settlement of the West as "a massive project of state building that had strong imperial impulses".[32] Federal legislation like the Northwest Ordinances allowed the government to assert authority over western lands by regulating settlement and landownership; the Homestead Act of 1862 encouraged migration by granting land to settlers who cultivated it for five years; and the Pacific Railway Act incentivized railroad construction by providing corporations with government bonds and extensive land grants. These measures show the federal government's central role in organizing and directing western expansion.

Western surveys were foundational to American nation-building and the projection of U.S. authority across the frontier. They mapped physical space, assessed natural resources, documented Indigenous populations, and laid the groundwork for settler colonialism. During the latter half of the nineteenth century, the government established federal agencies and bureaus including the Geological Survey, the Bureau of American Ethnology, and the Department of the Interior, which institutionalized these efforts in the West. The relationships between space, territorialization, and nation are central here. Only surveyed land could be controlled, parcellated, settled, and governed. Surveys also unified the nation by mapping lands according to a single standard of measurement and cartographic representation, producing a visually and conceptually consolidated U.S. territory.[33] In this way, the practices of geographers

---

29   Frederick Jackson Turner, "Geographical Interpretations of American History," Journal of Geography 4 (1905): 34–37.

30   Sexton, Monroe Doctrine, 32.

31   Brian Balogh, A Government out of Sight: The Mystery of National Authority in Nineteenth-Century America (Cambridge: Cambridge University Press, 2009); Paul Frymer, Building an American Empire: The Era of Territorial and Political Expansion (Princeton: Princeton University Press, 2017).

32   Hahn, Nation without Borders, 5.

33   See also: Livingstone, Geographical Tradition; and analogous for Switzerland: Gugerli and Speich, Topografien der Nation.

such as surveying facilitated westward expansion and contributed to the discursive construction of the United States as a coherent, knowable, and governable geographic entity.

Geographical societies actively participated in promoting and disseminating the knowledge generated by these state-sponsored efforts. An 1873 article in the *Overland Monthly* titled "Contributions to Physical Geography" announced that the AGS planned "to devote more attention to American exploration and to become the active agent in collecting and diffusing geographical information of a domestic character." After praising the collection and distribution of geographical information on the U.S. West, the society invited all "naval and military officers and civilians engaged in exploration" to contribute geographical knowledge, asserting that "nothing would conduce more to the unity, stability, and future greatness of our country" than documenting the resources between the Mississippi and the Pacific. The *Overland Monthly* endorsed this call and urged amateur geographers to contribute: "There are many energetic and intelligent travelers on the Pacific Coast, unconnected with scientific exploration whose observations, if recorded, would yet be of great value, and who would be adding to the sum of scientific knowledge by sending notes of the same to the American Geographical Society."[34] This call links geographical data collection by professionals and amateurs to national unity and greatness, illustrating the societies' role in mobilizing knowledge for nation-building and imperial expansion.

Naval Expeditions and Pacific Knowledge

Mapping the Pacific served not only scientific purposes, but also geopolitical motives. In the early nineteenth century, U.S. politicians worried that the nation depended on British maps to navigate even its own harbors. This sparked a sense of "hydrographic nationalism", which led to the establishment of the U.S. Coast Survey in 1807. Because accurate charts were viewed as essential for sovereignty, commerce, and naval defense, cartographic knowledge became explicitly linked to state power.[35] By 1853, oceanographer Matthew Fontaine

---

34   Clipping from *Overland Monthly* II, no. 5 Nov (1873), Box 42, Folder 3, AGS Archives.

35   D. Graham Burnett, "Hydrographic Discipline among the Navigators: Charting an Empire of Commerce and Science in the Nineteenth-Century Pacific," in *The Imperial Map: Cartography and the Mastery of Empire*, ed. James R. Akerman (Chicago: University of Chicago Press, 2009), 196.

Maury praised the U.S. government for systematically charting the Pacific, observing that "no maritime nation has heretofore undertaken a systematic search for [...] dangers which render navigation uneasy, if not unsafe".[36] This mapping served geopolitical and commercial objectives, transforming the Pacific from an uncharted area into a navigable and controllable space for American interests.

From the 1840s onward, politicians and naval strategists increasingly envisioned the Pacific Ocean as a space of national interest.[37] As early as the 1840s and 1850s, the U.S. Coast Survey and several Navy Exploring Expeditions charted the American Pacific coastline up to the Russian and Japanese coasts.[38] Between 1850 and 1900, the U.S. government dispatched 234 expeditions, many of which were naval missions into the Pacific.[39] Additionally, in 1867, the United States purchased Alaska and later acquired smaller Pacific islands such as Midway as naval coaling stations or strategic outposts.[40] These developments brought the Pacific more fully into the U.S. geopolitical imagination. As the nineteenth century progressed, these surveying and mapping activities in the Pacific became central to a new imperial vision well before the so-called "closing of the frontier". Throughout Western continental settlement, the Pacific remained a focus of American political and strategic ambitions.[41] Imperial advocates of the "large policy" of overseas expansion, such as Albert Beveridge, Henry Cabot Lodge, and Theodore Roosevelt, cited successful westward expansion to justify their vision of an overseas American Empire.[42]

Geographical societies amplified this connection between geography and naval power. An address delivered at the Eighth International Geographic Congress in 1904, titled "Early Geographers of the United States", claimed

---

36   Quoted in Rozwadowski, *Fathoming the Ocean*, 64.
37   Norman A. Graebner, *Empire on the Pacific: A Study in American Continental Expansion* (New York: The Ronald Press, 1955).
38   Perry, *Facing West*, 52.
39   Sally Gregory Kohlstedt, "Place and Museum Space: The Smithsonian Institution, National Identity, and the American West, 1846–1896," in *Geographies of Nineteenth-Century Science*, ed. Livingstone and Withers, 420–421.
40   Immerman, *Empire for Liberty*, 136.
41   Bruce Cumings, *Dominion from Sea to Sea: Pacific Ascendancy and American Power* (New Haven: Yale University Press, 2009).
42   David C. Hendrickson, *Union, Nation, or Empire: The American Debate over International Relations, 1789–1941* (Lawrence: University Press of Kansas, 2009), 285–286.

that the U.S. Navy was "one of the oldest, if not the oldest, of all the National Geographic Societies of this country".[43] The address by George W. Littlehales highlighted the parallel development of geographical knowledge acquisition and empire-building in the Pacific, starting with the Wilkes expedition (1838–1842), continuing with the "opening" of Japan, and culminating in the then-ongoing construction of the Panama Canal. The speaker's characterization of the Navy as a "Geographic Society" reveals how thoroughly military and scientific practices had become entangled with American imperial expansion. Similarly, in 1899, the AGS *Bulletin* published an article titled "The Navy as a Motor in Geographical and Commercial Progress", which praised Navy expeditions as "among the forceful agencies of the nineteenth century in extending the confines of knowledge to a wider horizon and in opening avenues through which the industries of the people have poured millions of treasures into the nation's lap." The article drew explicit connections between Wilkes's early Pacific expedition routes from Hawaii to the Philippines and contemporary U.S. imperial acquisitions, reframing earlier explorations as precursors to formal empire.[44] These examples show how geographical societies, especially through military and government members, promoted narratives linking state power, exploration, and imperial expansion.

This intensified focus on the Pacific stemmed from viewing the ocean as a new frontier. As Helen Rozwadowski argues, mid-century geophysical research transformed the imagination of the open sea from a wild, empty place to a knowable, ordered grid. Just as the West had once been seen as a frontier to be settled, the ocean was increasingly framed as the next domain of national expansion. Rozwadowski writes: "Observing, sampling, mapping, naming, and charting provided nineteenth-century explorers and scientists with tangible ways to demonstrate both personal and national claims to the atmosphere, mountains, and polar regions, as well as the sea. Between 1840 and 1880, the ocean was transformed from a mere highway and wasteland into a destination, a frontier, an uncivilized place ripe for conquest and exploitation."[45] Scientific motivations for charting the Pacific aligned with commercial shipping interests and strategic projects such as laying a submarine telegraph cable. To-

---

43   C. Chester, "Some Early Geographers of the United States," *NGM* 15 (1904): 392–394.

44   G. W. Littlehales, "The Navy as a Motor in Geographical and Commercial Progress," *Journal of the American Geographical Society of New York* 31, no. 2 (1899): 123–29.

45   Rozwadowski, *Fathoming the Ocean*, 62.

gether, these developments made geographical knowledge of the Pacific a matter of national importance.

This state-sponsored exploration and the conceptual shift of the Pacific into a knowable, controllable space, prepared the ground for how geographical societies would represent the Pacific in their publications and lectures. Drawing on knowledge produced through government expeditions and naval explorations, they developed spatial frameworks that made American expansion into the Pacific appear natural, beneficial, and necessary. The following section analyzes these representations in detail, demonstrating how geographical societies legitimized imperial ambitions in the Pacific.

6.3 Projecting American Empire: The Pacific, Infrastructure, and Geopolitics

Building on the concept of imaginative geographies and the historical context of U.S. expansion outlined earlier in this chapter, this section analyzes how geographical societies constructed and disseminated spatial representations that positioned the Pacific Ocean within the U.S. sphere of influence. The societies' engagement with imperial geopolitics is evident in their publications, illustrated clearly by this 1899 commentary from *National Geographic Magazine* on the partitioning of Samoa:

> "The arrangements for the disposition of the Samoan Islands entered into between the governments of Great Britain, Germany, and the United States may be considered as removing from the international chess-board these small islands [...]. Whether our European partners are satisfied with their share of the division, their geographical societies and foreign offices alone are in a position to say."[46]

Here, the writer positions the society – and other geographical societies abroad – not just as observers, but as actors equivalent to diplomats and foreign offices, institutions with both the expertise and the standing to weigh in on matters of geopolitical significance. The article's overt reference to the imperial 1899 division of Samoa between Britain, Germany, and the U.S. was no coincidence. This section argues that geographical societies deployed three

---

46   E. Morgan, "The Samoan Islands," *NGM* 12 (1900): 417.

mutually reinforcing representational strategies – commercial, infrastructural, and geopolitical – that transformed the Pacific from a vast expanse of water into an "American Ocean". Geographical societies deployed imaginative geographies to justify American imperial ambitions throughout the nineteenth century, with particular intensity in the 1890s and early 1900s.[47] Through analysis of their publications and lectures, it identifies three interconnected spatial arguments deployed by these societies: first, the Pacific was framed as a space of American commercial empire; second, they stressed the economic and strategic benefits of access to the Pacific by a transisthmian canal; and third, they represented the Pacific as a contested geopolitical space in which American imperialism was justified and naturalized.

Markets and Hubs: The Pacific as an American Commercial Space

Geographical societies consistently represented the Pacific as a natural space of American commercial empire, portraying the United States as ideally positioned to take advantage of the ocean's commercial potential.[48] This representation emerged decades before the annexation of Hawaii and the Philippines and only intensified after 1898. The islands acquired after the Spanish-American War, valued primarily for their strategic locations, were represented as ideal commercial outposts for future trade with Asia. The societies' commercial discourse operated through a spatial logic that transformed the Pacific from an obstacle (vast distances) into an opportunity (strategic positioning of islands).

The narrative of bringing the two American coasts closer together and opening up the Pacific for U.S. trade and influence was already prominent in the talks and articles of the early AGS, which discussed the construction of a transcontinental railroad and the Western surveys, in which the society's associated geographers were involved. At the AGS's first special meeting

---

47   Arguments not directly related to this topic, such as ideology, civilizing mission, race or others previously considered by historians will not be the primary focus in this analysis. See also historiographical overview of Empire in the introduction, relevant here are: Michael Hunt, *Ideology and U.S. Foreign Policy* (New Haven: Yale University Press, 2009); Paul Kramer, *The Blood of Government: Race, Empire, the United States, & the Philippines* (Chapel Hill: University of North Carolina Press, 2006); McCoy and Scarano, *Colonial Crucible.*

48   on the allure of the "China market", see Thomas McCormick, *China Market: America's Quest for informal Empire, 1893–1901* (Chicago: Quadrangle Books, 1967).

in 1851, Asa Whitney delivered a presentation on his proposed Pacific railroad to expedite trade with Asia, a project he avidly promoted.[49] In his 1870 address, printed in the AGS *Journal*, AGS President Charles P. Daly praised the completed First Transcontinental Railroad for bringing the East Coast "into direct connection with the wealth of China and the riches of India".[50] Historian Karen Morin has highlighted Daly's close ties to railroad interests during the 1870s and 1880s. Daly also used his influence to put the prospect of an interoceanic canal on the agenda of the society during that period, while he was an investor in the Nicaragua Canal Company.[51] This conflict of interest exemplifies how geographical societies could serve as vehicles for advancing members' commercial interests under the guise of scientific knowledge production. As established in Chapter 2, this was not an isolated case. The societies' financial reliance on wealthy patrons and members with direct investments in shipping, trade, and infrastructure created an incentive to produce and disseminate knowledge that supported projects such as the canal.

While historian Mona Domosh has analyzed the commercial motivations for Pacific expansion, the societies' specific spatial representations require further examination.[52] Society publications reveal three commercial-geographic arguments: proximity (the U.S. was "naturally" closer to Asia than Europe), centrality (the U.S. occupied the "center" of world trade routes), and destiny (the claim that geographic position predetermined commercial dominance). From the 1850s onward, numerous articles in the *Journal* of the AGS, also given as talks at society meetings, discussed the Pacific in relation to the United States' position in global trade. Its first issue in 1859 underscored the commercial significance of the Pacific by featuring a table listing sailing distances from U.S. ports to key Pacific ports, such as Shanghai, Canton, Calcutta, and Melbourne.[53] These distance calculations transformed abstract space into measurable commercial opportunity. Another article from the same year predicted that the United States was "destined to become [...] the greatest

49   Dave Benison, "The A.G.S. in the 1850s," manuscript, Box 43, Folder 5, AGS Archives.
50   Charles Daly, "Annual Address. Subject: Review of the Events of the Year, and Recent Explorations and Theories for Reaching the North Pole," *Journal of the American Geographical and Statistical Society* (1870): lxxxvi.
51   Morin, *Civic Discipline*, 19.
52   Domosh, *American Commodities*.
53   I. Stevens, "Northwest America," *Journal of the American Geographical and Statistical Society* (1859): 10.

grain market in the world; ready to assist Europe on the one hand and Asia on the other [because of] her commanding central position".[54] A further article emphasized the location of the newly acquired U.S. West Coast territories relative to Asia, stating that "the *position* of those great Territories, with their great resources, their splendid harbors, fronting on the world's greatest ocean, and over against the world's oldest and most populous nations, is indicative of their destiny" (emphasis in original).[55] The "fine geographical position" of San Francisco in particular was regarded as promising for future trade, due to its "magnificent harbor, excellent internal water communications, and its great railway systems, [it] possesses obvious advantages which, combined with the intelligence, foresight and energy of its merchants, and its greater proximity to the European and Atlantic markets, must place it above all of its possible rivals in the Pacific."[56]

The societies' commercial vision extended even to smaller Pacific territories. Shortly after the passage of the Guano Islands Act (1856), which authorized U.S. annexation of islands rich in guano, an AGS article argued for the strategic value of these islands as sources of high-quality fertilizer for U.S. agriculture.[57] Numerous other articles underscored the economic advantages of an American Empire in the Pacific. An 1859 piece on Siam expressed hopes that expanded trade between Siam and the United States would constitute a first step toward "the extension and development of our own empire on the Pacific".[58] An 1879 article recounted how the gold rush in California and the Mexican-American War of 1846–48 brought renewed attention to the Pacific's importance and suggested that with the "opening" of Japan came "the realization that

---

54   J. Jay, "American Agriculture. Part 1," *Journal of the American Geographical and Statistical Society* (1859): 55.

55   T. Hunt, "California, Oregon, and Washington," *Journal of the American Geographical and Statistical Society* (1859): 152.

56   Charles H. Stockton, "The Commercial Geography of the American Inter-Oceanic Canal," *Journal of the American Geographical Society of New York* 20 (1888): 85.

57   R. S. F.: "Statistics of Guano," *Journal of the American Geographical and Statistical Society* (1859): 181–189; Immerwahr, *How to Hide an Empire*, 51; for a history of guano in the Pacific, see: Gregory T. Cushman, *Guano and the Opening of the Pacific World: A Global Ecological History* (New York: Cambridge University Press, 2013).

58   D. King and Daly, "Notes on Siam," *Journal of the American Geographical and Statistical Society* (1859): 199.

Yokohama was the natural objective point for a line from California".[59] These writings naturalized American imperialism in the Pacific from the outset by presenting commercial expansion as an inevitable consequence of "natural" geographical positioning and destiny rather than a series of deliberate political choices.

After the Spanish-American War of 1898, the NGM emphasized the strategic location of newly acquired islands in the Pacific (the Philippines, Hawaii, Samoa, and Guam) as steppingstones for trade with Asia. An 1898 article, published two months after the United States' victory in Manila Bay, set the tone for the following coverage, arguing that the United States should retain control of the Philippines, then only partially-conquered. The article urged preemptive action before a European imperial power could annex the archipelago, declaring that "the times demand that we take our rightful position among the nations of the world, and especially in the unfolding commercial possibilities of the East." Its author argued that the Philippines' strategic location made it essential for controlling Pacific trade and advocated annexing the archipelago to exploit economic opportunities in Asia, predicting that "we shall be well repaid [for the Spanish-American War] in a very few years from the revenues to be derived from these several countries."[60]

Geographical societies consistently portrayed U.S. possession of Pacific territories as justified by, and evidence of, a natural geographic destiny. An 1899 article on the Philippines echoed these sentiments, characterizing Manila as the "most advantageously situated port and trading place in the East," and predicted its rise as a trade hub for China, Japan, and Australia.[61] Another article on the Philippines asserted that the United States had not "given sufficient attention to the remarkable position which they occupy in relation to other lands", which could position the archipelago as the key for controlling future commerce and politics in the region. The author used a spatial argument to spark the imagination of readers and to make imperial control seem necessary. Inviting the reader to "draw a circle on a radius of two thousand miles, with Manila as the center", the article enumerated several significant Russian, Japanese, Chinese and Australian ports in proximity to Manila. This cartographic exercise exemplified how societies taught readers to see space

---

59   A. Hayes, "Modern Ocean Highways," *Journal of the American Geographical Society of New York* (1879): 100.

60   C. Howe, "The Disposition of the Philippines," *NGM* 9 (1898): 304.

61   Max L. Tornow, Economic Conditions of the Philippines, *NGM* 10 (1899): 48.

through an imperial lens, which transformed geographic proximity into commercial and strategic opportunity. Thus, continued American control over the Philippines appeared as a logical necessity rather than a political choice. To take advantage of these commercial opportunities, the author explicitly recommended a continued American presence in the Philippines.[62] Even the small island of Samoa, partly annexed in 1899, was deemed insignificant in terms of direct trade, but "of first importance [...] for trans-Pacific commerce" due to its central position between the Americas and Australia. Samoa was described as "the key to Central Polynesia by reason of its geographical position – in the course of vessels from San Francisco to Auckland, from Panama to Sydney, and from Valparaiso to China and Japan".[63] These examples show the deployment of imaginative geographies that reduced complex places to strategic points on a commercial map, defined entirely by their utility to American interests, while erasing local contexts and populations in the process. The consistent framing of Pacific islands and peoples primarily in terms of their utility for American commerce (as resources, waystations, or markets) shows an instrumental geographical imagination produced by the societies' close ties to commercial and governmental elites, as detailed in earlier chapters.

A particularly systematic example of how geographical societies used imaginative geographies to justify imperial expansion appeared in a 1902 NGM article by O. P. Austin, Chief of the Bureau of Statistics. Austin's government position highlights the close relationship between state policy and geographical knowledge production. Austin's lecture before the NGS, later published as an article, presented a systematic spatial argument for American Empire in the Pacific. He identified the vast spatial extent of the Pacific as the main obstacle to trade. To alleviate this, the author recommended a continuation of American imperial policy in the Pacific, supported by a series of spatial arguments, each illustrated with a map. First, Austin pointed out that the United States already controlled Hawaii and the Philippines, the "chief way stations of commerce" in the Pacific, both located halfway to Asia from the U.S. West Coast. Second, he noted that the United States controlled the best route for a submarine cable across the Pacific, with Hawaii, Guam, and the Philippines forming a "line of great natural telegraph poles [...] protected by the American flag". Third, the Philippines were essential because of their

---

62   J. Barrett, "The Philippine Islands and their Environment," NGM 11 (1900): 1–14.

63   E. Morgan, "The Samoan Islands," NGM 11 (1900): 420.

position in the Western Pacific. The author illustrated this with a map displaying the trade statistics of nearby countries, including China, Japan, and Australia. He suggested that Manila could emerge as a distributing center akin to Singapore or Hong Kong, bringing American commodities spatially closer to Asia and thus helping to overcome the challenge posed by the vastness of the Pacific Ocean. Fourth, Austin argued that the location of the United States offered many alleged "natural advantages" for trade across the Pacific, including favorable water and air currents from the West Coast flowing past Hawaii, Guam and the Philippines.[64] The invocation of ocean currents as justification for empire demonstrates how some geographers mobilized even tenuous geographic phenomena to support political aims. Through these map-supported arguments, the article naturalized American imperial control by presenting it as geographically determined rather than politically chosen. Accordingly, both economic and strategic interests appeared to be reinforced by natural geographic conditions. The article closed by asserting the Pacific was "naturally" American: "Indeed, [...], we might almost claim the Pacific as essentially our own. Stretching along its eastern coast from the tropics to the Arctic, thence across its northern borders, then for more than a thousand miles on its western shore, in the Samoan group on the south, and in a line of islands across its very center, the American flag floats, and will continue to float, and by its presence, its ennobling purposes, and its power for civilization and advancement it proclaims, and will continue to proclaim, that the Pacific is, and will remain, an American ocean."[65] The specific cartographic choices – such as emphasizing U.S. possessions, drawing direct lines for cables and trade routes, and centering the perspective on American control – actively constructed this "American ocean" rather than merely illustrating it. Austin's systematic use of maps and spatial arguments exemplifies the "geopolitical gaze" identified by critical geopolitics, transforming the Pacific into an abstract space ordered by and for American power.

Interoceanic Access: Canal, Cable, and Coaling

Geographical societies presented the construction of an interoceanic canal through the Central American isthmus as a commercial necessity and a geopo-

---

64   O.P. Austin, "Problems of the Pacific – The Commerce of the Great Ocean," *NGM* 13 (1902): 311–317.

65   Austin, "Problems of the Pacific," 318.

litical imperative for the United States. They employed distance calculations, shipping tables, and strategic analyses to transform what was a political and commercial choice into an apparent geographical necessity. Their canal discourse rested on a paradox: societies celebrated U.S. continental expansion while simultaneously treating the continent's east-west breadth as a problem requiring technological solutions. They used spatial arguments to emphasize the nation's ideal position to profit economically and strategically from decreased interoceanic shipping distances.

In the wake of westward expansion, especially after the 1848 California Gold Rush, the idea of constructing a canal across the Central American isthmus to link the Atlantic and the Pacific gained prominence among U.S. policymakers and commercial interests. Although U.S. interest in a canal persisted throughout the second half of the nineteenth century (illustrated, for example, by the establishment of the Inter-Oceanic Canal Commission), it was a French company that secured the concession in 1881. However, challenges such as tropical diseases, financial troubles, and unforeseen engineering difficulties resulted in the company's bankruptcy in 1889. Following Panama's independence from Colombia in 1903, achieved with U.S. support, construction resumed under U.S. direction and was completed in 1914.[66] Yet for most of the nineteenth and early twentieth century, the canal project was far from guaranteed and geographical societies played an important role in framing it as a geographic inevitability.

The earliest society publications framed Central America as naturally predestined for canal construction. As early as 1859, the AGS *Journal* addressed interoceanic transport, characterizing Central America as a "natural" site for a canal. One article employed an imagined map to emphasize the United States' position between the oceans, asserting that "natural geographical conditions" made Central America the ideal location for canal construction. Its author claimed that a canal would bring large savings in distance and time for shipping, transforming North America into the main hub for global trade.[67]

---

66   Alexander Missal, *Seaway to the Future: American Social Visions and the Construction of the Panama Canal* (Madison: University of Wisconsin Press, 2009); Walter LaFeber, *The Panama Canal: The Crisis in Historical Perspective* (New York: Oxford University Press, 1989); John Major, *Prize Possession: The United States and the Panama Canal, 1903–1979* (Cambridge: Cambridge University Press, 1993).

67   J. Murphy, "The Isthmus of Tehuantepec. Its Inhabitants and Resources," *Journal of the American Geographical and Statistical Society* (1859): 165.

From the 1870s onwards, the AGS *Journal* published a continuous stream of articles advocating for an interoceanic canal. These pieces frequently reiterated the canal's economic potential, but this subsection focuses primarily on representations of space.[68] In 1876, an article depicted the proposed canal as reducing distances and travel times between the American West Coast, East Coast, and Europe, envisioning a division of future world trade between the Suez Canal and a Central American canal.[69] Taking a slightly different perspective, an 1879 article cautioned that the Suez Canal diverted trade away from the United States, thus reinforcing the necessity of a transisthmian canal. It praised the existing railroad across Panama as a step toward the "opening of the Pacific route to the Orient", explicitly linking canal construction to other

---

68   For more on the AGS's role in the evaluation of the different canal schemes in Central America, see Morin, *Civic Discipline*, 93–126; a non-exhaustive list of articles in question: Simon Stevens, J. G. Barnard, J. J. Williams, and Julius W. Adams, "The New Route of Commerce by the Isthmus of Tehuantepec," *Journal of the American Geographical Society of New York* 3 (1872): 300–342; Frederick Collins, "The Isthmus of Darien and the Valley of the Atrato Considered with Reference to the Practicability of an Interoceanic Ship-Canal," *Journal of the American Geographical Society of New York* 5 (1874): 138–65; Daniel Ammen, "Surveys and Reconnoissances from 1870 to 1875 for a Ship Canal across the American Isthmus," *Journal of the American Geographical Society of New York* 8 (1876): 188–203; Daniel Ammen, "The Interoceanic Ship Canal Meeting at Chickering Hall, December 9, 1879. The Proposed Interoceanic Ship Canal across Nicaragua," *Journal of the American Geographical Society of New York* 11 (1879): 113–52; "The Interoceanic Ship Canal, Special Meeting, December 29, 1879," *Journal of the American Geographical Society of New York* 11 (1879): 259–300.; A. G. Menocal, "Discussion upon the Proposed Interoceanic Ship Canal, Special Meeting, December 15, 1879," *Journal of the American Geographical Society of New York* 11 (1879): 186–218; H. C. Taylor, "The Nicaragua Canal," *Journal of the American Geographical Society of New York* 18 (1886): 95–126; Charles H. Stockton, "The Commercial Geography of the American Inter-Oceanic Canal," *Journal of the American Geographical Society of New York* 20 (1888): 75–93; George S. Morison, "The Panama Canal," *Bulletin of the American Geographical Society* 35, no. 1 (1903): 24–43; Emory R. Johnson, "The Panama Canal in Its Commercial Aspects," *Bulletin of the American Geographical Society* 35, no. 5 (1903): 481–91; Emory R. Johnson, "Comparison of Distances by the Isthmian Canal and Other Routes," *Bulletin of the American Geographical Society* 35, no. 2 (1903): 163–76. Edmund Otis Hovey, "The Isthmus of Tehuantepec and the Tehuantepec National Railway," *Bulletin of the American Geographical Society* 39, no. 2 (1907): 78–91; John W. Herbert, "The Panama Canal: Its Construction and Its Effect on Commerce," *Bulletin of the American Geographical Society* 45, no. 4 (1913): 241–54.

69   Daniel Ammen, "Surveys and Reconnoissances from 1870 to 1875 for a Ship Canal Across the American Isthmus," *Journal of the American Geographical Society of New York* 8 (1876): 201–2.

milestones in U.S. imperialism, including the Mexican-American War and the "opening" of Japan.[70] In 1888, yet another author declared that a transisthmian canal would surpass the Suez Canal in importance, as it would "open a direct route to the Pacific, an ocean of comparatively modern discovery".[71] The article also emphasized Hawaii's strategic location half-way between the canal and Asia, anticipating its future significance to American Empire.[72]

By the 1890s, geographical society publications shifted emphasis from commercial arguments toward increasingly naval strategic considerations. This shift reflected broader changes in U.S. geopolitical thinking as the nation transitioned from continental to overseas imperial expansion. An 1896 article made the case for building a transit route for ships at Tehuantepec (Mexico), based on a comparison of coast-to-coast distances via Tehuantepec with alternatives in Nicaragua and Panama.[73] The author pointed to the strategic value of the Tehuantepec route, citing Admiral Robert Wilson Shufeldt, who posited that proximity to the United States was the only criterion that mattered: "Each isthmus rises into importance as it lies nearer the center of American political and commercial influence, and the intrinsic value of this eminently national work ought to be based upon the inverse ratio of the distance from that center." Spatial proximity was presented as a natural justification for American control. Consequently, the usual economic arguments receded into the background, supplanted by an emphasis on the spatial advantages for American naval strategy: "A canal through the isthmus of Tehuantepec is an extension of the Mississippi river to the Pacific ocean. It converts the gulf of Mexico into an American lake. In time of war, it closes that gulf to all enemies. It is the only route which our Government can control. So to speak, it renders our own territory circumnavigable."[74] Through this imaginative geography, the author conceptually appropriated an international body of water and rebranded it as a national "American lake". In addition, two years before the Spanish-American War, the author made the imperial ambitions inherent in his argument explicit by expressing hope that Cuba would become part of the United States: "[...] when Cuba shall have become State of the Union, as it

---

70   A. Hayes, "Modern Ocean Highways," *Journal of the American Geographical Society of New York* 11 (1879):101–112.

71   Stockton, "American Inter-Oceanic Canal," 75.

72   Stockton, "American Inter-Oceanic Canal," 80–81.

73   E. Corthell, "The Tehuantepec Ship Railway," *NGM* 7 (1896): 68.

74   E. Corthell, "The Tehuantepec Ship Railway," *NGM* 7 (1896): 71.

may in the near future, we shall hold the entire circuit of this great sea."[75] An article in the AGS *Journal* used a similar spatial argument, suggesting that the Tehuantepec ship canal "would be the opening of the mouth of the Mississippi river in the Pacific ocean – another world of waters."[76] At the 1904 AGS semi-centennial, William Barclay Parsons of the *Isthmian Canal Commission* linked the Panama Canal's design to naval power and commercial utility, assuring guests that the canal should be built without locks so that "Capt. Mahan can send his largest battleships, and so that you gentlemen of commerce can send your largest passenger and freight steamers".[77]

By 1904, with the Panama Canal project effectively under U.S. control, arguments focusing on spatial and national unity became more pronounced. A NGM article by William Burr (Isthmian Canal Commission) emphasized not just the canal's strategic and commercial benefits, but also its symbolic impact on national cohesion. He contended that the spatial separation of the U.S. coasts would be alleviated by the canal which would "bring the Atlantic and Pacific shores of the United States into much closer communication than before, thus strengthening those bonds of mutual interest and natural sympathy which lie at the foundation of best national life."[78] This vision of national unity through infrastructure echoed earlier arguments about transcontinental railroads, indicating a persistent U.S. anxiety about continental vastness.[79] Similarly, at the International Geographic Congress in Washington in 1904, AGS President Robert Peary commended the ongoing construction of the Panama Canal and outlined the spatial advantages its completion would yield. He praised the canal's capacity to reduce time, distance, and cost in global shipping, envisioning a United States whose coasts were finally unified: "A few years hence and the commerce of the world will pass freely from the eastern

---

75   E. Corthell, "The Tehuantepec Ship Railway," *NGM* 7 (1896): 72.

76   Stevens, Simon, J. G. Barnard, J. J. Williams, and Julius W. Adams, "The New Route of Commerce by the Isthmus of Tehuantepec," *Journal of the American Geographical Society of New York* 3 (1872): 338. ; the same point was made by Stockton, "The Commercial Geography of the American Inter-Oceanic Canal," *Journal of the American Geographical Society of New York* 20 (1888): 75.

77   "Semi-Centennial of the American Geographical Society," *Bulletin of the American Geographical Society* 37, no. 1 (1905): 25; The question of a canal with or without locks was a technical debate among engineers at the time.

78   W. Burr, "The Republic of Panama," *NGM* 15 (1904): 61–73.

79   Richard White, *Railroaded: The Transcontinentals and the Making of Modern America* (New York: W. W. Norton, 2011).

sea to the western sea, traversing almost air lines from port to port, at an enormous saving of time and distance and expense, and this great orient-and-occident-facing Republic will rest content with coasts united from Eastport [Maine, East Coast] to the Straits of Fuca [near Seattle, West Coast]."[80]

As the Panama Canal neared completion in 1913, spatial arguments resurfaced in the AGS *Bulletin*, stressing the canal's ability to "bring together the remote sections of that immense country, assimilate its diverse interests, go far toward solving many difficult problems and make the United States still more united." The article posited that the canal would effectively "extend the coast line of the United States to the Isthmus of Panama" and stated that "one has but to glance at a map of the American hemisphere to be impressed with the wonderful economies of time and distance that will be accomplished." This claim that the U.S. coastline extended to Panama exemplified the American imperial geographical imagination by conceptually redrawing national boundaries to accommodate infrastructure projects. In addition, the geopolitical implications of a canal became ever more prominent alongside commercial considerations. While the canal initially was said to "benefit the commerce of the world," the American public allegedly recognized that "the time had come when the isthmian passage between the oceans had become a military necessity." The article concluded with a frank assessment of the canal's role in U.S. naval power: "Without the waterway across the Isthmus of Panama it would be necessary to maintain two squadrons when one of half the size will now suffice."[81]

Collectively, these spatial arguments demonstrate how U.S. geographical societies articulated the advantages of a transoceanic canal in terms of trade, national unity, and military strategy. The societies constructed the canal as a natural culmination of American expansion rather than a politically motivated imperial project, utilizing the apparently objective language of distance calculations and shipping routes. Through their imaginative geographies, societies not only rationalized imperial ambitions but also contributed directly to the reconfiguration of geopolitical space in American popular and scholarly thought.

---

80   R. Peary, "Address by Commander Robert E. Peary, U. S. N., on the Assembling of the Congress in Washington, September 8, 1904," *NGM* 15 (1904), 388.

81   John W. Herbert, "The Panama Canal: Its Construction and Its Effect on Commerce," *Bulletin of the American Geographical Society* 45, no. 4 (1913): 252–253.

Geopolitics of the Pacific: Bases and Rivalries

After the Spanish-American War, geographical societies increasingly represented the Pacific as a space of American imperial expansion and geopolitical
strategy. Their publications and lectures cultivated an imaginative geography
that framed U.S. imperialism as the inevitable extension of a "natural" American sphere of influence, obscuring its fundamentally political nature. They
also depicted the Pacific as a contested space of inter-imperial rivalry in a
global struggle for geopolitical and commercial supremacy. In particular, they
highlighted the strategic benefits of a continued U.S. presence in the Pacific,
especially in the Philippines and Hawaii.

The depiction of the Pacific advanced by geographical societies mirrored
the geopolitical vision of influential so-called "large policy" imperialists such
as Henry Cabot Lodge, Theodore Roosevelt, and Alfred Thayer Mahan. In his
widely read *The Influence of Sea Power upon History*, Mahan argued that commercial and strategic dominance of the seas went hand in hand: an expansive commercial empire required a strong navy supported by strategically placed overseas bases. The Spanish-American War had demonstrated that future conflicts
would increasingly take place at sea, far from the mainland. Consequently, the
modernization of the U.S. Navy and evolving naval strategies enhanced the
strategic significance of Hawaii and other Pacific islands as coaling stations
for steamships.[82] Mahan, speaking at the AGS Semi-Centennial celebration,
outlined his spatial conception of the Pacific: "And from our geographical position you will find that it must inevitably follow that the United States must
go on and cannot help going on with all that the United States stands for in
the matter of political liberty and political order, to impress itself upon the far-
ther borders of the Pacific, not by conquest, but by precept and example."[83] This
statement captures how geographical determinism was mobilized to present
imperial expansion as natural destiny, downplaying the overt political and military actions that had secured U.S. Pacific territories. Mahan's claim of expansion "not by conquest" stands in stark contrast with the actual military inter-
ventions that accompanied American imperialism in the Pacific.

At the same Semi-Centennial, the society's president, Robert Peary, articulated a complementary vision by linking the AGS's mission to the nation's im-

---

82   Hendrickson, *Union, Nation, or Empire*, 266.
83   "Semi-Centennial of the American Geographical Society," *Bulletin of the American Geographical Society* 37, no. 1 (1905): 25.

perial project: "There is ample work on land and sea for the Society, ample room for a closer association with the business and commercial interests of this great city, ample room for a closer affiliation with the increasing geographical expansion of the Nation."[84] Peary's remark, delivered from the same stage as Mahan's, underscores the fusion of geopolitical theory and institutional mission. The society was not just reflecting imperial ideas, but its leadership was actively co-producing them. Historian Robert Seager has argued that Mahan and other "New Navy" proponents were not so much innovators as codifiers of ideas already circulating in naval and political circles.[85] The discourse of U.S. geographical societies supports this assessment, showing that many spatial, commercial, and strategic arguments predated Mahan's formal articulation. In this way, geographical societies functioned as platforms for testing, refining, and popularizing geopolitical arguments before they achieved formal expression in policy circles.

Roosevelt, Mahan, and other imperialists deemed the annexation of Hawaii as imperative to preempt rival powers and ensure the security of the West Coast and the proposed interoceanic canal. Historian William Morgan has argued that a heightened appreciation of Hawaii's strategic location was the primary catalyst for its annexation.[86] After the Spanish-American War, attention turned to the Philippines, which – unlike Hawaii or the Caribbean islands – had not previously featured prominently in geopolitical discourse. This shift highlights the role played by geopolitical thought in American imperial expansion. Geographical societies were instrumental in making the Philippines legible to American audiences as a logical extension of Pacific expansion rather than a radical departure from existing American foreign policy traditions. The following paragraphs demonstrate more concretely how geographical societies translated and disseminated these geopolitical visions as accessible spatial representations for their members and wider audiences.

Publications of geographical societies frequently portrayed U.S. expansion as the natural continuation of the "Westward Movement" rather than as a new imperial departure. For Lodge and other imperialists, the annexation of Pacific islands represented a culmination of westward expansion and the opening of

---

84   "Semi-Centennial of the American Geographical Society," *Bulletin of the American Geographical Society* 37, no. 1 (1905): 23.

85   Robert Seager, "Ten Years Before Mahan: The Unofficial Case for the New Navy, 1880–1890," *The Mississippi Valley Historical Review* 40, no. 3 (1953): 491–512.

86   William Morgan, *Pacific Gibraltar* (Annapolis: Naval Institute Press, 2011), 221–26.

a new frontier for the U.S. civilizing mission.[87] Just one month after the Spanish-American War, WJ McGee, Vice President of the NGS, echoed this logic in an address titled "The Growth of the United States", delivered to a joint session of the NGS and the American Association for the Advancement of Science. McGee stressed a seamless spatial trajectory from the settlement of the American West to the expansion into the Pacific, insisting that "the growth of 1898 marks no new policy". By referencing earlier territorial gains – Louisiana, Oregon, Florida, Texas, and California – he sought to normalize the potential annexation of the Philippines, Hawaii, and Puerto Rico, which he characterized as "but a ripple on the stream of national progress".[88] McGee's arguments illustrate how geographical societies employed environmental determinism to naturalize imperial expansion, presenting territorial growth as a *natural* process rather than a political one by claiming it had been "shaped constantly by natural conditions rather than national policy".[89] This notion reflects a wider discourse of "naturalized geopolitics", in which imperialism appeared as an inevitable process dictated by geography rather than by policy.

By interpreting history as a process determined by geography, U.S. dominance appeared unavoidable. In an era defined by expanding empires and closing space, growth in population and area was considered vital by geographers worldwide.[90] Consistent with the ideology of Manifest Destiny, spatial stagnation was equated with national decline.[91] Through environmental determinism, imperialism appeared to result naturally from geographic conditions rather than political decisions, foregrounding "natural" borders rather than national ones. This allowed territorial expansion to seem both necessary and inevitable.[92] Prominent geographers actively advanced this naturalization of expansion in their interpretations of U.S. history and geography, most notably Frederick Jackson Turner in his influential essay, "The Significance of the Frontier in American History" (1893), and Ellen Semple in "American History and its

---

87   Richard H. Immerman, *Empire for Liberty: A History of American Imperialism from Benjamin Franklin to Paul Wolfowitz* (Princeton: Princeton University Press, 2010), 17.

88   WJ McGee, "The Growth of the United States," *NGM* 9 (1898): 379.

89   Ibid.

90   John Agnew and Stuart Corbridge, *Mastering Space: Hegemony, Territory and International Political Economy* (London: Routledge, 1995), 56–63.

91   Stephanson, *Manifest Destiny*, 97.

92   Jeremy Black, *Geopolitics and the Quest for Dominance* (Bloomington: Indiana University Press, 2016), 142.

Geographic Conditions" (1903).[93] Writing in the AGS *Bulletin* on the strategic significance of oceans in geography, Semple connected American interoceanic infrastructure projects to a global historical tradition, describing them as "a reversion to the old east-west path along the southern rim of Eurasia, now perfected by the Suez Canal, and to be extended in the near future around the world by the union of the Pacific with the Caribbean Sea at Panama."[94] Semple's framing thus situated U.S. expansion as part of a larger, historically inevitable geopolitical narrative.

A 1900 NGM article laid out the geopolitical rationale for annexing the Philippines, arguing that their central position in the Western Pacific made them strategically indispensable. The article declared the Philippines as the key to world power, stating that if the United States was to "hold there a position of commercial and strategic advantage for the advancement and protection of our vast growing interests in the Pacific and far East, we shall be forever the first power of the Pacific and of all the world". Conversely, withdrawal would inevitably lead to future war in the Pacific, given the "merciless race of nations for material and moral supremacy".[95] This perspective aligns with many other contemporary NGM articles evaluating U.S. imperial ambitions positively, while identifying rival empires, especially Britain and Germany, as potential threats.

Communications infrastructure was also portrayed as essential to American imperial control of the Pacific. One key geopolitical-imperial project was a U.S.-controlled telegraph cable across the Pacific, first promoted by entrepreneur Cyrus W. Field in the 1870s and later revived by President McKinley in 1898. This cable was intended as part of an imperial policy designed to assert U.S. influence in the Pacific by maintaining an information advantage over enemies who could not securely use a U.S. telegraph system.[96] Some articles in geographical society publications were written with a more technical tone, discussing the hydrography and practical challenges of laying a trans-

93 Frederick Jackson Turner, "The Significance of the Frontier in American History," a paper read at the meeting of the American Historical Association in Chicago, 1893, *Report of the American Historical Association for 1893* (1893): 199–227; Ellen C. Semple, *American History and its Geographic Conditions* (New York: Houghton, Mifflin, 1903).

94 Ellen Churchill Semple, "Oceans and Enclosed Seas: A Study in Anthropo-Geography," *Bulletin of the American Geographical Society* 40, no. 4 (1908): 208.

95 J. Barrett, "The Philippine Islands and their Environment," *NGM* 10 (1900): 14.

96 Simone Müller, *Wiring the World: The Social and Cultural Creation of Global Telegraph Networks* (New York: Columbia University Press, 2016), 169–77.

Pacific telegraph cable on the ocean floor.[97] Others were more overt in their political support for the cable, which they underlined with spatial-geopolitical arguments. In a 1901 article, Captain George Squier of the U.S. Signal Corps, argued that the Spanish-American War had demonstrated the "dominating influence of submarine cable communications in the conduct of a naval war". The author emphasized that submarine cables could "close space" by linking distant territories, but only if control remained exclusive. An uninterrupted, secure "colonial telegraph system" of U.S. telegraph cables across the Pacific, would require possession of Hawaii, Midway Island, Samoa, Guam, and the Philippines. Squier's vision illustrates how technological infrastructure and territorial possession became mutually reinforcing in the imperial imagination. The article closed with a sweeping claim on oceans, geopolitics, and space, highlighting the spatial advantages of naval bases and telegraph cables in the Pacific: "The sea is usually considered as the great international highway, belonging equally to all nations; this, however, is no longer true. The real political boundaries of states are no longer defined and restricted by the land, but involve such portions of the high seas as a nation can, by her commercial and naval vessels, and her submarine cables, reach out and secure."[98] In this way, Squier's geopolitical argument explicitly linked technological infrastructure to the spatial expansion of national power beyond traditional territorial limits, transforming international waters into spaces to be partitioned through technological and military dominance.

The strategic importance of Hawaii featured prominently in geographical societies' publications, with authors frequently emphasizing its position as essential for American naval power in the Pacific. As early as 1888, an AGS *Journal* article highlighted Hawaii's "position as a mid-way point of call" on the routes from an interoceanic canal to Asia,[99] while an article a year later pointed out that Hawaii was "within a fortnight's journey from the city of New York".[100] In 1898, following the annexation of Hawaii, the AGS *Journal* featured an article

97   G. W. Littlehales, "Recent Advances in Geographic Knowledge Accomplished by the United States Hydrographic Office at Washington," *Journal of the American Geographical Society of New York* 30 (1898): 124–26.

98   G. Squier, "The Influence of Submarine Cables upon Military and Naval Supremacy," *NGM* 12 (1901): 2–12.

99   Charles H. Stockton, "The Commercial Geography of the American Inter-Oceanic Canal," *Journal of the American Geographical Society of New York* 20 (1888): 92.

100   Titus Munson Coan, "The Hawaiian Islands: Their Geography, Their Volcanoes, and Their People," *Journal of the American Geographical Society of New York* 21 (1889): 150.

on the significance of "The United States Mid-Pacific Naval Supply Station", a coaling and repair station on the Hawaiian island of Oahu, advocating its potential development as a full-scale military harbor for the U.S. Navy.[101] A 1908 NGM article reiterated these arguments, asserting that Hawaii's location made it ideal for guarding the Panama Canal, protecting trans-Pacific trade, and securing the U.S. West Coast. Drawing a parallel between the U.S. role in the Pacific and the dominance of the British Empire in the Mediterranean, the article stressed Hawaii's geopolitical significance and the importance of establishing a strong naval presence in the Pacific, implying that oceans were now battlefields: "The relation of a strategic point like Hawaii to the safety of the nation is illustrated by the relation of Gibraltar and Malta to the safety of Great Britain. The control of the Mediterranean is essential to England, as thereby she dominates the coasts of all the adjacent countries and controls hostile movements." Using this imperial parallel, the author called on Congress to fund the construction of a naval base at Pearl Harbor.[102] Such comparisons also served to normalize American imperial ambitions by framing them within established European precedents.

This expansionist vision was remarkably consistent across geographical societies' publications, a fact underscored by the professional affiliations of the authors. Several contributors to the NGM or the AGS *Bulletin* cited in this chapter were also central figures in the professionalization of U.S. geography. Influential contributors such as O. P. Austin, WJ McGee, Ellen C. Semple, and G. W. Littlehales were not only members of AGS or NGS, but also charter members of the *Association of American Geographers* (AAG). This overlap complicates simplistic distinctions between popular and professional geography regarding U.S. imperialism. Rather, it reveals a widely shared pro-imperial consensus within the geography community, endorsed and disseminated by figures across the institutional spectrum. Thus, the vision of the Pacific as an "American Ocean" cannot be dismissed as a popular distortion, but rather represented a viewpoint supported and disseminated by many of the discipline's leading figures.

---

101   G. W. Littlehales, "The United States Mid-Pacific Naval Supply Station," *Journal of the American Geographical Society of New York* 30, no. 4 (1898): 277–80.

102   G. Perkins, "The Key to the Pacific," *NGM* 19 (1908): 295–298.

Regional Societies and the Pacific Imagination

The imperial representation of the Pacific was not limited to major national societies. Similar discourses permeated smaller regional societies, demonstrating that imperial spatial representations were widely disseminated across geographical societies of varying sizes. Their lectures and publications disseminated similar narratives, shaped by the same networks of knowledge production discussed in previous sections.[103]

Regional societies sometimes articulated imperial visions as openly as their national counterparts. For instance, the Alaska Geographical Society explicitly included a commercial mission focusing on the Pacific alongside its other objectives: "to foster commerce and navigation; to promote the great industrial, educational and material interests of Alaska and the islands and countries of the Pacific."[104] This theme was taken up in one of the society's first lectures, delivered by Colonel P. H. Ray, formerly in command of the Department of Alaska. Drawing on two decades of service in Alaska, Ray stressed Alaska's strategic significance for the "development of the commerce of the Pacific" and urged the U.S. government to "fortify some harbor in the Aleutian Islands to protect this interest in case of war."[105] In their focus on the economics and geopolitics of the Pacific, these statements echoed arguments put forth by the larger national geographical societies.

On the West Coast, the Geographical Society of the Pacific in San Francisco was particularly active in representing the Pacific as an American commercial space.[106] Founded by George Davidson of the U.S. Coast and Geodetic Survey,

---

103   The AGS also invited many lecturers to speak on the Pacific and other aspects of American Empire, many of them already quoted in this chapter, see: "List of lecturers, 1888–1951", Box 230, Folder 30, AGS Archives. The lectures were: 1894, William Libbey jr., "The Hawaiian Islands"; 1898, Titus Munson Coan, "The Hawaiian Islands"; 1899, Herbert H. Wilson, "Porto Rico"; 1899, Robert T. Hill, "Cuba"; 1900, J.G Schurman, "The Philippine Islands"; 1901, George P. Becker, "Conditions requisite to our success in the Philippine Islands"; 1902, George S. Morrison, "The Panama Canal"; 1914, James W. Erwin "Hawaii: our Mid-Pacific Outpost"; 1914, Hon. Dean Conant Worcester, "The Philippines: Our Far-Pacific Outpost"; several lectures were also given on the topic of an interoceanic canal in 1876, 1879, and 1886.

104   "Front matter," *Bulletin of the Alaska Geographical Society* (October 1900).

105   P. H. Ray, "Alaska," *Bulletin of the Alaska Geographical Society* (October 1900).

106   "Front matter," *Transactions and Proceedings of the Geographical Society of the Pacific,* 1, no. 2 (1892)

it had several hundred members and published a semi-regular magazine.[107] Between 1881 and 1891, the society hosted numerous lectures on regions far from California, including discussions of the proposed canal routes and the economic potential of Pacific-adjacent areas such as Alaska, Japan, China, Korea, and Hawaii. Even Samoa, a relatively minor subject for the larger societies before 1898, featured in multiple talks during the 1880s.[108] The society's magazine also covered a range of Pacific-related topics, featuring articles on "South Polar Expeditions", the "Bishop Expedition in Hawaii", the "U.S. Steamer 'Albatross' among the Fauna of the Hawaiian and Philippine Island Waters" and on the "Survey of the Philippine Archipelago".[109] An 1891 article speculated on Korea's strategic importance for colonial powers in the Pacific and declared that control of Korea represented the "command of the Pacific trade of America and the China Seas."[110] Another article on "Oriental Trade" recapitulated commercial themes familiar from the AGS and NGS regarding the Pacific Ocean's role. It highlighted San Francisco's position as an asset for trade, noting that the U.S. cities on the Pacific coast "consider that from their location they should enjoy the greater part of this trade" and that San Francisco would become "the center of America's trade with the Orient and the isles of the Malaysian Seas". The article concluded with a statement of support for American Empire, declaring that "the acquisition of the Philippines has helped wonderfully to further our interests in that direction", followed by a table listing the growth of U.S. trade with several Asian countries adjoining the Pacific.[111]

An article by the society's secretary, C. Mitchell Grant, offers insight into the Geographical Society of the Pacific's ties to government agencies. He noted that most of the society's lectures and papers were authored by individuals affiliated with the federal government: "Taking into consideration that most of the explorers of the Pacific Coast are Government Officers sent out from Washington, and that their duty is to report first at headquarters, it will be found

---

107   Gary S. Dunbar, "The Rival Geographical Societies of 'Fin-de-Siècle' San Francisco," *Yearbook of the Association of Pacific Coast Geographers* 40 (1978): 58.
108   "Papers read before the Geographical Society of the Pacific," *Transactions and Proceedings of the Geographical Society of the Pacific*, 1, no. 2 (1892).
109   "The Hawaiian Islands": 51–52, "Albatross": 52, "Philippines" 55–56; in: *Transactions and Proceedings of The Geographical Society of the Pacific*, 2, no. 1 (1902).
110   "Corea – the Hermit Nation," *Transactions and Proceedings of The Geographical Society of the Pacific* 1, no. 2 (1891): 1–20.
111   "Oriental Trade," *Transactions and Proceedings of The Geographical Society of the Pacific* 2, no. 1 (1902): 56–58.

that the Council has been very successful in obtaining papers of interest."[112] This observation confirms the pattern seen nationally: close ties to government personnel facilitated access to information aligned with state interests. Similarly, the San Francisco-based Geographical Society of California emphasized in its objectives the city's geopolitical and commercial significance, referring to it as "the capital of the West, occupying such an advantageous position on the Pacific Coast, and destined at no remote period to rank amongst the most renowned cities". The society's stated purpose was to acquire and disseminate geographical knowledge, explicitly prioritizing knowledge about the Pacific.[113]

East Coast societies such as the Geographical Society of Philadelphia also participated in disseminating imperial perspectives on the Pacific, hosting lectures by many of the same figures who spoke at the larger national societies. The society published multiple articles on proposed canal routes across Central America and hosted numerous lectures on the islands acquired by the United States following the Spanish-American War.[114] Many of these talks were delivered by geographers who wrote and lectured for the NGS and AGS, which highlights the circulation of their spatial imperial representations between regional and national geographical societies. In 1899 alone, the Geographical Society of Philadelphia featured lectures on the Philippines, the proposed Nicaragua Canal, and Puerto Rico.[115] This trend continued in the following years, including a lecture by John Barrett, a frequent NGM contributor cited earlier in this section, on "America in the Philippines and the Far East" (1900) and another lecture by A. W. Greely, also a prolific writer for the NGM, on "Glimpses of the Philippines" (1902). Additional lectures on proposed canal routes across Central America were delivered by Angelo Heilprin (1901) and Emory R. Johnson

---

112   C. Mitchell Grant, "Notes by the Secretary," *Transactions and Proceedings of The Geographical Society of the Pacific* 1, no. 2 (1891): xxi.

113   "Objects of the Society," *Bulletin of the Geographical Society of California* 2 (1894), 2.

114   Angelo Heilprin, "The Shrinkage of Lake Nicaragua," *Bulletin of the Geographical Society of Philadelphia* 3, no. 1 (1901): 1–12; Angelo Heilprin, "The Water Supply of Lake Nicaragua," *Bulletin of the Geographical Society of Philadelphia* 3, no. 1 (1901): 13–20; Angelo Heilprin, "The Nicaragua Canal in its geographical and geological relation," *Bulletin of the Geographical Society of Philadelphia* 2, no. 5 (1900): 87–107.

115   Geographical Society of Philadelphia, *Charter, By-Laws, List of Members*, May 1899, 6–7; the lectures in 1899 included: Raymon Reyes Lala: "Philippines"; Lewis M. Haupt "The Nicaragua Canal: Topography and Geography of the Isthmus"; and 1899 Robert T. Hill: "The Island of Porto Rico".

(1903).[116] Although the full transcripts are unavailable, their titles and speakers strongly suggest the same pro-imperial, spatial-geopolitical focus found in their published works circulating through other geographical society venues.

The consistency of Pacific representations across geographical societies of different sizes and regions demonstrates how thoroughly imperial spatial discourses permeated American geographical thought. The regional geographical societies contributed significantly to spreading a distinct form of imperial geographical knowledge about the Pacific. By hosting prominent geographers and discussing trade routes, commercial opportunities, and the strategic significance of the Pacific Ocean and an interoceanic canal, these regional societies helped transform the Pacific into a space of American economic and geopolitical interest. Their activities complemented those of larger societies, reinforcing and extending the imperial discourse on geography that underpinned U.S. expansion in the long nineteenth century.

In summary, U.S. geographical societies produced and disseminated spatial representations of the Pacific that naturalized American imperial expansion. Through their lectures and publications, they represented the Pacific as a space of American empire, positioning Hawaii, Guam, and the Philippines as steppingstones toward Asian trade. They advocated consistently for the construction of an interoceanic canal, depicting it as vital to facilitating East Coast trade with Asia, and reinforced these claims with spatial arguments centered on distance and strategic advantage. These three strategies – commercial, infrastructural, and geopolitical – transformed the Pacific from a vast maritime area into an "American Ocean", as one NGS geographer proclaimed. The commercial framework established the economic rationale, the canal discourse provided the technological solution, and the geopolitical arguments supplied the strategic justification. Together, they shaped a vision of U.S. Pacific dominance that appeared not as a deliberate political choice, but as a geographical destiny. Notably absent from the extensive society publications and lectures on the Pacific was any sustained anti-imperialist perspective, a silence that underscores their function as institutions for consensus-building among political and economic elites committed to imperial expansion.

---

116   Lectures in: Geographical Society of Philadelphia, *Charter, By-Laws, List of Members,* 1902, 6: Heilprin "The Nicaragua and the Panama Canal routes contrasted" (1901); Geographical Society of Philadelphia *Charter, By-Laws, List of Members,* December 1903 lists Emory R. Johnson, "The Scenic and Geographic Aspects of the Panama Canal" and 1902 Greely, "Glimpses of the Philippines".

Conclusion: Geography, Authority, Empire

By the close of the long nineteenth century, governments increasingly relied on geographical expertise in matters of war, nation-building, and empire. In the United States, this reliance is evident in the participation of leading members of geographical societies in President Wilson's wartime think tank (The Inquiry, which met at the AGS headquarters) and later as authoritative experts at the Paris Peace Conference. The societies' political authority represented the culmination of decades of institutional development that transformed them from modest learned associations into influential mediators of spatial knowledge: organizational networks connected societies to government provided infrastructure for The Inquiry; professionalization battles established credentialed expertise; and circulation networks had accumulated the global knowledge that negotiators required. This study has traced the evolution of U.S. geography from its roots in natural history through early institutionalization in learned societies to the politically authoritative science it became by the early twentieth century. Crucially, this analysis emphasizes that geographical knowledge was historically contingent, shaped by specific practices, influential actors, and particularly the institutions that granted legitimacy and significance to geographers' work.

Unlike studies focused on individual geographers or published texts alone, this institutional analysis highlights how geographical societies built their authority by managing relationships between different knowledge communities. Examining this institutional "middle ground" – the space where scientific claims were forged, contested, and legitimized – clarifies that scientific authority rested not only on pure intellectual merit, but also on institutional mediation and alignment with state power.

The organization and professionalization of U.S. geography were shaped by the national context, particularly continental expansion and a decentralized scientific infrastructure. Geographical societies emerged later in the United

States than in Europe and developed distinctive national characteristics. The three major societies – the AGS, NGS, and AAG – pursued the dissemination of geographical knowledge, each influencing the development of geography in distinct ways. Numerous regional societies emphasized local knowledge and commercial geography, thereby connecting regional priorities to national trends. These local societies also fostered geography as a "civic science", embedding the discipline in local communities and linking geographical knowledge to nation-building efforts.

The spatial distribution of these societies reflected and reinforced existing power structures. The dominance of Northeastern commercial centers in the scientific landscape and the gradual development of Washington, D.C. as a hub for scientists and government agencies significantly influenced the growth, financial viability, and agendas of geographical societies, and by extension, the discipline itself. Westward expansion facilitated the establishment of local societies in the West, while the South remained largely disconnected from this scientific infrastructure before 1914. The locations of the major societies influenced their membership compositions – primarily government, military, and business elites – and thus the knowledge produced and prioritized. Since most societies relied on membership dues, they had to cater to their members' interests, which often meant presenting popular lectures or publishing on topics of immediate geopolitical and economic significance, such as the Pacific after 1898. In the absence of a strong academic tradition in geography, amateurs and practitioners associated with government or commerce contributed their first-hand knowledge of strategic regions, which societies then disseminated. These structural dependencies underscore that U.S. geographical societies were not neutral knowledge brokers. Rather, their organizational structures frequently aligned scientific endeavors with the strategic aims of an expanding nation.

The effort to professionalize geography emerged from a national aspiration to establish scientific institutions rivaling those of European colonial powers. When William Morris Davis founded the AAG in 1904, he steered the organization toward professionalization, particularly emphasizing physical geography. Early academic geography had its roots in the Western surveys, initially dependent on geology and amateur fieldwork. As the discipline consolidated, professional geographers needed to demarcate their field to secure authority. Through "boundary-work", the societies delineated the scope of geography and determined which subfields belonged at the center of the discipline and which aspects were relegated to its margins. Geology was gradually excluded, commercial geography was initially marginalized, and popularization had only a peripheral place in the AAG's vision. As popularization and professionalization intensified in the early twentieth century, competition and cooperation among societies simultaneously increased. Rivalry for members, high-profile lecturers, and high-quality articles for their journals caused friction between societies, while events such as the 1904 International Geographic Congress necessitated cooperation.

The persistent tension between professional exclusivity and geography's amateur origins and popular appeal shaped professionalization strategies and outcomes. The AAG maintained strict membership standards, positioning itself as the elite professional alternative by prioritizing original scholarship and limiting membership to a small group of academics, government experts, and survey professionals. Nevertheless, the AAG strategically relaxed these standards to forge alliances, attract influential politicians, or benefit from the publicity generated by celebrity explorers. The turn of the century thus saw ongoing negotiation between competing visions of what geography should be and who should practice it, reflecting the simultaneous development of three distinctive yet interconnected trends: the professionalization of geography as a scientific discipline, the popularization of geographical knowledge for mass consumption, and the preservation of amateur traditions. Geographical societies mediated these tensions, especially as specialization and academization intensified.

These dynamics structured knowledge circulation, orchestrated by geographical societies acting as "centers of calculation". Throughout the nineteenth and early twentieth centuries, these societies built global networks for gathering, validating, and disseminating information. They accumulated knowledge through their libraries, government reports, ex-officio members, and international publication exchanges. Connections with government officials were particularly vital for ensuring a steady supply of materials, facilitating recruitment of ex-officio members who sent geographical materials by diplomatic mail, and enabling foreign expeditions. Expedition sponsorship represented a significant mechanism for controlling knowledge production. Societies expected to receive credible, high-quality results for incorporation into publications and lectures. They closely oversaw expeditions to ensure that field-gathered data arrived at headquarters in the prescribed format. Standardized practices bolstered the credibility and suitability of knowledge, stabilizing it in transit from field to metropole.

As their repositories grew, geographical societies became the principal institutions for disseminating geographical information in the United States.

Periodical publications signaled prestige while increasing visibility, funds, and membership. They also enabled participation in international publication exchanges, which ensured a steady influx of reliable foreign sources and promoted U.S. geographical research abroad. The AGS's evolving publication strategy balanced professional standards with popular appeal. The AGS's *Bulletin* expanded in volume and frequency, incorporating more accessible articles and maps while preserving a core of high-quality research. This hybrid approach predated the NGS's more aggressive phase of popularization after 1899. Lectures followed a similar dual structure: specialist talks were reserved for members and visually engaging public lectures for broader audiences. As the NGS's membership and revenue soared, competition intensified. By the 1910s, the divide had solidified: the professional AAG stood at one end of the spectrum, the popular NGS at the other, with the AGS navigating the contested middle ground.

By reframing U.S. geographical societies as mediating institutions, this study links the history of knowledge, state formation, and empire, demonstrating how spatial expertise became a tool of power. U.S. geographical societies promoted, naturalized, and legitimized American empire-building in the Pacific during the nineteenth and early twentieth centuries. Through "imaginative geographies", Pacific islands were depicted as strategic stepping-stones toward Asia, emphasizing their relative proximity to the U.S. West Coast. This framing made the Pacific knowable, accessible, and seemingly destined for integration into the U.S. imperial sphere. These imaginative geographies resulted from the institutional mechanisms traced in previous chapters: societies' dependence on commercial and military elites (Chapter 2) created institutional bias toward representing spaces as strategic opportunities; their competition for members and readers (Chapters 3, 5) incentivized dramatic imperial narratives; and their circulation networks (Chapter 4) privileged government and military sources, making state perspectives appear as objective geography. Through their maps, lectures, and articles, societies portrayed the Pacific as a "naturally" American ocean, a frontier for commerce, and an arena of geopolitics. This was a discursive project of appropriation: even before formal political or military control was exercised, the ocean was mapped, narrated, and effectively claimed through the geographical imagination.

Imperial ambitions decisively influenced the U.S. geographical knowledge system during the nineteenth century. Close institutional connections and personal networks linking geographical societies to political leaders and imperialist thinkers directed these societies along a trajectory similar to that of their European counterparts, aligning geography with imperial interests. This alignment resulted in a symbiotic relationship between geography and empire: empire provided geographers with subject matter, research opportunities, and institutional significance, while geographers provided spatial arguments and legitimating narratives for imperial expansion. Geographical societies mediated this mutually reinforcing relationship, balancing the state's need for imperial knowledge with the discipline's desire for scholarly legitimacy and funding. By blurring the line between scientific observation and imperial ambition, they presented empire-building as inevitable, natural, and scientifically destined.

Yet, this alignment was not automatic. The organizational framework of these geographical societies – how they operated, the audiences they sought to reach, and what knowledge they prioritized – influenced the character and political implications of U.S. geographical knowledge. By structuring how knowledge was produced and disseminated, these societies also shaped the geopolitical awareness of U.S. citizens. As societies intertwined with the state and commercial interests, they became powerful mediators of imperial knowledge. Importantly, as emphasized throughout this study, they did not function simply as passive conduits for geography. Rather, they actively selected and framed geographical knowledge relevant to territorial expansion, transformed it into compelling narratives, and validated these accounts through claims to scientific objectivity, thereby reinforcing both elite and public backing for imperial ambitions. Yet, this trajectory developed amidst internal debates over geography's definition, professional standards, and public role. The societies' alignment with national goals was the result of negotiations, compromises, and institutional rivalries, rather than a unified, predetermined strategy. While external factors such as "large policy" geopolitical strategies, economic pressures or ideological justifications of a civilizing mission certainly drove American empire-building, these forces required a specific geographical language to achieve their full political effectiveness.

Ultimately, the authority of U.S. geographical societies derived less from purely objective scientific methods than from their institutional practices, extensive network building, and explicit alignment with state and commercial power. These factors simultaneously secured and undermined their claims to neutrality. The expertise displayed at the Paris Peace Conference emerged from decades of organizational growth, disciplinary boundary-work, and alignment with national priorities. The history of these societies thus illuminates

the relationship between scientific institutions and state power, the mechanisms through which expert knowledge achieves legitimacy, and the enduring
influence of spatial discourses in constructing national identities and legitimizing geopolitical actions. By tracing how geography became instrumental
to empire, this study also underscores the importance of interrogating how
spatial knowledge is produced, framed, and legitimized. The geographical
knowledge produced and circulated by these societies was not merely descriptive, but an active force in constructing the imperial realities it claimed simply
to represent. These findings thus remind us that ostensibly neutral scientific
practices are deeply embedded in historical power structures, and that these
structures leave lasting epistemic, political, and cartographic traces long after
empires fade.

Bibliography

Archives Consulted

Chicago, Illinois

Chicago Historical Society, Abakanowicz Research Center
Geographic Society of Chicago Miscellaneous
University of Chicago Library, Hanna Holborn Gray Special Collections Research Center
Rollin D. Salisbury Papers, 1880–1922

Milwaukee, Wisconsin

University of Wisconsin-Milwaukee Libraries, American Geographical Society Library
American Geographical Society of New York Records, 1723–2010
American Geographical Society Library Records, 1851–2013
Association of American Geographers Records, 1879–2013

Primary Published Sources

Adams, Julius W., J. G. Barnard, Simon Stevens, and J. J. Williams. "The New Route of Commerce by the Isthmus of Tehuantepec." *Journal of the American Geographical Society of New York* 3 (1872): 300–342.

"Albatross." *Transactions and Proceedings of The Geographical Society of the Pacific* 2, no. 1 (1902): 52.

Ammen, Daniel. "Surveys and Reconnoissances from 1870 to 1875 for a Ship Canal across the American Isthmus." *Journal of the American Geographical Society of New York* 8 (1876): 188–203.

Ammen, Daniel. "The Interoceanic Ship Canal Meeting at Chickering Hall, December 9, 1879. The Proposed Interoceanic Ship Canal across Nicaragua." *Journal of the American Geographical Society of New York* 11 (1879): 113–52.

"Amended Charter." *Journal of the American Geographical Society of New York* 11 (1879): ix–x.

"Annual Proceedings." *Bulletin of the Geographical Society of California* 2, no. 2 (1894): 3–10.

Austin, O. P. "Problems of the Pacific – The Commerce of the Great Ocean." *National Geographic Magazine* 13, no. 8 (1902): 303–318.

Barrett, J. "The Philippine Islands and their Environment." *National Geographic Magazine* 11, no. 1 (1900): 1–14.

Brigham, Albert P. "The Association of American Geographers, 1903–1923." *Annals of the Association of American Geographers* 14, no. 3 (1924): 109–116.

Burr, W. "The Republic of Panama." National Geographic Magazine 15, no. 2 (1904): 57–73.

Chester, C. "Some Early Geographers of the United States." *National Geographic Magazine* 15, no.10 (1904): 392–404.

Coan, Titus Munson. "The Hawaiian Islands, Their Geography, Their Volcanoes, and Their People." *Journal of the American Geographical Society of New York* 21, no. 2 (1889): 149–166.

Collins, Frederick. "The Isthmus of Darien and the Valley of the Atrato Considered with Reference to the Practicability of an Interoceanic Ship-Canal." *Journal of the American Geographical Society of New York* 5 (1874): 138–65.

"Corea – the Hermit Nation." *Transactions and Proceedings of The Geographical Society of the Pacific* 1, no. 2 (1891): 1–20.

Corthell, Elmer L. "The Tehuantepec Ship Railway." *National Geographic Magazine* 7, no. 2 (1896): 64–72.

Cowles, Henry C. *The Plant Societies of Chicago and Vicinity*, Geographic Society of Chicago Bulletin, no. 2. Chicago: Geographic Society of Chicago, 1901.

Cox, Henry J., and J. Paul Goode, eds. *Lantern Slide Illustrations for the Teaching of Meteorology – prepared by a Committee of the Geographic Society of Chicago*, Geographic Society of Chicago Bulletin, no. 3. Chicago: Geographic Society of Chicago, 1906.

Cox, Henry J., and John H. Armington. *The Weather and Climate of Chicago*, Geographic Society of Chicago Bulletin, no. 4. Chicago: Geographic Society of Chicago, 1914.

Daly, Charles. "Annual Address. Subject: Review of the Events of the Year, and Recent Explorations and Theories for Reaching the North Pole." *Journal of the American Geographical and Statistical Society* 2, no. 2 (1870):lxxxiii-cxxvi.

Davis, William Morris. "Geography in the United States." *Science* 19, no. 473 (1904): 121–132.

Davis, William Morris. "The Opportunity for the Association of American Geographers." *Bulletin of the American Geographical Society* 37, no. 2 (1905): 84–86.

"The Discovery of the Pole." *National Geographic Magazine* 20, no. 10 (1909): 889–912.

Dodge, Richard E. "Notes on Geographical Education." *Journal of the American Geographical Society of New York* 32, no. 1 (1900): 55–60.

Fenneman, Nevin M. "The Circumference of Geography." *Geographical Review* 7, no. 3 (1919): 168–175.

"Front Matter." *Journal of the American Geographical Society of New York* 11 (1879): i–lv.

"Front Matter." *Bulletin of the Alaska Geographical Society* (October 1900).

"Front Matter." *Transactions and Proceedings of the Geographical Society of the Pacific* 1, no. 2 (1891).

"Geographical Record." *Bulletin of the American Geographical Society* 46, no. 9 (1914): 679–687.

Geographical Society of Philadelphia. *Charter, By-Laws, List of Members.* Philadelphia: The Society, May 1899.

Geographical Society of Philadelphia. *Charter, By-Laws, List of Members.* Philadelphia: The Society, 1902.

Geographical Society of Philadelphia. *Charter, By-Laws, List of Members.* Philadelphia: The Society, December 1903.

Geographic Society of Chicago. *Geographic Society of Chicago Handbook 1934–35.* Chicago: The Society, 1934.

Geographic Society of Chicago. *Geographic Society of Chicago Year Book 1912–1913.* Chicago: The Society, 1913.

Geographic Society of Chicago. *Geographic Society of Chicago Year-Book 1919–21.* Chicago: The Society, 1921.

Geographic Society of Chicago. *Geographic Society of Chicago Year Book 1922–1924.* Chicago: The Society, 1924.

Geographic Society of Chicago. *Preliminary Announcement 1907–08.* Chicago: The Society, 1907.

Geographic Society of Chicago. *Preliminary Announcement 1908–09*. Chicago: The Society, 1908.

Geographic Society of Chicago. *The Rivers and Harbors of Chicago, Geographical Excursion Bulletin* 1. Chicago: The Society, 1911.

Geographic Society of Chicago. *The Rock River, between Rockford and Dixon*, Geographic Society of Chicago Excursion Bulletin 2. Chicago: The Society, 1911.

Geographical Society of Philadelphia. *History 1891–1960*. Philadelphia: The Society, 1960.

Gilbert, G. K. "Earthquake Forecasts." *Science* 29, no. 734 (1909): 121–38.

Grosvenor, Gilbert H. "Seven Principles." *National Geographic Magazine* 27, no. 3 (1915): 318–320.

Grosvenor, Gilbert H. "The National Geographic Society." *National Geographic Magazine* 14, no. 3 (1912): 272–275.

"The Hawaiian Islands." *Transactions and Proceedings of The Geographical Society of the Pacific* 2, no. 1 (1902): 51–52.

Hayes, A. "Modern Ocean Highways." *Journal of the American Geographical Society of New York* 11 (1879): 97–112.

Heilprin, Angelo. "The Shrinkage of Lake Nicaragua." *Bulletin of the Geographical Society of Philadelphia* 3, no. 1 (1901): 1–12.

Heilprin, Angelo. "The Water Supply of Lake Nicaragua." *Bulletin of the Geographical Society of Philadelphia* 3, no. 1 (1901): 13–20.

Heilprin, Angelo. "The Nicaragua Canal in its geographical and geological relation." *Bulletin of the Geographical Society of Philadelphia* 2, no. 5 (1900): 87–107.

Herbert, John W. "The Panama Canal: Its Construction and Its Effect on Commerce." *Bulletin of the American Geographical Society* 45, no. 4 (1913): 241–54.

"History Highlights." Geographic Society of Chicago. Accessed May 20, 2023. https://www.geographicsociety.org/about/history-highlights/.

Hovey, Edmund Otis. "The Isthmus of Tehuantepec and the Tehuantepec National Railway." *Bulletin of the American Geographical Society* 39, no. 2 (1907): 78–91.

Howe, C. "The Disposition of the Philippines." *National Geographic Magazine* 9, no. 6 (1898): 304.

Hunt, T. "California, Oregon, and Washington." *Journal of the American Geographical and Statistical Society* 1, no. 5 (1859): 137–52.

Jay, J. "American Agriculture. Part 1." *Journal of the American Geographical and Statistical Society* 1, no. 2 (1859): 50–57.

Johnson, Emory R. "Comparison of Distances by the Isthmian Canal and Other Routes." *Bulletin of the American Geographical Society* 35, no. 2 (1903): 163–76.

Johnson, Emory R. "The Panama Canal in Its Commercial Aspects." *Bulletin of the American Geographical Society* 35, no. 5 (1903): 481–91.

King, D., and Charles Daly. "Notes on Siam." *Journal of the American Geographical and Statistical Society* 1, no. 7 (1859): 193–199.

Littlehales, G. W. "Recent Advances in Geographic Knowledge Accomplished by the United States Hydrographic Office at Washington." *Journal of the American Geographical Society of New York* 30, no. 2 (1898): 124–126.

Littlehales, G. W. "The Navy as a Motor in Geographical and Commercial Progress." *Journal of the American Geographical Society of New York* 31, no. 2 (1899): 123–29.

Littlehales, G. W. "The United States Mid-Pacific Naval Supply Station." *Journal of the American Geographical Society of New York* 30, no. 4 (1898): 277–80.

Lumholtz, Carl. "The American Cave-Dwellers: The Tarahumaris of the Sierra Madre." *Journal of the American Geographical Society of New York* 26, no. 1 (1894): 299–325.

McGee, WJ. "The Growth of the United States." *National Geographic Magazine* 9 (1898): 377–385.

"Members of the National Geographic Society." *National Geographic Magazine* 14, no. 1 (1903): appendix.

Menocal, A. G. "Discussion upon the Proposed Interoceanic Ship Canal, Special Meeting, December 15, 1879." *Journal of the American Geographical Society of New York* 11 (1879): 186–218.

"Mexican Archaeology." *Science* 17, no. 429 (1891): 232.

Mikkelsen, Ejnar. "The Mikkelsen-Leffingwell Expedition." *Bulletin of the American Geographical Society* 39, no. 4 (1907): 224–31.

Mikkelsen, Ejnar. "Report of the Mikkelsen-Leffingwell Expedition." Bulletin of the American Geographical Society 39, no. 10 (1907): 607–20.

Morgan, E. "The Samoan Islands." *National Geographic Magazine* 11 (1900): 417–426.

Morison, George S. "The Panama Canal." *Bulletin of the American Geographical Society* 35, no. 1 (1903): 24–43.

Murphy, J. "The Isthmus of Tehuantepec. Its Inhabitants and Resources." *Journal of the American Geographical and Statistical Society* 1, no.6 (1859): 162–77.

"The National Geographic Society." *National Geographic Magazine* 14, no. 3 (1912): 272–275.

"Notes by the Secretary." *Transactions and Proceedings of The Geographical Society of the Pacific* 1, no. 2 (1891): xxi-xxiv.

"Objects of the Society." *Bulletin of the Geographical Society of California* 2 (1894): 1–2.

"Oriental Trade." *Transactions and Proceedings of The Geographical Society of the Pacific* 2, no. 1 (1902): 56–58.

"Papers read before the Geographical Society of the Pacific." *Transactions and Proceedings of the Geographical Society of the Pacific* 1, no. 2 (1891): xxiv-xxvi.

Peary, R. "Address by Commander Robert E. Peary, U. S. N., on the Assembling of the Congress in Washington, September 8, 1904." *National Geographic Magazine* 15, no. 10 (1904): 387–404.

Perkins, G. "The Key to the Pacific." *National Geographic Magazine* 19, no. 4 (1908): 295–298.

"Philippines." *Transactions and Proceedings of The Geographical Society of the Pacific* 2, no. 1 (1902): 55–56.

Ray, P. H. "Alaska." *Bulletin of the Alaska Geographical Society* (October 1900): 8–11.

R. S. F. "Statistics of Guano." *Journal of the American Geographical and Statistical Society* 1, no. 6 (1859): 181–189.

Salisbury, Rollin D., and William C. Alden. *The Geography of Chicago and its Environs*, Geographic Society of Chicago Bulletin no. 1. Chicago: Geographic Society of Chicago, 1899.

Sauer, Carl O., Gilbert H. Cady and Henry C. Cowles. *Starved Rock State Park and its Environs*, Geographic Society of Chicago, Bulletin no. 6. Chicago: Geographic Society of Chicago, 1918.

"Semi-Centennial of the American Geographical Society." *Bulletin of the American Geographical Society* 37, no. 1 (1905): 1–29.

Semple, Ellen Churchill. *American History and its Geographic Conditions*. New York: Houghton, Mifflin, 1903.

Semple, Ellen Churchill. "Oceans and Enclosed Seas: A Study in Anthropo-Geography." *Bulletin of the American Geographical Society* 40, no. 4 (1908): 193–209.

Shelford, Victor E. *Animal Communities in Temperate America – as illustrated in the Chicago Region*, Geographic Society of Chicago Bulletin no. 5. Chicago: Geographic Society of Chicago, 1913.

"Sir Ernest Shackleton Receives the Cullum Geographical Medal." *Bulletin of the American Geographical Society* 42, no. 4 (1910): 241–43.

Squier, G. "The Influence of Submarine Cables Upon Military and Naval Supremacy." *National Geographic Magazine* 12, no. 1 (1901): 1–12.

Stevens, I. "Northwest America." *Journal of the American Geographical and Statistical Society* 1, no. 1 (1859): 3–10.

Stockton, Charles H. "The Commercial Geography of the American Inter-Oceanic Canal." *Journal of the American Geographical Society of New York* 20, no. 1 (1888): 75–93.

Tarr, Ralph S. "Glaciers and Glaciation of Alaska." *Annals of the Association of American Geographers* 2 (1912): 3–122.

Tarr, Ralph S. "The Malaspina Glacier." *Bulletin of the American Geographical Society* 39, no. 5 (1907): 273–85.

Tarr, Ralph S., and Lawrence Martin. "Glaciers and Glaciation of Yakutat Bay, Alaska." *Bulletin of the American Geographical Society* 38, no. 3 (1906): 145–67.

Taylor, H. C. "The Nicaragua Canal." *Journal of the American Geographical Society of New York* 18 (1886): 95–126.

"The Interoceanic Ship Canal, Special Meeting, December 29, 1879." *Journal of the American Geographical Society of New York* 11 (1879): 259–300.

Tornow, Max L. "Economic Conditions of the Philippines." *National Geographic Magazine* 10, no. 2 (1899): 33–64.

Transactions and Proceedings of The Geographical Society of the Pacific 2, no. 2 (1902).

"The Transcontinental Excursion." New York Times, October 19, 1912.

Turner, Frederick Jackson. "The Significance of the Frontier in American History." *Report of the American Historical Association for 1893* (1893): 199–227.

Turner, Frederick Jackson. "Geographical Interpretations of American History." *Journal of Geography* 4 (1905): 34–37.

"Washington Letter." *Journal of the American Geographical Society of New York* 30, no. 1 (1898): 69–71.

Secondary Sources

Abramson, Howard S. *National Geographic: Behind America's Lens on the World.* New York: Crown Publishing, 1987.

Agnew, John. "The Origins of Critical Geopolitics." In *The Ashgate Research Companion to Critical Geopolitics*, edited by Klaus Dodds, Merje Kuus, and Joanne Sharp, 19–32. London: Ashgate, 2013.

Agnew, John, and Stuart Corbridge. *Mastering Space: Hegemony, Territory and International Political Economy.* London: Routledge, 1995.

Agnew, John A., and David N. Livingstone, eds. *The Sage Handbook of Geographical Knowledge.* Los Angeles: Sage, 2011.

Akerman, James R., ed. *The Imperial Map: Cartography and the Mastery of Empire.* Chicago: University of Chicago Press, 2009.

Allen, David E. "Amateurs and Professionals." In *The Cambridge History of Science*, vol. 6, edited by Peter J. Bowler and John V. Pickstone, 24–43. Cambridge: Cambridge University Press, 2009.

Anderson, Benedict. *Imagined Communities: Reflections on the Origin and Spread of Nationalism*. London: Verso, 1983.

Ash, Mitchell. "Wissenschaft und Politik als Ressourcen füreinander." In *Wissenschaften und Wissenschaftspolitik: Bestandsaufnahmen zu Formationen, Brüchen und Kontinuitäten in Deutschland des 20. Jahrhunderts*, edited by Rüdiger vom Bruch and Brigitte Kaderas, 32–51. Stuttgart: Franz Steiner, 2002.

Ayala, César J., and Rafael Bernabe. *Puerto Rico in the American Century: A History since 1898*. Chapel Hill: University of North Carolina Press, 2007.

Balogh, Brian. *A Government out of Sight: The Mystery of National Authority in Nineteenth-Century America*. Cambridge: Cambridge University Press, 2009.

Bates, Ralph Samuel. *Scientific Societies in the United States*. Cambridge, MA: MIT Press, 1965.

Beckinsale, Robert P. "W. M. Davis and American Geography." In *The Origins of Academic Geography in the United States*, edited by Brian W. Blouet, 107–122. Hamden: Archon Books, 1981.

Bell, Morag, Robin A. Butlin, and Michael Heffernan, eds. *Geography and Imperialism, 1820–1940*. Manchester: Manchester University Press, 1995.

Bemis, Samuel Flagg. *A Diplomatic History of the United States*. New York: Henry Holt and Company, 1936.

Bender, Thomas. *A Nation among Nations: America's Place in World History*. New York: Hill and Wang, 2006.

Bennett, Brett M., and Joseph M. Hodge, eds. *Science and Empire: Knowledge and Networks of Science across the British Empire, 1800–1970*. Basingstoke: Palgrave Macmillan, 2011.

Benson, Keith, and Jane Maienschein. "Introduction: AAAS Narrative History." In *The Establishment of Science in America: 150 Years of the American Association for the Advancement of Science*, edited by Sally G. Kohlstedt, Michael M. Sokal, and Bruce V. Lewenstein, 6–11. New Brunswick: Rutgers University Press, 1999.

Binnema, Theodore. *Enlightened Zeal: The Hudson's Bay Company and Scientific Networks, 1670–1870*. Toronto: University of Toronto Press, 2014.

Black, Jeremy. *Maps and History: Constructing Images of the Past*. New Haven: Yale University Press, 1997.

Black, Jeremy. *Geopolitics and the Quest for Dominance*. Bloomington: Indiana University Press, 2016.

Bloom, Lisa. *Gender on Ice: American Ideologies of Polar Expeditions*. Minneapolis: University of Minnesota Press, 1993.

Blouet, Brian W. "Preface." In *The Origins of Academic Geography in the United States*, edited by Brian W. Blouet, ix-xii. Hamden: Archon Books, 1981.

Blouet, Brian W., ed. *The Origins of Academic Geography in the United States*. Hamden: Archon Books, 1981.

Bruce, Robert V. "A Statistical Profile of American Scientists, 1846–1876." In *Nineteenth-Century American Science: A Reappraisal*, edited by George H. Daniels, 63–94. Evanston: Northwestern University Press, 1972.

Bruce, Robert V. *The Launching of Modern American Science, 1846–1876*. New York: Alfred A. Knopf, 1987.

Brückner, Martin. The *Geographic Revolution in Early America: Maps, Literacy, and National Identity*. Chapel Hill: University of North Carolina Press, 2006.

Bryan, Courtlandt. *The National Geographic Society: 100 Years of Adventure and Discovery*. New York: Abrams, 1987.

Burke, Peter. *What is the History of Knowledge?* Cambridge: Polity Press, 2016.

Burke, Peter. *Die Explosion des Wissens*. Berlin: Wagenbach, 2014.

Burnett, D. Graham. "Hydrographic Discipline among the Navigators: Charting an Empire of Commerce and Science in the Nineteenth-Century Pacific." In *The Imperial Map: Cartography and the Mastery of Empire*, edited by James R. Akerman, 185–259. Chicago: University of Chicago Press, 2009.

Burnett, D. Graham. *Masters of All They Surveyed: Exploration, Geography, and a British El Dorado*. Chicago: University of Chicago Press, 2000.

Butlin, Robin A. *Geographies of Empire: European Empires and Colonies, c. 1880–1960*. Cambridge: Cambridge University Press, 2009.

Cantor, Geoffrey, and Sally Shuttleworth, eds. *Science Serialized: Representations of the Sciences in Nineteenth-Century Periodicals*. Cambridge: MIT Press, 2004.

Carter, Paul. *The Road to Botany Bay: An Exploration of Landscape and History*. Minneapolis: University of Minnesota Press, 1987.

Cooper, Alix. "From the Alps to Egypt (and Back Again): Dolomieu, Scientific Voyaging, and the Construction of the Field in Eighteenth-Century Natural History." In *Making Space for Science*, edited by Crosbie Smith and Jon Agar, 39–63. New York: St. Martin's Press, 1998.

Craggs, Ruth. "Situating the imperial archive: The Royal Empire Society Library, 1868–1945." *Journal of Historical Geography* 34, no. 1 (2008): 48–67.

Cumings, Bruce. *Dominion from Sea to Sea: Pacific Ascendancy and American Power*. New Haven: Yale University Press, 2009.

Cushman, Gregory T. *Guano and the Opening of the Pacific World: A Global Ecological History*. New York: Cambridge University Press, 2013.

Dalby, Simon. "Critical Geopolitics: Discourse, Difference, and Dissent." *Environment and Planning D: Society and Space* 9, no. 3 (1991): 261–83.

Daston, Lorraine. "The History of Science and the History of Knowledge." *KNOW: A Journal on the Formation of Knowledge* 1, no. 1 (Spring 2017): 131–154.

Daum, Andreas W. *Wissenschaftspopularisierung im 19. Jahrhundert: bürgerliche Kultur, naturwissenschaftliche Bildung und die deutsche Öffentlichkeit, 1848–1914*. 2nd ed. München: Oldenbourg, 2002.

Daunton, Martin. "Introduction." In *The Organisation of Knowledge in Victorian Britain*, edited by Martin Daunton, 1–28. Oxford: Oxford University Press, 2005.

Dick, Steven J. *Sky and Ocean Joined: The U.S. Naval Observatory, 1830–2000*. Cambridge: Cambridge University Press, 2003.

Dodds, Klaus, and James Derrick Sidaway. "Locating Critical Geopolitics." *Environment and Planning D: Society and Space* 12, no. 5 (1994): 515–24.

Domosh, Mona. *American Commodities in an Age of Empire*. New York: Routledge, 2006.

Döring, Jörg, and Tristan Thielmann. *Spatial Turn. Das Raumparadigma in den Kultur- und Sozialwissenschaften*. Bielefeld: transcript, 2015.

Dritsas, Lawrence. "From Lake Nyassa to Philadelphia: A Geography of the Zambesi Expedition, 1858–64." *British Journal for the History of Science* 38, no. 1 (2005): 35–52.

Driver, Felix. "Geography's Empire: Histories of Geographical Knowledge." *Environment and Planning D: Society and Space* 10 (1992): 23–40.

Driver, Felix. *Geography Militant: Cultures of Exploration and Empire*. Oxford: Blackwell, 2001.

Driver, Felix. "Imaginative Geographies." In *Introducing Human Geographies*, 3rd ed., edited by Paul Cloke, Philip Crang and Mark Goodwin, 245–261. London: Routledge, 2014.

Driver, Felix, and Gillian Rose. *Nature and Science*. Cheltenham: Historical Geography Research Group, 1992.

Dunbar, Gary S. "Credentialism and Careerism in American Geography." In *The Origins of Academic Geography in the United States*, edited by Brian W. Blouet, 71–88. Hamden: Archon Books, 1981.

Dunbar, Gary S. "The Rival Geographical Societies of 'Fin-de-Siècle' San Francisco." *Yearbook of the Association of Pacific Coast Geographers* 40 (1978): 55–67.

Dupree, A. Hunter. *Science in the Federal Government: A History of Policies and Activities to 1940*. Cambridge: Belknap Press of Harvard University Press, 1957.

Dzudzek, Iris. "Räumliche Repräsentationen als Element des Politischen – Konzeptionelle Grundlagen und Untersuchungsperspektiven der Humangeographie." In *Die Politik räumlicher Repräsentationen – Beispiele aus der empirischen Forschung*, edited by Iris Dzudzek, Paul Reuber and Anke Strüver, 3–23. Münster: LIT Verlag, 2011.

Edney, Matthew H. *Mapping an Empire: The Geographical Construction of British India, 1765–1843*. Chicago: University of Chicago Press, 1997.

Ferguson, Niall. *Colossus: The Rise and Fall of the American Empire*. London: Penguin, 2005.

Finnegan, Diarmid A. "The spatial turn: Geographical approaches in the history of science." *Journal of the History of Biology* 41, no. 2 (2008): 369–388.

Finnegan, Diarmid A. *Natural History Societies and Civic Culture in Victorian Scotland*. London: Pickering & Chatto, 2009.

Finnegan, Diarmid A., ed. *Spaces of Global Knowledge*. Farnham: Ashgate, 2015.

Fleck, Ludwik. *Entstehung und Entwicklung einer wissenschaftlichen Tatsache: Einführung in die Lehre vom Denkstil und Denkkollektiv*. Basel: Schwabe, 1935.

Foucault, Michel. *The Order of Things: An Archaeology of the Human Sciences*. London: Tavistock, 1970.

Foucault, Michel. *The Archaeology of Knowledge*. New York: Vintage Books, 1982.

Friis, Herman R. "The Role of Geographers and Geography in the Federal Government: 1774–1905." In *The Origins of Academic Geography in the United States*, edited by Brian W. Blouet, 35–60. Hamden: Archon Books, 1981.

Frymer, Paul. *Building an American Empire: The Era of Territorial and Political Expansion*. Princeton: Princeton University Press, 2017.

Gerstner, Patsy A. "The Academy of Natural Sciences of Philadelphia, 1812–1850." In *The Pursuit of Knowledge in the Early American Republic: American Learned and Scientific Societies from Colonial Times to the Civil War*, edited by Alexandra Oleson and Sanborn C. Brown, 174–192. Baltimore: Johns Hopkins University Press, 1976.

Geyer, Michael, and Charles Bright. "World History in a Global Age." *The American Historical Review* 100, no. 4 (1995): 1034–60.

Gieryn, Thomas F. "Boundary-Work and the Demarcation of Science from Non-Science: Strains and Interests in Professional Ideologies of Scientists." *American Sociological Review* 48, no. 6 (1983): 781–95.

Go, Julian. *Patterns of Empire: The British and American Empires, 1688 to the Present*. Cambridge: Cambridge University Press, 2011.

Godlewska, Anne, and Neil Smith, eds. *Geography and Empire*. Oxford: Black-well, 1994.

Godlewska, Anne, and Neil Smith. "Introduction: Critical Histories of Geography." In *Geography and Empire*, edited by Anne Godlewska and Neil Smith, 1–8. Oxford: Blackwell, 1994.

Golinski, Jan. *Making Natural Knowledge: Constructivism and the History of Science*. Cambridge: Cambridge University Press, 1998.

Górny, Maciej. *Vaterlandszeichner: Geografen und Grenzen im Zwischenkriegseuropa*. Osnabrück: fibre, 2019.

Graebner, Norman. *Empire on the Pacific: A Study in American Continental Expansion*. New York: The Ronald Press, 1955.

Gräbel, Carsten. *Die Erforschung der Kolonien: Expeditionen und koloniale Wissenskultur deutscher Geographen, 1884–1919*. Bielefeld: transcript, 2015.

Gregory, Derek. *Geographical Imaginations*. Cambridge, MA: Blackwell, 1994.

Grosvenor, Gilbert, and John La Gorce. *The National Geographic Society and its Magazine: A History*. Washington: National Geographic Society, 1957.

Gugerli, David, and Daniel Speich. *Topografien der Nation. Politik, kartografische Ordnung und Landschaft im 19. Jahrhundert*. Zürich: Chronos-Verlag, 2002.

Guldi, Jo, and David Armitage. *The History Manifesto*. Cambridge: Cambridge University Press, 2014.

Günzel, Stephan. *Raum. Eine kulturwissenschaftliche Einführung*. Bielefeld: transcript, 2017.

Hahn, Steven. *A Nation Without Borders: The United States and Its World in an Age of Civil Wars, 1830–1910*. New York: Viking, 2016.

Hall, Stuart. *Representation: Cultural Representations and Signifying Practices*. London: Sage, 1997.

Haraway, Donna. "Situated Knowledges: The Science Question in Feminism and the Privilege of Partial Perspective." *Feminist Studies* 14, no. 3 (1988): 575–99.

Harley, J. Brian. "Maps, Knowledge, and Power." In *Geographic Thought: A Praxis Perspective*, edited by George L. Henderson & Marvin Waterstone, 129–48. London: Routledge, 2009.

Harvey, David. "Between Space and Time: Reflections on the Geographical Imagination." *Annals of the Association of American Geographers* 80, no. 3 (1990): 418–34.

Harvey, David. *The Condition of Postmodernity: An Enquiry into the Origins of Cultural Change*. Oxford: Blackwell, 1989.

Hawkins, Stephanie L. *American Iconographic: National Geographic, Global Culture, and the Visual Imagination*. Charlottesville: University of Virginia Press, 2010.

Heffernan, Michael. "Learned Societies." In *The Sage Handbook of Geographical Knowledge*, edited by John A. Agnew and David N. Livingstone, 111–125. Los Angeles: Sage, 2011.

Heggie, Vanessa. "Why Isn't Exploration a Science?" *Isis* 105, no. 2 (2014): 318–34.

Hendrickson, David C. *Union, Nation, or Empire: The American Debate over International Relations, 1789–1941*. Lawrence: University Press of Kansas, 2009.

Hobsbawm, Eric. *The Age of Empire: 1875–1914*. New York: Pantheon Books, 1987.

Hunt, Michael. *Ideology and U.S. Foreign Policy*. New Haven: Yale University Press, 2009.

Husseini de Araújo, Shadia. *Jenseits vom "Kampf der Kulturen": imaginative Geographien des Eigenen und des Anderen in arabischen Printmedien*. Bielefeld: transcript, 2011.

Immerman, Richard H. *Empire for Liberty: A History of American Imperialism from Benjamin Franklin to Paul Wolfowitz*. Princeton: Princeton University Press, 2010.

Immerwahr, Daniel. *How to Hide an Empire: A History of the Greater United States*. New York: Farrar, Straus and Giroux, 2019.

James, Preston E. "Geographical Ideas in America, 1890–1914." In *The Origins of Academic Geography in the United States*, edited by Brian W. Blouet, 319–326. Hamden: Archon Books, 1981.

James, Preston Everett, and Geoffrey J. Martin. *The Association of American Geographers: The First Seventy-Five Years, 1904–1979*. Easton: Association of American Geographers, 1978.

Jansen, Axel. *Alexander Dallas Bache: Building the American Nation through Science and Education in the Nineteenth Century*. Frankfurt: Campus, 2011.

Johnson, Nuala. "Grand design(er)s: David Moore, natural theology and the Royal Botanic Gardens in Glasnevin, Dublin, 1838–1879." *Cultural Geographies* 14, no. 1 (2007): 29–55.

Jones, Max. "Measuring the World: Exploration, Empire and the Reform of the Royal Geographical Society, c. 1874–93." In *The Organisation of Knowledge in Victorian Britain*, edited by Martin Daunton, 313–336. Oxford: Oxford University Press, 2005.

Jöns, Heike. "Academic travel from Cambridge University and the formation of centres of knowledge, 1885–1954." *Journal of Historical Geography* 34, no. 2 (2008): 338–362.

Kennedy, Dane. *The Last Blank Spaces: Exploring Africa and Australia.* Cambridge: Harvard University Press, 2013.

Kern, Stephen. *The Culture of Time and Space, 1880–1918.* Cambridge: Harvard University Press, 1983.

Kohler, Robert E., and Kathryn M. Olesko. "Introduction: Clio Meets Science." *Osiris* 27, no. 1 (2012): 1–16.

Kohlstedt, Sally Gregory. "Savants and Professionals: Scientific Societies in the Nineteenth-Century United States." In *The Establishment of Science in America: 150 Years of the American Association for the Advancement of Science*, edited by Sally G. Kohlstedt, Michael M. Sokal, and Bruce V. Lewenstein, 297–317. New Brunswick: Rutgers University Press, 1999.

Kramer, Paul. "Power and Connection: Imperial Histories of the United States in the World." *The American Historical Review* 116, no. 5 (2011): 1348–91.

Kramer, Paul. *The Blood of Government: Race, Empire, the United States, & the Philippines.* Chapel Hill: University of North Carolina Press, 2006.

LaFeber, Walter. *The New Empire: An Interpretation of American Expansion, 1860–1898.* Ithaca: Cornell University Press, 1963.

LaFeber, Walter. "A Note on the 'Mercantilist Imperialism' of Alfred Thayer Mahan." *Mississippi Valley Historical Review* 48, no. 4 (1962): 674–85.

LaFeber, Walter. *The Panama Canal: The Crisis in Historical Perspective.* New York: Oxford University Press, 1989.

Landwehr, Achim. "Das Sichtbare sichtbar machen. Annäherungen an 'Wissen' als Kategorie historischer Forschung." In *Geschichte(n) der Wirklichkeit*, edited by Achim Landwehr, 61–89. Augsburg: Wißner-Verlag, 2002.

Lane, K. Maria D. *Geographies of Mars: Seeing and Knowing the Red Planet.* Chicago: The University of Chicago Press, 2011.

Latour, Bruno. *Science in Action: How to Follow Scientists and Engineers through Society.* Cambridge, MA: Harvard University Press, 1987.

Latour, Bruno, and Steve Woolgar. *Laboratory Life: The Social Construction of Scientific Facts.* Los Angeles: Sage, 1979.

Lentz, Sebastian, and Ferjan Ormeling. *Die Verräumlichung des Welt-Bildes: Petermanns Geographische Mitteilungen zwischen 'explorativer Geographie' und der 'Vermessenheit' europäischer Raumphantasien.* Stuttgart: Steiner, 2008.

Lightman, Bernard. *Victorian Popularizers of Science: Designing Nature for New Audiences.* Chicago: University of Chicago Press, 2007.

Livingstone, David N. *The Geographical Tradition: Episodes in the History of a Contested Enterprise*. Oxford: Blackwell, 1992.

Livingstone, David N. *Putting Science in Its Place: Geographies of Scientific Knowledge*. Chicago: University of Chicago Press, 2003.

Livingstone, David N. "Environmental Determinism." In *The Sage Handbook of Geographical Knowledge*, edited by John A. Agnew and David N. Livingstone, 368–380. Los Angeles: Sage, 2011.

Livingstone, David N., and Charles W. J. Withers, eds. *Geography and Enlightenment*. Chicago: University of Chicago Press, 1999.

Livingstone, David N., and Charles W. J. Withers, eds. *Geography and Revolution*. Chicago: University of Chicago Press, 2005.

Livingstone, David N., and Charles W. J. Withers, eds. *Geographies of Nineteenth-Century Science*. Chicago: University of Chicago Press, 2011.

Lossau, Julia. *Die Politik der Verortung: eine postkoloniale Reise zu einer anderen Geographie der Welt*. Bielefeld: transcript, 2002.

Löw, Martina. *Raumsoziologie*. Frankfurt am Main: Suhrkamp, 2001.

Lowenthal, David. "Fruitful Liaison or Folie à Deux? The AAG and the AGS." *The Professional Geographer* 57, no. 3 (2005): 468–473.

Lucier, Paul. "The Professional and the Scientist in Nineteenth-Century America." *Isis* 100, no. 4 (2009): 699–732.

Lutz, Catherine A., and Jane L. Collins. *Reading National Geographic*. Chicago: University of Chicago Press, 1993.

Maier, Charles S. "Consigning the Twentieth Century to History: Alternative Narratives for the Modern Era." *The American Historical Review* 105, no. 3 (2000): 807–31.

Major, John. *Prize Possession: The United States and the Panama Canal, 1903–1979*. Cambridge: Cambridge University Press, 1993.

Malich, Lisa. "Eine Zukunft der Wissenschaftsgeschichte liegt in der Institution." *Berichte zur Wissenschaftsgeschichte* 41, no. 4 (2018): 395–98.

Marchand, Suzanne. "How Much Knowledge is Worth Knowing? An American Intellectual Historian's Thoughts on the Geschichte des Wissens." *Berichte zur Wissenschaftsgeschichte* 42, no. 2–3 (2019): 126–149.

Martin, Geoffrey J. "Paradigm of Change: A Study in the History of Geography in the United States, 1892–1925." *Organon* 20/21 (1984/1985): 275–282.

Martin, Geoffrey J. *American Geography and Geographers: Toward Geographical Science*. New York: Oxford University Press, 2015.

Martin, Geoffrey J., and James E. Preston. *All Possible Worlds: A History of Geographical Ideas*. New York: Wiley, 1993.

McCormick, Thomas. *China Market: America's Quest for Informal Empire, 1893–1901.* Chicago: Quadrangle Books, 1967.

McCoy, Alfred W., and Francisco A. Scarano, eds. *Colonial Crucible: Empire in the Making of the Modern American State.* Madison: University of Wisconsin Press, 2009.

McCoy, Alfred W., Francisco A. Scarano, and Courtney Johnson. "On the Tropic of Cancer: Transitions and Transformations in the U.S. Imperial State." In *Colonial Crucible: Empire in the Making of the Modern American State,* edited by Alfred W. McCoy and Francisco A. Scarano, 3–33. Madison: University of Wisconsin Press, 2009.

McManis, Douglas R. "Leading Ladies at the AGS." *Geographical Review* 86, no. 2 (1996): 270–77.

Meusburger, Peter, David N. Livingstone, and Heike Jöns, eds. *Geographies of Science.* Dordrecht: Springer, 2010.

Mikesell, Marvin W. "Continuity and Change." In *The Origins of Academic Geography in the United States,* edited by Brian W. Blouet, 1–18. Hamden: Archon Books, 1981.

Miller, David Philip. "Joseph Banks, Empire, and 'Centers of Calculation' in Late Hanoverian London." In *Visions of Empire: Voyages, Botany, and Representations of Nature,* edited by David Philip Miller and Peter Hanns Reill, 21–37. Cambridge: Cambridge University Press, 1996.

Missal, Alexander. *Seaway to the Future: American Social Visions and the Construction of the Panama Canal.* Madison: University of Wisconsin Press, 2009.

Mitchell, Timothy. *Colonising Egypt.* Berkeley: University of California Press, 1991.

Monk, Janice. "Women's Worlds at the American Geographical Society." *Geographical Review* 93, no. 2 (2003): 237–257.

Monmonier, Mark. *How to Lie with Maps.* Chicago: University of Chicago Press, 1991.

Monmonier, Mark. *Mapping It Out.* Chicago: University of Chicago Press, 1993.

Morgan, William. *Pacific Gibraltar.* Annapolis: Naval Institute Press, 2011.

Morin, Karen M. *Civic Discipline: Geography in America, 1860–1890.* Farnham: Ashgate, 2011.

Müller, Simone. *Wiring the World: The Social and Cultural Creation of Global Telegraph Networks.* New York: Columbia University Press, 2016.

Naylor, Simon. *Historical Geographies of Science.* Cambridge: Cambridge University Press, 2005.

Naylor, Simon. "Introduction: Historical geographies of science – places, contexts, cartographies." *The British Journal for the History of Science* 38, no. 1 (2005): 1–12.

Neem, Johann N. "Civil Society and American Nationalism, 1776–1865." In *Politics and Partnerships: The Role of Voluntary Associations in America's Political Past and Present*, edited by Elisabeth S. Clemens and Doug Guthrie, 29–53. Chicago: University of Chicago Press, 2011.

Ninkovich, Frank. *The United States and Imperialism*. Malden: Blackwell, 2001.

Nugent, Walter. *Habits of Empire: A History of American Expansion*. New York: Vintage Books, 2009.

Oleson, Alexandra. "Introduction: To Build a New Intellectual Order." In *The Pursuit of Knowledge in the Early American Republic: American Scientific and Learned Societies from Colonial Times to the Civil War*, edited by Alexandra Oleson and Sanborn C. Brown, xv-xxv. Baltimore: Johns Hopkins University Press, 1976.

Oleson, Alexandra, and Sanborn C. Brown, eds. *The Pursuit of Knowledge in the Early American Republic: American Scientific and Learned Societies from Colonial Times to the Civil War*. Baltimore: Johns Hopkins University Press, 1976.

Ophir, Adi, and Steven Shapin. "The Place of Knowledge: A Methodological Survey." *Science in Context* 4, no. 1 (1991): 3–21.

Osterhammel, Jürgen. "Die Wiederkehr des Raumes: Geopolitik, Geohistorie und historische Geographie." *Neue Politische Literatur* 43, no. 3 (1998): 374–97.

Östling, Johan. "Circulation, Arenas, and the Quest for Public Knowledge: Historiographical Currents And Analytical Frameworks." *History and Theory* 59, no. 4 (2020): 111–126.

Ó Tuathail, Gearóid. "Geopolitical Discourses: A New Geopolitics Series." *Geopolitics* 5, no. 1 (2000): 125–128.

Ó Tuathail, Gearóid. *Critical Geopolitics: The Politics of Writing Global Space*. London: Routledge, 1996.

Passoth, Jan-Hendrick. "Aktanten, Assoziationen, Mediatoren: Wie die ANT das Soziale neu zusammenbaut." In *Dimensionen und Konzeptionen von Sozialität*, edited by Gert Albert, Rainer Greshoff, and Rainer Schützeichel, 309–316. Wiesbaden: VS Verlag für Sozialwissenschaften, 2010.

Pattinson, William D. "Rollin Salisbury and the Establishment of Geography at the University of Chicago." In *The Origins of Academic Geography in the United States*, edited by Brian W. Blouet, 151–164. Hamden: Archon Books, 1981.

Pauly, Philip J. "The World and All That is in It: The National Geographic Society, 1888–1918." *American Quarterly* 31, no. 4 (1979): 517–532.

Pérez, Louis A., Jr. *The War of 1898: The United States and Cuba in History and Historiography*. Chapel Hill: University of North Carolina Press, 1998.

Perry, John Curtis. *Facing West: Americans and the Opening of the Pacific*. Westport: Praeger, 1994.

Pickering, Andrew, ed. *Science as Practice and Culture*. Chicago: University of Chicago Press, 1992.

Poole, Robert M. *Explorers House: National Geographic and the World it Made*. New York: Penguin Press, 2004.

Pratt, Mary Louise. *Imperial Eyes: Travel Writing and Transculturation*. London: Routledge, 1992.

Reingold, Nathan. "Definitions and Speculations: The Professionalization of Science in America in the Nineteenth Century." In *The Pursuit of Knowledge in the Early American Republic: American Learned and Scientific Societies from Colonial Times to the Civil War*, edited by Alexandra Oleson and Sanborn C. Brown, 33–69. Baltimore: Johns Hopkins University Press, 1976.

Reingold, Nathan. "American Indifference to Basic Research: A Reappraisal." In *Nineteenth-Century American Science: A Reappraisal*, edited by George H. Daniels, 38–62. Evanston: Northwestern University Press, 1972.

Reingold, Nathan. "Reflections on 200 Years of Science in the United States." In *The Sciences in the American Context: New Perspectives*, edited by Nathan Reingold, 9–13. Washington: Smithsonian Institution Press, 1979.

Reingold, Nathan. *Science in Nineteenth-Century America: A Documentary History*. Chicago: University of Chicago Press, 1964.

Reingold, Nathan. *Science in America: A Documentary History, 1900–1939*. Chicago: University of Chicago Press, 1981.

Renn, Jürgen. "From the History of Science to the History of Knowledge – and Back." *Centaurus* 57, no. 1 (2015): 37–53.

Robic, Marie-Claire. "Geography." In *The Cambridge History of Science*, edited by Theodore M. Porter and Dorothy Ross, vol. 7, 379–400. Cambridge: Cambridge University Press, 2003.

Robinson, Michael F. *The Coldest Crucible: Arctic Exploration and American Culture*. Chicago: University of Chicago Press, 2006.

Rothenberg, Tamar Y. *Presenting America's World: Strategies of Innocence in National Geographic Magazine, 1888–1945*. London: Routledge, 2007.

Rozwadowski, Helen M. *Fathoming the Ocean: The Discovery and Exploration of the Deep Sea*. Cambridge, MA: Belknap Press, 2005.

Rudwick, Martin J. S. *The Great Devonian Controversy*. Chicago: University of Chicago Press, 1985.

Ruiz, Ernesto. "Geography and Diplomacy: The American Geographical Society and the 'Geopolitical' Background of American Foreign Policy, 1848–1861." PhD diss., Northern Illinois University, 1975.

Ryan, James R. *Picturing Empire: Photography and Visualization of the British Empire*. Chicago: University of Chicago Press, 1997.

Said, Edward W. *Orientalism*. New York: Vintage, 1993.

Said, Edward W. *Culture and Imperialism*. New York: Knopf, 1993.

Said, Edward W. "Representing the Colonized: Anthropology's Interlocutors." *Critical Inquiry* 15, no. 2 (1989): 205–225.

Sarasin, Philipp. "Was ist Wissensgeschichte?" *Internationales Archiv für Sozialgeschichte der deutschen Literatur* 36, no. 1 (2011): 159–72.

Schenk, Winfried. *Allgemeine Anthropogeographie*. Gotha: Klett-Perthes, 2005.

Schillings, Pascal. *Der Letzte Weiße Flecken: Europäische Antarktisreisen um 1900*. Göttingen: Wallstein, 2016.

Schlögel, Karl. *Im Raume lesen wir die Zeit: Über Zivilisationsgeschichte und Geopolitik*. München: Hanser, 2003.

Schlögel, Karl. "Kartenlesen, Augenarbeit. Über die Fälligkeit des spatial turn in den Geschichts- und Kulturwissenschaften." *In Was sind Kulturwissenschaften? 13 Antworten*, edited by Heinz Dieter Kittsteiner, 261–83. München: Fink, 2004.

Schneider, Ute. *Die Macht der Karten: Eine Geschichte der Kartographie vom Mittelalter bis heute*. Darmstadt: Primus, 2004.

Schröder, Iris. *Das Wissen von der ganzen Welt: globale Geographien und räumliche Ordnungen Afrikas und Europas 1790–1870*. Paderborn: Schöningh, 2011.

Schulten, Susan. *The Geographical Imagination in America, 1880–1950*. Chicago: University of Chicago Press, 2001.

Schwarz, Angela. *Der Schlussel zur modernen Welt: Wissenschaftspopularisierung in Großbritannien und Deutschland im Übergang zur Moderne (ca. 1870–1914)*. Stuttgart: Steiner, 1999.

Seager, Robert. "Ten Years Before Mahan: The Unofficial Case for the New Navy, 1880–1890." *The Mississippi Valley Historical Review* 40, no. 3 (1953): 491–512.

Secord, James A. "Knowledge in transit." *Isis* 95, no. 4 (2004): 654–672.

Secord, James A. *Victorian Sensation: The Extraordinary Publication, Reception, and Secret Authorship of Vestiges of the Natural History of Creation*. Chicago: University of Chicago Press, 2000.

Seegel, Steven. *Mapping Europe's Borderlands: Russian Cartography in the Age of Empire*. Chicago: University of Chicago Press, 2012.

Sexton, Jay. *Monroe Doctrine: Empire and Nation in Nineteenth-Century America.* New York: Hill & Wang, 2011.

Shapin, Steven. "Placing the View from Nowhere: Historical and Sociological Problems in the Location of Science." *Transactions of the Institute of British Geographers* 23 (1998): 5–12.

Shapin, Steven. *Never Pure: Historical Studies of Science as If It Was Produced by People with Bodies, Situated in Time, Space, Culture, and Society, and Struggling for Credibility and Authority.* Baltimore: Johns Hopkins University Press, 2010.

Shapiro, Henry D. "The Western Academy of Natural Sciences of Cincinnati and the Structure of Science in the Ohio Valley." In *The Pursuit of Knowledge in the Early American Republic: American Scientific and Learned Societies from Colonial Times to the Civil War,* edited by Alexandra Oleson and Sanborn C. Brown, 219–247. Baltimore: Johns Hopkins University Press, 1976.

Sheets-Pyenson, Susan. "Popular Science Periodicals in Paris and London: The Emergence of a Low Scientific Culture, 1820–1875." *Annals of Science* 42, no. 6 (November 1985): 549–72.

Smith, J. Russell. "American Geography, 1900–1904." *The Professional Geographer* 4, no. 4 (1952): 5–15.

Smith, Crosbie, Jon Agar, and Gerald Schmidt, eds. *Making Space for Science: Territorial Themes in the Shaping of Knowledge.* New York: St. Martin's Press, 1998.

Smith, Neil. *American Empire: Roosevelt's Geographer and the Prelude to Globalization.* Berkeley: University of California Press, 2003.

Soja, Edward. *Postmodern Geographies: The Reassertion of Space in Critical Social Theory.* London: Verso, 1989.

Stafford, Mary Peary. "History of the Society." In *History 1891–1960: Geographical Society of Philadelphia,* edited by Geographical Society of Philadelphia, 5–15. Philadelphia: The Society, 1960.

Stafford, Robert A. "Scientific Exploration and Empire." In *The Oxford History of the British Empire: Volume III: The Nineteenth Century,* edited by Andrew Porter and William Roger Louis, 294–319. Oxford: Oxford University Press, 1999.

Stephanson, Anders. *Manifest Destiny: American Expansion and the Empire of Right.* New York: Hill and Wang, 1995.

Stoddart, David R. "The RGS and the 'New Geography': Changing Aims and Changing Roles in Nineteenth Century Science." *The Geographical Journal* 146, no. 2 (1980): 190–202.

Veysey, Laurence R. *The Emergence of the American University.* Chicago: University of Chicago Press, 1965.

White, Richard. *"It's Your Misfortune and None of My Own": A History of the American West*. Norman: University of Oklahoma Press, 1991.

White, Richard. *Railroaded: The Transcontinentals and the Making of Modern America*. New York: W. W. Norton, 2011.

Wigen, Kären, and Martin Lewis. *The Myth of Continents: A Critique of Metageography*. Berkeley: University of California Press, 1997.

Winichakul, Thongchai. *Siam Mapped: A History of the Geo-Body of a Nation*. Honolulu: University of Hawaii Press, 1997.

Withers, Charles W. J. "Place and the 'Spatial Turn' in Geography and in History." *Journal of the History of Ideas* 70, no. 4 (2009): 637–58.

Withers, Charles W. J. "Towards a History of Geography in the Public Sphere." *History of Science* 37, no. 1 (1999): 45–78.

Withers, Charles W. J., and David N. Livingstone. "Thinking Geographically about Nineteenth-Century Science." In *Geographies of Nineteenth-Century Science*, edited by Charles W. J. Withers and David N. Livingstone, 1–19. Chicago: The University of Chicago Press, 2011.

Withers, Charles W. J., and Diarmid A. Finnegan. "Natural History Societies, Fieldwork and Local Knowledge in Nineteenth-Century Scotland: Towards a Historical Geography of Civic Science." *Cultural Geographies* 10, no. 3 (2003): 334–353.

Withers, Charles W. J. "Geographies of Science and Public Understanding? Exploring the Reception of the British Association for the Advancement of Science in Britain and in Ireland, c.1845–1939." In *Geographies of Science*, edited by Peter Meusburger, David N. Livingstone, and Heike Jöns, 185–197. Dordrecht: Springer, 2010.

Withers, Charles W. J. *Geography, Science, and National Identity: Scotland since 1520*. Cambridge: Cambridge University Press, 2001.

Wright, John Kirtland. *Geography in the Making: The American Geographical Society, 1851–1951*. New York: American Geographical Society, 1952.

Acknowledgements

This book began as my dissertation project at Ludwig-Maximilian-Universität München in 2016, but it has grown into something far richer thanks to the generous contributions of many people and institutions. Writing about the historical situatedness of science has made me acutely aware of my own position in this network of collaboration and support.

My deepest gratitude goes to my academic mentors, whose guidance shaped this work and my development as a scholar. Ursula Prutsch's encouragement, patience, and gift for sparking intellectual curiosity were foundational to everything that followed. Michael Hochgeschwender provided thoughtful guidance that kept me grounded as I navigated postmodern and postcolonial theory. Martin H. Geyer's teaching strengthened my conviction that rigorous historical scholarship must engage seriously with theory. I am also grateful to Charlotte Lerg and Kärin Nickelsen, who kindly stepped in as examiners when the need unexpectedly arose.

The Hanns-Seidel-Stiftung provided essential financial support throughout this project, and early funding from the Amerika-Institut Alumni Association helped get the research off the ground. Will Jackson deserves special mention for first opening my eyes to the entanglements of geography and empire during my time at the University of Leeds. I am grateful to the EU's Erasmus program for making that experience possible.

Several institutions provided support for this research. My employer, the Deutsches Museum (Digital), graciously provided not only the flexibility for week-long writing retreats, but also a daily reminder of the importance of making complex knowledge accessible to a wider audience. Although the COVID-19 pandemic curtailed my planned research trip to the Library of Congress in Washington, exceptional archival holdings and dedicated archivists elsewhere more than compensated. No institution was more foundational to this book than the American Geographical Society Library at the

University of Wisconsin-Milwaukee; its collections and dedicated staff made this research possible. I also thank the University of Chicago Library and the Chicago Historical Society for access to their archival materials.

The intellectual community of colleagues sustained this project from start to finish. All the regular LMU Amerika-Institut Oberseminar participants, particularly Jonas, Sabrina and Lisa, provided a stimulating environment for critical feedback, tough questions, and fair, fruitful debate. The 2017 ENIUGH Budapest panel on the history of geography reassured me that other scholars shared my passion for the field. Colleagues like Maximilian Georg, Ute Wardenga, Charles Withers, and many others offered valuable perspectives that enriched my work.

Beyond the world of academia, friends and family provided the counterbalance to scholarly intensity through emergency proofreading, reality checks, and patient tolerance of my long preoccupation with nineteenth-century geography. While I cannot name everyone, your support sustained me through the inevitable difficulties. Toni, Fred, Jasper, and Timur were my most trusted sounding boards from beginning to end. My family, especially Monika and Daniel, provided unwavering encouragement and faith in this project. Above all, this book is dedicated to Katja, whose support makes her the most important actor of knowledge in bringing this book to life.

I have done my best to acknowledge my many debts, but for any contributions inadvertently overlooked, please accept my sincere gratitude. For any errors, shortcomings or views expressed in the text, I alone am responsible.